"In *Targeted*, Deepa Fernandes exposes the immigr
She follows the money of the DHS-funded companies that profit, and tells the stories of the immigrants who ultimately pay. This well-researched book documents the perfect storm of white nationalist policy, corporate greed, and the privatized war on terror. As an immigrant herself twice-over, Fernandes writes movingly about the experiences of 'brown people in white countries,' and shows that when anyone is diminished, we all lose."

—Amy Goodman, host of *Democracy Now!*

"*Targeted* lays bare the complex struggle for human rights that have no borders. With haunting personal stories, Deepa Fernandes deftly guides the reader through the hidden and fascinating debate that captivates our nation."

—Dalia Hashad, USA Program Director, Amnesty International

"Deepa Fernandes has written a truly brilliant book. She goes to the heart of current U.S. immigration policy—a policy centered on criminalizing and policing black and brown bodies. But just as superexploited immigrant labor has been—and continues to be—the source of huge profits for U.S. capital, now the repressive apparatus created to police the border and those who cross over has become the latest capitalist dream. If we really want immigration policies geared toward social justice, we must read this book."

—Robin D. G. Kelley, author of
Freedom Dreams: The Black Radical Imagination

"Immigrants are dying for jobs. . . . Hundreds suffocate every year in the Arizona desert. Recycled Halliburton air strips make up the wall. That's the bottom line few recognize like Deepa Fernandes. She portrays not only the human dimension, but how an immigration-industrial complex profits at all our expense."

—Tom Hayden, former California delegate
to the U.S.-Mexico Border Commission

"Many people talk about the immigration system and those that benefit from it. But most immigrant rights organizers are frustrated by how many people underestimate the size and the significance of the current enforcement system. In the past decade over 1.5 million people have been deported, thousands have died at the border, and scores of families have been torn apart. At the same times prison corporations, county jails, and private phone companies see immigrants as a fresh source of income. Deepa Fernandes' *Targeted* paints a picture that helps us understand just why we have to commit ourselves to the fight of our lives."

—Subhash Kateel, Families for Freedom

"Deepa Fernandes has created a powerful text of stories, interviews, research, and facts to dramatize the inanity of a war the United States government is waging against the immigrant poor in the guise of fighting terrorism. Economic realities are forcing people to leave their homes for an uncertain, exploitative, and often deadly journey to this country. *Targeted* is a much-needed sobering look at what is really going on in the midst of anti-immigrant hysterics and jingoism emanating from the halls of Congress to the desert borderlands."

—Luis J. Rodriguez, author of
Always Running: La Vida Loca: Gang Days in L.A.

"The most comprehensive book on post-9/11 attack on immigrants in the U.S. From the desert sands of the U.S.-Mexican border to detention centers in NYC, and from the decades old writings of right wing ideologues to the draconian anti immigrant legislations of the last few years, Fernandes has woven together an in depth story of the current state of U.S. immigration policy; its origins, its arbitrariness, its contradictions, and its ineffectiveness. If you wish to understand contemporary America, this book is a must read."

—Biju Mathew, author of *Taxi!: Cabs and Capitalism in New York City*

"Deepa Fernandes' extensive and serious research about immigration policies, homeland security business and the elites that profit from both, offers solid information and facts in contrast with the constant flow of prejudice, misinformation and outright lies that seem to frame the debate in our current 'talk show' culture."

—Pancho Argüelles. co-author of *BRIDGE:
Building a Race and Immigration Dialogue in the Global Economy*

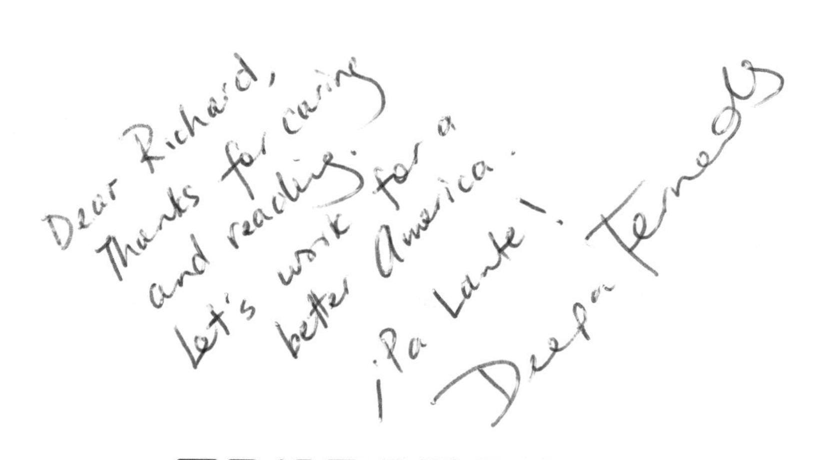

Targeted

Homeland Security and the Business of Immigration

DEEPA FERNANDES

FOREWORD BY HOWARD ZINN

seven stories press
NEW YORK • TORONTO • LONDON • MELBOURNE

Copyright © 2007 by Deepa Fernandes
Foreword copyright © 2007 by Howard Zinn

A Seven Stories Press First Edition

All rights reserved. No part of this book may be reproduced, stored in a retrieval system, or transmitted in any form or by any means, including mechanical, electric, photocopying, recording, or otherwise, without the prior written permission of the publisher.

Seven Stories Press
140 Watts Street
New York, NY 10013
http://www.sevenstories.com

In Canada: Publishers Group Canada, 250A Carlton Street, Toronto, ON M5A 2L1

In the UK: Turnaround Publisher Services Ltd., Unit 3, Olympia Trading Estate, Coburg Road, Wood Green, London N22 6TZ

In Australia: Palgrave Macmillan, 627 Chapel Street, South Yarra, VIC 3141

College professors may order examination copies of Seven Stories Press titles for a free six-month trial period. To order, visit http://www.sevenstories.com/textbook or send a fax on school letterhead to (212) 226-1411.

Book design by Phoebe Hwang

Library of Congress Cataloging-in-Publication Data
Fernandes, Deepa.
Targeted : homeland security and the business of immigration / Deepa Fernandes ; foreword by Howard Zinn. — 1st ed.
p. cm.
Includes index.
ISBN-13: 978-1-58322-728-2 (pb : alk. paper)
ISBN-10: 1-58322-728-8 (pb : alk. paper)
1. United States—Emigration and immigration—Government policy. 2. United States—Emigration and immigration—Economic aspects. 3. National security—United States. I. Title.

JV6483.F47 2006
325.73—dc22

2006019078

Printed in Canada
9 8 7 6 5 4 3 2 1

•

To Abba John, my gentle and patient grandfather, who lived and died with the fear of being deported from Australia when all he wanted to do was live his later years close to his children and grandchildren.

To Nana Teresa, my loving and generous grandmother.
May your wish to acquire permanent residence status, after eleven years of waiting in the "queue," be granted soon.

•

CONTENTS

ACKNOWLEDGMENTS

This book is the product of the genius of my very dearest friend Greg Ruggiero. Back when nobody was talking about immigration, when few cared enough to even commission an article on it, Greg wanted this story told. I am blessed that he has been with me as my editor and friend at every stage of this process. For his love and enthusiastic encouragement, this book owes him a great debt.

Many thanks to the crew at Seven Stories—Dan, Ria, Ruth, Crystal, and especially Theresa—for their valuable input and advice as this daily news journalist tackled her first book.

Sincere thanks to Jessica Silver-Greenberg and Nell Abram, my dedicated and probing research assistants, who managed to dig up many incredible pieces of information without which this book would be much less.

Mil gracias to my congressional advisor, researcher, and dear friend Mitch Jeserich of Pacifica Radio. Mitch's daily reporting for Free Speech Radio News from Capitol Hill was nothing short of exceptional, and I am thankful for his patience and help as I navigated the complex world of bills, acts, and subcommittees.

This has been, especially in the final haul, a collaborative effort. While the end product is mine, and I take full responsibility for any errors within, critical groundwork and research were contributed by Ting Ting Cheng, Nell Geiser, Pratap Chatterjee, Eddy Becker, Tricia Wang, and Monica López.

Heartfelt thanks to those who gave up so much time to read drafts of this book and give me valuable feedback: Joe Fernandes, Mike Walsh, Matt Rogers, Biju Mathew, Nell Abram, Jee Kim, Benita Jain, and Aaron Hanna.

To the immigration attorneys who gave me countless hours of their time, especially Benita Jain. Also to Jack Wallace, Traci Hong, Marc Seitles, Marisa Dersey, Heather Rogers, Steven Forester, and Ira Kurzban.

And then there are the folks who live these issues every single day and whose work forms the basis of this book: Subhash Kateel, Adem Carroll, Bobby Khan, Biju Mathew, Karla Quiñonez, Vijay Prasad, Benita Jain, Kat Rodriguez, Michelle Karshan, Aarti Shahani, Eric Tang, and Monami Maulik. Your wisdom, thinking, and years of community-organizing work around immigrant issues has been so critical.

To my Haiti confidantes and travel buddies Kody Emmanuel and Sacajawea Hall. Thanks for showing me your Haiti and helping me learn your history. And to my dear friend Errol Maitland, thank you for teaching me so much and for being, as the inmates of Prison Civile so aptly named you, our Papa Noel. The mangoes were good. Let's go back soon.

Gracias to Joshua Chaffin for teaching me the wonders of a FOIA request.

To the Pacifica Radio family; our network is a treasure, and I feel blessed to be a part of it. Special thanks to those at WBAI who mentored, taught, and guided me.

To my aunty Daphne Gonzalvez, my high school writing coach, and my uncle Dom Gonzalvez, who has always believed I had a book or a screenplay in me. This book would never have been possible without the years of love and encouragement you both channeled toward my reading, writing, and critical-thinking abilities. Special thanks to the one writer in our family who constantly reminds me by her work that good writing always keeps the reader turning the page: my godchild, Meera Fernandes.

To the intelligent, inspiring, and beautiful women who have been so important in my life outside of Australia and who have taught me so much: Dena, Flora, Sharan, Louise, Catherine, Anurima, Karlita, Lydia, Amycita, Nell, Ama, Monica, Norma, Makani, Riene, Suzy, and Hilda. We have laughed and cried together, and you have all helped shape who I am and what I believe. I hope you see some of our conversations represented here.

This book would never have been written if I did not have a dedicated and selfless crew to lean on so heavily. To my absolutely inspiring *Wakeup Call* and People's Production House coworkers who have carried my weight and taken on so much more while I have been in the depths of this book. I am especially grateful to Sharan Harper and Kat Aaron: I learn from you both every single day and feel blessed to have you both as such dear, dear friends. To Sylvia Guerrero, Mitch Jeserich, Errol Maitland, Samori Benjamin, Leigh Ann Caldwell, and Saki Hall, mil gracias. Your work is incredible, and I am forever indebted. You all are my heroes.

To my family who span the globe, your love and nurturing over the years, regardless of borders and country of residence, has made me the person I am today. Thank you all. To my family in this country, especially Liz and Bill Rogers, and Eben and Heather, your support has been incredible, and all those *San Francisco Chronicle* immigration articles that periodically arrived in the mail kept the West Coast well represented in the book.

My deepest thanks to my parents, Joe and Sylvie, for their constant love and encouragement. Dad, as my first reader and editor, from those sixth-grade essays to the chapters of this book, I thank you for helping me find and sharpen my voice. And Mum, your fierce determination to always stand up for what is right is why I am who I am today.

To Sujatha, my sister, my best friend, my intellectual sparring partner, I learn from you and know that I would never have been thinking or caring about these issues if it was not for you showing me the way. And to my brother Mike, thank you so much for the amount of careful time you have put into reading and editing this book. This book would have been half of what it is if it was not for your wisdom, edits, rewrites, and the sheer love that you brought to the manuscript. And that you were such a huge daily support for me when you were going through such a devastating loss is simply incredible to me. I hope I can do the same for you one day.

And finally to my sweet Matt. You nourished me when I was empty, you were silly and playful when I was overwhelmed, and you gave me love and encouragement every step of the way. I couldn't wish for a better partner in life.

FOREWORD

Howard Zinn

This book by Deepa Fernandes comes at the right time. There is a simmering controversy in the United States about the status of immigrants. There are loud cries from nationalist ideologues, but also from ordinary citizens who feel threatened by the influx of people who don't speak English, especially from Mexico. Vigilantes sit at the borders, guns on their laps, looking for those who might cross over. President Bush promises to deploy thousands of National Guardsmen who will be sent to do the same.[1]

Roused by the increasing hostility, immigrants and their advocates all over the country, but especially in places like California and Arizona, have been demonstrating by the hundreds of thousands for the rights of foreign-born people, whether here legally or illegally. One sign is seen in every demonstration: "No Human Being Is Illegal."

At the same time, members of Congress, conscious of their political fortunes, are trying to both assuage the anti-immigrant feelings of many of their constituents—while also meeting the needs of businessmen who want to profit from cheap labor. As they debate legislation to deal with the situation, they want to make some show of adherence to the ideal of generosity toward the foreign born.

Discrimination against the foreign born, often to the point of hatred, is graphically brought to our attention in *Targeted*. It has a long history, going back to the beginning of the nation.

In the late eighteenth century, the United States, having just gone through its own revolution, was ironically fearful of having revolutionaries in its midst. The French had recently overthrown its monarchy, Irish rebels were protesting British rule, and the new U.S. government was conscious of "dangerous foreigners"—Irish and French—in the country. In the year 1798, in a climate of "cold war" with France, Congress passed legislation lengthening the residence requirement for becoming a citizen from five to fourteen years. It also authorized the President to deport any alien he regarded as dangerous to public safety.

There was virulent anti-Irish sentiment in the 1840s and 1850s, especially after the failure of the potato crop in Ireland killed one million people and drove millions more abroad, most of them to the United States. "No Irish Need Apply," a phrase that often appeared in employment ads, symbolized the prejudice that existed against Irish immigrants. It was part of a long tradition of irrational fear in which an earlier generation of immigrants, once partly assimilated, reacted with hatred toward the next generation of immigrants. The Irish-born Dennis Kearney, for example, became a spokesman for anti-Chinese prejudice. His political ambitions led him and the California Workingmen's Party to adopt the slogan "The Chinese Must Go."

In the 1860s the Chinese had been welcome as cheap labor for the building of the transcontinental railroad, but a decade later they were seen—especially after the economic crisis of 1873—as taking away jobs from the native born. This sentiment was turned into law with the Chinese Exclusion Act of 1882, which for the first time in the nation's history created the category of "illegal" immigrants. Before this, there was no border control. Chinese, desperate to find a better life in the United States, tried to evade the act by crossing into the United States from Mexico. Some learned to say *Yo soy Mexicano,* Spanish for *I am Mexican*. But violence against them continued, as whites, seeing their jobs go to ill-paid Chinese, reacted with fury. In Rock Springs, Wyoming, in the summer of 1885, whites attacked five hundred Chinese miners, massacring twenty-eight of them in cold blood.

Europeans, on the other hand, were welcome, especially on the East Coast, where they were needed as laborers, stonecutters, ditchdiggers, or as workers in garment factories, textile mills, and mines. Immigrants poured in from southern and eastern Europe, from Italy, Greece, Poland, Russia, and the Balkans. There were five million immigrants in the 1880s, four million in the 1890s. From 1900 to 1910, eight million more arrived.

Newcomers faced vicious hostility. A typical comment in the *Baltimore Sun*: "The Italian immigrant would be no more objectionable than some others were it not for his singularly bloodthirsty disposition and frightful temper and vindictiveness." New York City's police commissioner, Theodore Bingham, insisted that "half of the criminals" in New York City in 1908 were Jews.

There was widespread opposition when the U.S. entered World War I. To suppress antiwar sentiment, the government adopted legislation—the Espionage Act and the Sedition Act, for example—which led to the imprisonment of almost a thousand people. Their crime was to protest, by speech or in writing, the United States' entrance in the war. Another law provided for the deportation of aliens who opposed organized government or advocated the destruction of property.

After the war, the lingering superpatriotic atmosphere led to more hysteria against the foreign born, intensified by the Bolshevik Revolution of 1917. In 1919, after the explosion of a bomb in front of the house of Attorney General A. Mitchell Palmer, a series of raids were carried out against immigrants. Palmer's agents picked up 249 noncitizens of Russian birth—many of whom had lived in this country a long time—put them on a ship, and deported them to Soviet Russia. Anarchists Emma Goldman and Alexander Berkman were among those deported. J. Edgar Hoover, at that time a young agent of the Department of Justice, personally supervised the deportation.

Shortly after the Palmer raids, in January 1920, four thousand people in thirty-three cities were rounded up and detained in seclusion for long periods of time. They were subjected to secret hearings, and more than five hundred of them were deported. In Boston, Department of Justice agents, aided by local police, arrested six hundred people by raiding meeting halls and by invading private homes in the early morning. They were handcuffed, chained together, and marched through the city streets. It was in this atmosphere of jingoism and antiforeign hysteria that the Italian immigrants Nicola Sacco and Bartolomeo Vanzetti were put on a trial after a robbery and murder at a Massachusetts shoe factory, found guilty by an Anglo-Saxon judge and jury, and sentenced to death.

The rise in nationalist and antiforeign sentiment during World War I led to the passage of the National Origins Quota Act in 1924. The act set quotas that encouraged immigration from England, Germany, and Scandinavia and strictly limited immigration from eastern and southern Europe.

Following World War II, the cold war atmosphere of anti-Communist hysteria brought about the McCarran-Walter Act of 1952. The Act permitted immigrants from the United Kingdom, Ireland, and Germany to fill 70 percent of the total annual immigration quota, but set quotas of one hundred immigrants for each country in Asia. The act also revived, in a particularly virulent way, the antialien legislation of 1798, creating ideological grounds for the exclusion of immigrants and the treatment of all foreign-born residents, who could be deported for any "activities prejudicial to the public interest" or "subversive to national security." Noncitizens suspected of radical ideas were rounded up and deported.

The great social movements of the 1960s led to a number of legislative reforms, including voting rights for African Americans and health care for senior citizens and for the poor. Among these was a law abolishing the

National Origins Quota system and allowing a maximum of twenty thousand immigrants to enter the United States from each country.

Although the Cold War presumably ended with the disintegration of the Soviet Union, the atmosphere of militarism and war continued. Panama was invaded in 1989 and Iraq in 1991.

When the Federal Building in Oklahoma City was bombed in 1995, killing 168 people, the two men convicted of the crime were native-born Americans. Nevertheless, the following year President Bill Clinton signed into law the Antiterrorism and Effective Death Penalty Act, which contained especially harsh provisions for foreign-born people. For immigrants as well as for citizens, the act reintroduced the McCarthy-era principle of "guilt by association." That is, people could be put in jail or, if foreign born, deported, not for what they actually did, but for lending support to any group that the secretary of state designated as "terrorist." Visas could also be denied to people wanting to enter the United States if they were members of any such group, even if the actions of the group the individual supported were perfectly legal. Under the new law, a person marked for deportation had no rights of due process and could be deported on the basis of secret evidence.

Clinton's signing of this act sent a clear message: targeting immigrants and depriving them of constitutional rights were not only characteristic of Republican right-wingers, but also of the Democratic Party, which in the military atmosphere of World War II and the Cold War had joined a bipartisan attack on the rights of both the native and foreign born.

In the wake of the 9/11 attacks on the Pentagon in Washington, DC, and Twin Towers in New York, President George W. Bush declared a "war on terrorism." A climate of fear spread across the nation in which any foreign-born person became an object of suspicion. The government was now armed with new legal powers by the USA PATRIOT Act of 2001, which gave the Attorney General the power to detain any foreign-born person he declared a suspected terrorist. He doesn't need to show proof—he merely needs to say the word. The act established that any such detained persons may be held indefinitely, with no burden of proof on the government and no hearing required. The act was passed with both Democratic and Republican support; only Senator Russ Feingold (D-Wisconsin) voted against it.

In the anxious atmosphere created by 9/11 and the war on terrorism, there were, predictably, numerous cases of violence against foreign-born people. For instance, just four days after 9/11, a forty-nine-year-old Sikh-American, who was doing landscaping work outside his gas station in Mesa, Arizona, was shot and killed by a man shouting, "I stand for America all the way!" In February

2003 a group of teenagers in Orange County, California, used bats and golf clubs to attack Rashid Alam, an eighteen-year-old Lebanese-American. He suffered a broken jaw, stab wounds, and head injuries.

Shortly after 9/11, as documented by the Center for Constitutional Rights and Human Rights Watch, Muslims from various countries were picked up, held for various periods of time in tiny, windowless cells, and often beaten and abused. As the *New York Times* has since reported on more than one occasion, "hundreds of Muslim immigrants . . . were swept up in the weeks after the 2001 terror attacks and held for months before they were cleared of links to terrorism and deported."[2]

Incidents continue to occur. For instance, on October 23, 2003, according to a report by the Meiklejohn Civil Liberties Institute, federal agents raided sixty Wal-Mart stores in twenty-one states across the country and arrested 250 janitors employed by Wal-Mart contractors for alleged violations of immigration law. In a series of raids that began on May 26, 2006, swarms of federal agents arrested more than two thousand immigrants across the country.[3]

Muslims became a special target of surveillance and arrest. Thousands were detained. *New York Times* columnist Anthony Lewis told of one man who, even before 9/11, was arrested on secret evidence. When a federal judge found that there was no reason to conclude the man was a threat to national security, the man was released. However, after 9/11 the Department of Justice, ignoring the judge's finding, imprisoned him again, held him in solitary confinement twenty-three hours a day, and didn't allow his family to see him.

Since the passage of the Antiterrorism and Effective Death Penalty Act of 1996, 1.5 million people have been deported from the United States. And after the immigration protests of May 2006, U.S. authorities have stepped up their raids, arrests, and deportations. Missing from much of the debate about the rights of immigrants are the voices and the experiences of the immigrants themselves. This, the human story, is what Deepa Fernandes supplies in this gripping book.

As of summer 2006, Republicans and Democrats are attempting to arrive at a "compromise" on the rights of immigrants. But in none of their proposals is there a recognition that immigrants deserve the same rights as everyone else. Forgetting, or rather ignoring, the indignation of liberty-loving people at the building of the Berlin Wall and the exultation that greeted its fall, the government plans to build a wall at the southern borders of California and Arizona. I doubt that any national political figure will point out that this wall is intended to keep Mexicans out of the land that was violently taken from Mexico in the war of 1846–48.

Only demonstrators in cities across the country are reminding us of the words on the Statue of Liberty in New York harbor:

Give me your tired, your poor,
Your huddled masses yearning to breathe free,
The wretched refuse of your teeming shore.
Send these, the homeless, tempest-tossed to me:
I lift my lamp beside the golden door.

In the wave of anger against government action in the 1960s, cartoons were drawn showing the Statue of Liberty blindfolded. The blindfold remains, if only symbolically, until we begin to act as if, yes, *no human being is illegal.*

Note: Many names have been changed throughout the book to protect the identity of those interviewed.

PREFACE

Immigration is a multifaceted process, and there are distinct ways for foreigners to enter the United States. I call them immigration tracks. Part one of *Targeted* explores some of these immigration tracks, looking at how each one has changed over the past decade.

The book begins at the southern border, perhaps the most controversial immigration track in the United States today. For decades immigrants have crossed into the United States from Mexico via the shared border. Nothing is different today, except perhaps that it is a more dangerous trip. Chapter one straddles border towns in San Diego-Tijuana and Tucson-Nogales-Altar. There we find thousands of people risking their lives every day, engaged in a northward journey in the hope of crossing into a future with more opportunities for themselves and their families. For those who make it, the first opportunities come as grueling low-wage jobs that form the basis of the U.S. economy. Over the past decade, the government's answer to this undocumented immigration has been to lock down the southern borders, military style. The anti-immigration lobby, which advocates that the government do more to thwart undocumented immigration, has gained notoriety for its citizen patrols of the border. This lobby has garnered the support of some border residents and local elected officials, and during the two terms of the Bush administration, funding for policing the border has dramatically increased. In the post-9/11 years this has been justified in the name of homeland security. Yet the numbers of those crossing have not decreased, nor have the increased apprehensions dissuaded the crossers. So why do they come?

The first chapter of *Targeted* chronicles stories of the "illegals"—overwhelmingly a people who are crossing into the U.S. as a last resort. In their home countries, and often due to U.S. economic and trade policies, these undocumented immigrants have been stripped of land, work, and political power, and forced into a migratory pattern in search of a job to survive. When they come to the U.S., they are welcomed with a smorgasbord of low-wage work opportunities and criminalized for seeking this livelihood.

Chapter one also examines the profitable nature of the border crackdown.

From the unmanned drones that cost millions and frequently break down to the stadium lights and ground sensors that are more useful in disrupting the ecosystem than in apprehending criminals, the southern border has seen significant amounts of money spent on new technologies that target work-seeking immigrants. Yet the bloated budget is justified on the grounds that it is securing the homeland against infiltration and attack.

In the second chapter, I look at the detention and deportation arsenal of the government. In the aftermath of 9/11, a deliberate sweep through immigrant communities was sanctioned by the government. Thousands of noncitizens were arrested and detained, and when no terrorism connections could be found, the government used past immigration violations to hold and then deport an untold number. However, the machinery of detention and deportation—an underexamined element of U.S. immigration policy—had been well oiled long before 9/11. Chapter two looks at the many ways in which noncitizens end up in immigration custody, it examines how so-called administrative detention impacts immigrants and lines the pockets of the profitable corrections industry, and it delves into the almost inevitable result of removal from the country. I highlight the Caribbean nation of Haiti as a case study of what deportees face on return and ask whether the United States can be allowed to deport people into situations that it acknowledges are dangerous and potentially life threatening.

Asylum seekers arriving at U.S. ports of entry have been treated harshly over the past decade. The 1996 immigration laws allowed for the incarceration of all arriving foreigners without a visa, and this overwhelmingly affected people seeking political asylum in the U.S. For the past decade, from their immigration prison cells, asylum seekers have had to prove that they will be persecuted if they are sent back home. Chapter three looks at immigration's asylum track. It illustrates how the 1996 laws impacted asylum seekers and explores what the post-9/11 climate has meant for foreign nationals fleeing persecution. Again, I use Haiti as a case study when examining the asylum track over the past ten years. While successive U.S. governments have had a separate system for dealing with arriving Haitians, in the current climate, the special treatment has only intensified. Chapter three takes on the dual purpose of exposing discriminatory treatment and warning that these policies could be used against all immigrants, while highlighting the particular abuses against Haitian nationals.

Chapter four considers two immigration tracks that encompass the majority of temporary residents: foreign students and foreign workers. Foreign students will often become foreign workers upon completion of their studies. And after a long stint as a foreign worker, some manage to change their status to legal permanent resident either because their company sponsored them or because they married a U.S. citizen. Chapter four traces the new challenges of the post-9/11 years that have made life much harder for both foreign students and foreign workers. These are also the immigrants most likely to make it to the final step and naturalize, a process that can be quick and cheap if the green-card holder goes to Iraq to serve.

Chapter four illustrates that despite the zero-tolerance practiced in immigration today, those immigrants who are deemed more valuable are dealt with differently. However, within a system that has been clamping down on immigrant rights, even these most favored immigrants are targeted.

In the second part of *Targeted* (chapters five and six), I look at the primary forces that are driving immigration policy in the United States. The Republican Party, which has been behind all the key immigration legislation of the past ten years, is split over the issue. On one side there are big-business interests that profit from cheap undocumented labor and cheap skilled labor. On the other side are the anti-immigrationists who pursue a white nationalist agenda and whose ultimate goal is a complete moratorium on immigration to the United States.

Chapter five exposes the industrial complex that has been built up around immigration. In the aftermath of 9/11, the big business interests that have always driven immigration policy dramatically increased their participation in the enforcement of immigration law through lucrative federal contracts. With the creation of the Department of Homeland Security (DHS) in 2003, the Bush administration invited businesses of all stripes not only to help chart DHS's future course, but also to do much of the work. Technology-driven systems and devices were invented and sold to the government to help secure the nation against another attack. From fingerprinting machines to computer systems that track and store information about suspicious persons, from digital helmet-cams for border patrol officers to privately run immigration jails, there has been a boom in contracts aimed at securing the homeland. As chapter five illustrates, there are numerous examples documenting the massive amounts of tax dollars that have been spent on contracts that are negligently executed, ineffective in protecting against terrorism, and that simply end up netting the wrong fish: migrants in search of a better life.

The final chapter looks at the state of the legislation that governs immigration and the lives of noncitizens, and follows white nationalists and hate groups from the margins of American society into the mainstream. It illustrates how these individuals and groups, whose prime agenda is to halt all immigration to the United States, have led a calculated and quiet campaign to sway the public debate firmly into their camp. By infiltrating Congress, these white nationalist groups have been behind every key piece of legislation that has passed in the last decade. The final chapter is part exposé, part warning; it exposes the tactics and motives of those driving anti-immigration networks and warns of what their white nationalist agendas could mean for present and future immigrants and noncitizens if it is not actively opposed.

Throughout the process of writing this book, I was extremely surprised by how little most people know about the nation's immigration policies, and yet how knowledgeable many claim to be. As illustrated by President Bush's immigration speech in Arizona at the end of 2005, over the past few years the Right has successfully reconsolidated immigration into just two issues: amnesty and terrorism. Both drive immigration spending and policies and both have very little to do with the country's current immigration realities.

Yet while immigrants have been successfully cast as a national security threat in the post-9/11 years, they continue to be pitted against those who have traditionally occupied the lowest paying jobs in the country, as their willingness to work for even lower wages has escalated a race to the bottom. Many citizens have been pushed out of the workforce as immigrant labor is plentiful, cheaper, and with few basic worker rights. When combined with the government's war on terror on the home front, which has directly cast immigrants as the threat, there exists today greater—and growing—resentment against immigrants as a whole.

So why did I write this book? And what do I hope you will take from it? It's funny that television talk-show host Oprah Winfrey comes to mind when I think about what it is this book hopes to do. I picture Oprah looking directly into the camera, as she does when she has a message for the audience, and saying with seriousness and moral conviction: "Folks. What is going on here just breaks my heart. We, as a nation that has proven that we care about justice, have a big problem here. And if we don't each take some personal action soon, we may just find ourselves a truly alienated nation. We have to start treating immigrants right. We have to stop exploiting their labor, stop locking them up, and most certainly, we have to stop ripping their families apart by mercilessly throwing them out of the country. This country is richer for its immigrants, and what is happening today is just plain wrong."

I am an immigrant, twice over. I was born in India, migrated to Australia as a baby with my parents, and then to the U.S. in my twenties. Mine is a family of immigrants, brown-skinned people in white countries. My grandparents, who came to Australia on tourist visas, attempted to change their status to permanent resident so they could live out their later years with their five Australian-citizen children. However, their applications were denied because my grandfather was in the early stages of degenerative Parkinson's disease, and the Australian government deemed that he would become a drain on the public health system. My family decided it was best they stay in Australia, as they had no one to return to in their home city of Bombay. Though the Australian government proceeded to threaten to deport my elderly grandparents, it never took steps to detain them. This allowed them to continue living with their family. Eventually we were able to get them temporary visas and put them on a path to regularizing their status.

If this had happened in the United States, their past visa violation would today have been enough to throw my grandparents in jail to await deportation. Neither of my grandparents were ever criminals.

The people in this book have not been so lucky. These are their stories.

PROLOGUE

"Yo, I'm begging you sis, just get me outta here. *Please.* I'm dying in here," Marc pleaded, his sunken cheeks pressed up against the chain-link fence that separated us inside of Haiti's most notorious jail. "They treat us worse than dogs here," he whispered. "Don't leave me here, I don't want to die in here."[4] Those were the last words I heard as my visit with inmates of Haiti's Prison Civile was terminated by the prison warden. About thirty men, all of them black, gaunt, and dripping with sweat from the Port-au-Prince heat, clung onto the fence that locked them into a jail they had little hope of getting out of any time soon.

"The prison guards beat me so bad they broke my arm," Marc complained. "And they gave me no medical treatment," he added, as he waved his deformed arm. The men I met in Haiti's Prison Civile were separated from the rest of the inmate population because they shared one thing in common: they were noncitizen Americans of Haitian origin who had been deported by the U.S. government. On arrival in Haiti these criminal deportees were immediately jailed. "Why am I here? What did I ever do to the Haitians?" Marc pleaded with me. Not one of the imprisoned Haitian-Americans had been charged with a crime by the Haitian government, nor had any gone before a judge or received a sentence. They hailed from Brooklyn, Tallahassee, and East L.A., and now they were at the mercy of Haitian prison officials. The week before my December 2005 visit, three inmates had died at the Prison Civile from beriberi,[5] an easily preventable disease. A few years ago, a massacre had occurred in the prison—then called the National Penitentiary—in which guards opened fire on inmates and killed dozens. "This place is crazy dangerous. I have never been this scared before," Marc said during my visit.

The inmates I met had all landed in the Haitian prison because of U.S. immigration policy. Their crimes in the U.S., for which each had fully served his sentence, ranged from domestic violence to shoplifting to drug possession. It was during a reporting trip to Haiti in 2004, when President Jean-Bertrand Aristide was removed from the country, that I first discovered the gravity of U.S. deportation policies.

"I wish I had fought my case harder in the U.S., got a good lawyer or something, because now that I am here, they are telling me I can never go back. Ever. All for smoking a joint." When Marc was transferred to an immigration jail in Miami upon the termination of his criminal sentence, he did not know that his pending deportation to Haiti meant another indefinite jail term on arrival. Nor did he know at the time of his conviction for possession of a small amount of marijuana that he would be deported from the U.S., the country where he had spent the majority of his life, to Haiti, a country where he had only one old uncle and barely spoke the language.

The U.S. government bought Marc a one-way ticket out of the country and took away his green card. "If I make it out of here alive, I'm gonna start an electronics business or maybe export Haitian products to the U.S." The reality is that U.S. deportees are also targeted outside of prison walls in Haiti, blamed by the government and the media for the country's many problems. And because U.S. immigration laws have gotten so harsh, it is likely that Marc will never set foot in the U.S. again.

Since 1996 almost 1.5 million noncitizens like Marc have been deported from the U.S. It is time these policies are examined and their impact on immigrant communities *and* U.S. citizens given thorough consideration.

Immigration has become a hot-button issue, one that's not going to go away anytime soon. Polls indicate that following Iraq and the economy, immigration is the next most pressing issue to people living in the United States. In direct response to harsh immigration legislation that has been enacted over the last ten years and to protest the even harsher pending legislation, massive numbers took to the streets around the country to rally for immigrant rights in Spring 2006. Congress is inundated with bills that seek to regulate immigration procedures and immigrants' lives. Yet for a country that is so preoccupied with immigration, there is little understanding of the complex issues and real-life implications of these distinctly anti-immigrant policies and proposals.

Since 9/11 many punitive actions have been justified in the name of national security. In Afghanistan and Iraq, the U.S. government has pursued devastating preemptive assaults, in part as retribution and in part as a warning against a future attack. On the home front, dark-skinned immigrants have been targeted. Immigration was successfully framed by the Right as an issue of homeland security that should be dealt with using law enforcement practices and tools.

Marc's situation exemplifies the state of immigration and immigrant-citizen relations in the United States today. Although he has nothing to do with terrorism and does not pose a national security threat, he was still targeted by a system with little empathy for immigrants and noncitizens. Prior to its 2003 transition to multiple agencies within the Department of Homeland Security, the Immigration and Naturalization Service (INS) regulated immigration matters from within the Justice Department. Given the direct connections that have been made in the media between immigrants and terrorists, the fact that the government now treats immigration as an issue of homeland security is barely questioned. Ironically, it may be more baffling to ponder why the former INS was an agency of the Department of Justice. Yet whether it is part of the DOJ or DHS, it is clear that immigration has been a law enforcement issue for decades, if not generations.

As this book goes to press, there are numerous immigration bills being negotiated and renegotiated in Washington. Most would enhance the mechanisms for criminalizing and permanently removing immigrants with and without legal status. Some bills would further limit the number of immigrants allowed into the U.S., while others would restrict access to naturalization. Immigration is a convenient scapegoat for a bad economy and for dealing with the ongoing fear of terrorism.

When President Bush gave his November 2005 speech on immigration, his promises to protect the nation framed immigration squarely as an issue of security. Bush's speech captured the national spotlight, and few immigrants or their advocates got sound bites in edgewise. Immigrants and their advocates did speak up, and they spoke loudly and passionately, but their only political representation in Congress—the Democratic Party—had years ago lost the debate on immigration and been relegated to the margins.

To fulfill corporate hunger for low-wage labor, Bush proposed a guest-worker program that would allow for the temporary legalization of some of the millions of undocumented immigrants in the country. For this he was called a *moderate*. On the one hand, his guest-worker proposal was a gift of cheap and subservient labor to the big-business wing of his Republican Party. On the other, the increased budget for border patrol, fences, detention beds, and immigration jails appeased the anti-immigration wing of Bush's support base. This growing lobby wants a complete moratorium on immigration. What is decidedly lost in the way the debate is framed is that Bush is by no means a moderate when it comes to immigration. As is documented in the pages ahead, Bush is at the head of some of the harshest and most inhumane immigration policy in modern U.S. history.

But this book is not an indictment of just the current administration and its immigration policies. The law enforcement apparatus dealing with immigration and immigrants was set in place long before Bush took power. In fact, President Clinton signed into law various bills in 1996 that were punitive against both new immigrants and legal permanent residents. President Clinton deepened the legal divide between citizens and noncitizens, furthering the process whereby the rights that all U.S. citizens take for granted could be stripped from any noncitizen, no matter how many years they have been living in the country as a legal permanent resident.

Despite the fact that some of the bills floating in Congress are referred to as amnesty bills, this book does not delve into the issue because amnesty is not currently a real political possibility—at least not as articulated by the bills under consideration. The last amnesty for undocumented immigrants was in 1986. Portrayed by the anti-immigration movement as rewarding illegal behavior and endangering the lives of U.S. citizens, the 1986 amnesty caused such a backlash that most politicians have since endorsed the criminalization of undocumented entrants. Current proposals that promise to legalize those in the country with no legal status have such stringent clauses attached to them that they cannot be seriously considered amnesty.

Politicians on both sides of the aisle regularly claim that undocumented immigration is out of control and that undocumented migrants should simply come to the U.S. legally. As this book documents, this line of argument is false. Firstly, and contrary to popular opinion, there is no easy way to come to the U.S. legally, especially for people from developing countries. Yet perhaps more disingenuous still is that for immigrants who have managed to navigate the system and attain some kind of legal status, the country's immigration policies *still* target them.

Over the past decade, noncitizens—be they legal permanent residents, temporary visa holders, immigrants awaiting a change of status, or undocumented workers—have been lumped together and so thoroughly dehumanized that cruel and brutal immigration polices have been allowed to pass. The majority of deportations occur for a visa violation or an old criminal conviction. Yet an immigration violation that could permanently remain on one's record and qualify a person for deportation could be as simple as dropping a class from a full-time student load. In fact, in 2002 over thirty thousand foreign students unwittingly became removable from the U.S. for simply dropping a class from their full-time schedule.[6]

As I delved into past and present immigration policy, I learned that one cannot divorce real people and their stories from the policy. I have therefore documented the actual experiences of immigrants, noncitizens, and immigration workers to illustrate the impact of the policies. Only by understanding their impact can one evaluate who is benefiting from them, and if they are serving their intended purpose. It is my sincere hope that by giving voice to those who are most directly affected, civic demand for greater tolerance, justice, and fairness in this country's relationship with its immigrants will grow and achieve real results.

PART I

Chapter I

THE BORDER CRACKDOWN

New York City, 1999

Maria is a mother of six, a devout Catholic, and a resident of East Harlem, New York. She did not make it past the second grade and finds it difficult to read and write. Her three eldest children were born in Mexico in the town of Tlapa where Maria herself was born and raised. She describes herself and her family as "dirt poor."[7] But Maria, like most people, is generally a happy, positive person, trying to make the best of her lot in life.

My first impression of Maria was that she is a feisty woman—a woman who will do what she has to do to get what she needs. I met her in a Manhattan restaurant. She was wearing a white chef's apron, and seeing me alone at a table, she barreled right up. "¿Hablas español?" she asked me. I did speak Spanish, and there began a long friendship.

Maria wanted to know where she could get a job better than her current one chopping vegetables ten hours per day, six days per week for which she earned two hundred dollars. Maria had just arrived in New York from Mexico. She and her boyfriend had paid a guide—better known as a *coyote*—one thousand dollars each to bring them across the border, and two weeks after leaving her home in Mexico, Maria landed in the Big Apple. I was visiting New York and had little idea about the job market, let alone the prospects for a non-English speaker. But I was immediately endeared by Maria's determination to work hard and make a better life for her three children whom she had left behind in Mexico. During our conversations her immigration status never came up. In the middle of a city of immigrants, I didn't think to ask and Maria didn't tell.

Years later, in the course of my work as a journalist, I discovered the harrowing details of Maria's life. She had arrived in the U.S. illegally, crossing from Altar-Sasabé in Mexico back in 1999. Her sole reason for coming to the U.S. was to find work. With the money she earned, Maria first paid back what it cost to hire the coyote who guided her through her desert crossing. She also regularly sent money to her mother who was looking after her children. If she was lucky, Maria told me, she might even save enough money to return to Mexico and set up a small business that would provide her with a stable and modest income to raise her family. "Qué sueño,"[8] Maria sighed wistfully; this was undoubtedly a dream with little chance of being realized.

For a single mother who speaks no English and has little education, Maria said it was next to impossible to get a work visa to come to the United States. So she weighed her options and chose to cross coyote-style. Maria was lucky; she made it the first time and did not suffer too much during the journey. Today it's a different story.

Arizona-Mexico Border, April 2005

It's ninety-one degrees Fahrenheit at lunch time in the just-south-of-the-border town of Nogales, a bustling town in northern Mexico that borders Arizona. In Mexico, Nogales is known for its once-abundant walnut trees, its Olympic medal–winning sprinter who clinched Mexico's only medal in the 2004 Athens games, and its thriving tax-free factories (companies like Motorola and Samsonite enjoy the cheap labor and low overheads). Perhaps lesser known is that Nogales currently serves as the United States' busiest deportation point for Mexicans being returned to Mexico.

U.S. Customs and Border Protection (CBP) drop off around one thousand mostly poor, mostly indigenous, mostly work-seeking Mexicans at Nogales's dusty border port each day. In some sense, they are the lucky ones whom CBP has decided not to prosecute. They have all signed a document known as a "voluntary return status," in which they agree to be fingerprinted and entered into a CBP database and then bused to the border where they walk through a gate designed just for deportees. But as many will tell you, they are in fact extremely *unlucky*. They have just signed themselves into a lifetime of debt by not making it to a U.S. city where a job in construction, house cleaning, a chicken factory, or in the back of a restaurant awaited them. Their attempts to cross into the U.S. and find work probably set them back somewhere between fifteen hundred and three thousand dollars—a staggering sum to earn and save in Mexico.

Less than one mile from the border gate on the Mexican side is the brightly colored office of Grupo Beta, a Mexican government agency that provides services to migrants who have just been deported. On any given day, their office sees between three hundred and five hundred deported Mexicans and offers them a bed, a meal, and a discount bus ticket back to their hometown. In stark contrast to the U.S. side, where undocumented immigrants are treated as criminals, Grupo Beta's mission is to educate Mexicans about the risks of attempting the border crossing and to provide critical services to the often-penniless deportees.

At any given moment, thousands of migrants are in various stages of the northward move all across the two thousand miles of the U.S.-Mexico border. Since President Bush came to power there has been a solid boosting of resources to police the border. In 1986 the annual spending on border enforcement was $151 million.[9] In 1993, the year before the implementation of Operation Gatekeeper, Border Patrol's annual budget was about $361 million.[10] Since 9/11, CBP's budget has grown by 34 percent.[11] In 2006, it is slated to jump even higher to a mammoth $6.7 billion.[12] This windfall has yet to translate into the apprehension of a single terrorist along the Mexican border, but it has ensured that CBP looks like a well-oiled military machine and that a steady flow of undocumented immigrants are picked up each day.

In 1994, the chain-link fence that residents of Nogales say allowed them to cross back and forth to shop or work was replaced with a twenty-foot cement and metal wall topped with razor wire. Part of this wall is constructed with landing mats that were used on U.S. Navy ships during the Gulf War.[13] The wall is monitored by video cameras and stadium floodlights. Vibration sensors were installed in the ground along the border to alert Border Patrol to possible traffic. For residents of Nogales on both sides of the border, this was the beginning of a hypervigilant policing operation.

When I visited the Nogales branch of Grupo Beta, there were ten people sitting listlessly on the front steps staring out into the dusty parking area. Bright orange and blue trucks periodically drove up and unloaded groups of people. All of them were deportees. Inside the offices a television was blaring in the corner as still more people, mostly men, stared blankly at the game show that roared wealth and good fortune at them, neither of which these people possessed.

Information about every newly arrived deportee is processed into a computer, and each is informed of their options. Most carry a simple backpack and some have nothing at all. The place filled up as they waited for their bus home or tried to decide what to do next. Many reattempt to cross the border. As they waited, I was told that the day was as good a sample of what deportees experience as any. And then their stories flowed out.

First were Miguel and his wife, Ana. They are from the easternmost state of Quintana Roo. Two weeks earlier they had left their three daughters with Ana's parents as they began their journey to Los Angeles. Miguel and Ana are in their late thirties, and in their hometown, Ana could not find a job and Miguel worked as a welder on construction sites, which was irregular. When he could find work, he earned ten to twelve dollars per day. Neither Miguel nor Ana had made it past the sixth grade. Their options were few. Ana did not want to talk to me, and Miguel bowed his head as he told his story.

"It was the hardest decision we had to make, to leave our young daughters and come to America. But we did it for them, because we cannot provide them with even the basics with the money I earn in Mexico."[14] The trip from Quintana Roo to Altar in northern Mexico was easy enough. In Altar Miguel and his wife met up with their coyote, paid one thousand dollars up front, and were told the trip would take two days. They would reach Phoenix and then be flown to Los Angeles. From Altar, Miguel and Ana were jammed into a small van along with fifteen others and driven to the northernmost town in Mexico before the U.S. border. From there they transferred into the back of a pickup truck and began the treacherous journey to Phoenix.

After driving for one hour, the truck dropped them off in the desert. It was the middle of the day and extremely hot. Miguel, Ana, and their group began walking. Some hours later they were accosted by a group of bandits who demanded money. Miguel wondered how anyone could have found them out in the middle of nowhere. When no one in the group actually had any money to give, the bandits decided to strip and cavity search every member of the group. Humiliating as this was, it was nothing compared to the forced naked march the bandits then sent the group on in retaliation for the lack of money. Ana cried the whole way. Some hours later their clothes were returned to them. The walking continued for days, and the coyote thought they were close to Tucson when they were apprehended by CBP. The group spent four hours in a Tucson jail before they were processed and then dropped off at the border. Miguel says they were given no food or water in that time. He and Ana were waiting in the Grupo Beta office for a bus to go back home to be with their daughters. While they had lost more money than they could earn in three years, the humiliation was too great to attempt the crossing again. Miguel was barely audible as he finished telling his story. His face and shoulders crumpled into uncontrollable, heaving sobs.

Mario was sitting alongside Miguel in the Grupo Beta office and watching the game show, occasionally exclaiming something in English. He did not want to talk, but he wanted advice. Mario seemed in deep shock. As his story spilled out, it was clear that he was one of those to get caught up in the dragnet without due process. Mario said he had lived in California for fifteen years and was married to a U.S. citizen.[15] His paperwork was in process, and he had gone to Phoenix for a routine immigration appointment. As he tells it, he was all but a green-card holder. Because he spoke little English, Mario seemed suspicious to the immigration officials who handed him over to Border Patrol. Mario said he was not allowed to make a phone call to his wife or a lawyer. He had his paperwork taken from him and was summarily put on a bus and sent back to Mexico. Mario was waiting for his cell phone battery to charge so he could call his wife in California. Luckily, she had copies of all the immigration paperwork that Mario said proved his right to be in the United States legally.

One of the commonly held myths about the U.S. immigration system is that marriage to a U.S. citizen means an immigrant is home-free. For many, this couldn't be further from the truth. While the wait to be granted a green card in some immigrant-dense cities is five years, even having a green card these days does not guarantee much.[16] Nearly 40 percent of families in California are of mixed status, 20 percent in New York City, and 10 percent nationwide.[17] A mixed-status family is one where one parent is a U.S. citizen, the other is a green-card or visa holder, and the children are citizens because they were born in the United States.

Sadly, especially in the aftermath of 9/11, families are increasingly torn apart as immigration laws are used to supposedly root out terrorists. In the case of the Mexican border, Mario is a prime example of being trapped in the system. Mario should have insisted on his right to see an immigration judge, but unfortunately no one told Mario about his rights. Because he accepted a "voluntary return" (he says he was given no other option), his green-card application is technically void. To leave the country with a pending change-of-status application without prior permission from U.S. Citizenship and Immigration Services (USCIS), called "advance parole," nullifies any pending application because this act is considered an abandonment of the claim to change status.[18] Mario's case for reentry and his dream of returning to his wife, his home, and his job in California had just got a whole lot harder to win.

Next to tell his story in the dusty heat of the Grupo Beta office was fifteen-year-old José. His callused hands and tired eyes made him seem much older. José's voice was barely audible as he began his tale. Having left his home in Mexico City with his father, leaving behind three younger sisters and his mother, José and his father were headed to New York to stay with a relative. "I was following my dream to earn enough money so my family would not be poor. I only wanted to go to work; if I could earn that money here in Mexico, I would not want to go to the U.S."[19] This relative had promised that both could find work in construction making what he made—up to $150 per day. With their combined incomes, José and his father could earn in New York in one day what it would take one of them a whole month to earn in Mexico City. After completing much the same route as the other deportees (Altar to Sasabé, then walking for days to cross the border and finally reach Phoenix), José, his father, and their group arrived in Arizona's capital city four days later.

They were the smart ones. Having already been caught and deported three times in the previous two weeks, José and his father had sought out a guide that they would pay only on arrival in Phoenix. However, the initial relief and joy at arriving in Phoenix was quickly forgotten when the group realized they had been sold by their coyote to four men who proceeded to hold them hostage for four days. Each person had to have fifteen hundred dollars wired via Western Union to the account of the men who held them. They were threatened each day at gunpoint; if the money did not arrive soon, they would be taken and dumped in the desert where they would surely die. Or worse, they would just be shot. José and his father had their relative wire the money, but still they were not allowed to go. After four days of this torture, the Phoenix riot police arrived and arrested everyone. It took authorities three days to figure out that José and his father were not the kidnappers. While they were in custody, they were fed only one burrito per day at lunchtime. "When we asked for water," José said, "immigration officers told us we were in the country illegally and did not have the right to ask for anything."[20]

José was lucky to be captured with his father, because the consequences for unaccompanied minors are steep. In 2004, the number of undocumented minors apprehended at ports of entry was 6,478, up almost 17 percent over the previous year.[21] The U.S. government does not simply fingerprint and drop off at a border gate a person who is under eighteen. Instead, the minor gets placed in a children's jail. Juvenile immigrant jails dot the southwest with an average yearly population of five thousand.[22] The old INS came under much criticism for its treatment of minors because of its multiple and conflicting roles as jailer, guardian, and ultimately judge. In 2002, Congress passed the Homeland Security Act, which created the Office of Refugee Resettlement (ORR) within the Department of Health and Human Services, transferring all basic care and custody away from the INS. On any given day, ORR is responsible for five hundred to eight hundred minors.[23] The rest are still subject to DHS guardianship despite the Homeland Security Act.

While conditions have greatly improved for the nation's detained children since ORR took over from the INS, children's advocates say they are still not good enough. In the Globe Jail in Phoenix, children are put into solitary confinement for twenty-four hours on arrival, a process that children's advocates say causes great trauma. Jailers reportedly use solitary confinement on a regular basis with the youth population. The Florence Project, a nonprofit organization that provides legal advice and counsel to detained minors in Phoenix, says the children it works with in the Globe facility experience weight loss, sleeplessness, anxiety attacks, and mental breakdowns.

Anti-immigration critics say the government is being too easy on the children, providing a summer camp–like environment for the detained. These critics also decry ORR's handing over of undocumented minors to undocumented relatives who are in the U.S.[24] Victoria López, Executive Director of the Florence Project, counters that the treatment of minors is far from idyllic and charges that authorities use children as bait to catch their undocumented relatives. "Currently the Bureau of Immigration & Customs Enforcement (BICE)[25] will release a child to an undocumented family member but will issue a Notice to Appear which ensures that the family member who came forward for the child will also be placed in removal proceedings."[26] This doesn't give parents or relatives much of an option.

In the course of Maria's years in East Harlem, she has had three more children. It is a struggle to pay the rent and raise her youngest American-born children. In 2001 Maria decided to bring her oldest child from Mexico to New York to help her with childcare; her seventeen-year-old daughter Lupita would be a free and trustworthy babysitter. So Maria paid a coyote fifteen hundred dollars to get Lupita from Tlapa to New York. "I am not a bad mother," Maria told me. "Of course I know there are many risks in sending my young daughter across the desert all by herself, but what choice do I have? I cannot go and pick her up myself."[27] Maria is like tens of thousands of other desperate and impoverished parents who are forced by circumstances to gamble with their children's lives. Lupita had a very tough time making the crossing. Maria fears she was sexually abused, being young and pretty and at the mercy of the coyote. But she made it. Maria did not know that if her daughter were caught, Lupita would be put in jail because she is a minor.

In 2003 Maria paid a coyote to bring her second child, Juan, to New York, and then in 2004, on the eve of the presidential election, Maria went the coyote route again for her final child, thirteen-year-old Javier. Javier's trip proved the most grueling of all of Maria's family. This slight child, who looks no more than six years old, spent three weeks in transit. Maria says that in the rare moments that Javier speaks, he has told stories of dead bodies, days without food or water, and of being passed from coyote to coyote. One year after his arrival, Javier still barely utters a word.

In March 2005 the Bush administration launched the second phase of its controversial Arizona Border Control Initiative (ABC). A multiagency program, the ABC initiative has formalized much of Arizona's border policy. In fiscal year 2004, the Department of Homeland Security claimed that the initiative was a resounding success with increased numbers of border patrol officers reporting for duty, increased use of technology such as the introduction of Black Hawk helicopters, and increased prosecutions at the state and federal levels.[28]

One of the ABC initiative's biggest claims is that it is successfully going after the smugglers and thug rings that make the crossing both possible and dangerous for so many migrants. However, immigrant advocate and Tucson public defender Isabel García compares the pursuit of smugglers to the way the War on Drugs is being fought—where the government goes after the low-level user and street pusher and does not address the bigger, systemic cause of the drug industry. "We don't have what in Mexico they call the '*autor intelectual*'—the intellectual author—the real people behind this who are making all the money."[29] To go after the coyotes does not mean the flow of crossers will lessen, it just means that the crossing may get more dangerous as people attempt to cross without a guide. As critics of the War on Drugs claim that the "war" should be a matter of public health rather than law enforcement, similarly García believes protection of the borders cannot be accomplished through law enforcement, but only by due consideration of economic and labor issues.

The Tohono O'odham Nation, whose communities straddle the Arizona-Mexico border, has fallen into the middle of the U.S. crackdown on undocumented border crossers. With the 1853 Gadsden Purchase, this indigenous nation was split between two countries. Since then, visiting family, attending ceremonies, or conducting business has been difficult for the peoples of this sovereign nation. All such actions require providing birth certificates or visas, or having their sacred bundles searched as they cross back and forth. In the recent years of increased Border Patrol presence and increased use of technology, life for the Tohono O'odham Nation has become like living in a military zone: unmanned drones fly overhead constantly, sometimes crashing on Indian land; armed agents regularly stop residents asking for proof of status; and with the twenty-four-hour floodlights, many nocturnal creatures have left the area, changing the ecosystem dramatically.[30]

The Arizona Border Control Initiative proposes a Mexico-Arizona border fencing project that will stretch 330 miles across the entire Arizona-Mexico border. This wall is slated to cross seventy-four miles of Tohono O'odham lands, which will be viewed twenty-four hours a day by 145 surveillance cameras. The fence, which has been touted by Border Patrol as America's Berlin Wall, will consist of two walls. The first will be made of steel rails and steel sheets and will be constantly lit by four hundred stadiumlike floodlights. The secondary fence will be topped with razor coils. Between the two fences will be a paved road patrolled by Homeland Security armed forces.

It must be noted that many nonindigenous residents in the border areas have called for tough border policies because they say that crossing migrants do much damage to their property and are dangerous. The Tohono O'odham people, on the other hand, also experience a large amount of crossers but consider militarizing border policies their single greatest problem. José García, Lt. Governor of the Tohono O'odham Nation, has said that outside of border patrol, the Nation's loss of land due to "encroachment by squatters, ranchers, mining companies and cattle companies"[31] is another main concern—not undocumented immigrant traffic.

In late November 2005, the day after President Bush gave a landmark speech on immigration that outlined increases to the budget for building the wall, hiring more Border Patrol officers, and increasing technology to assist officers, a court case began in which a Tohono O'odham family accused CBP of running over and killing their nineteen-year-old son, Bennett Patricio. Angelita Reino Ramon, mother of Patricio, told me the day the trial began that the Border Patrol agents were "out of control" and that she had never experienced any ill from the undocumented crossers. "It is the Border Patrol that make our lives hell, not the migrants who cross."[32]

Back in the Nogales office of Grupo Beta, José said it was a great relief to have his first real meal in nearly two weeks. He and his father were headed home after this third unsuccessful crossing attempt. Washing wealthy people's cars and windows in Mexico City for ten dollars per day would have to suffice until they could repay their debts for the attempted crossing. José had no idea how his family would survive. He predicted his sisters would have to leave middle school and become housemaids, which is exactly what he wanted to prevent by going to the U.S. to work. José told me that he just wants his sisters to stay in middle school and maybe even finish high school, something no one in his family has yet done.[33]

In Mexico, it is mandatory to attend school until only the sixth grade. Studying beyond the sixth grade is relatively expensive, and the majority of aspiring families simply cannot afford it. The cheapest high school fees range from $50 to $100 per month. Add to that the cost of uniforms and textbooks, and a basic high school education becomes a luxury. A working-poor family in rural Mexico earns $200 to $300 per month, the combined income of both parents and possibly even one of the children. Rent takes more than half that sum, and the rest is spent on food, transportation, medical expenses, and schooling for the younger children. Doing the math makes it clear why families would be willing to lose a father, brother, or mother for a few years *el norte* where the earning potential is just so much greater.

Recent analysis of census figures by the Urban Institute, a nonpartisan research institute, reports that there are 9.3 million undocumented workers in the U.S.,[34] though other estimates range as high as 12 million.[35] Two-thirds of that number are said to actively participate in the labor force. The Pew Hispanic Center estimates that more than 1 million undocumented immigrants are employed in manufacturing, 1 million in services, 600,000 in construction, and 700,000 work in restaurants.[36] Perhaps one of the largest single industries that relies on undocumented labor is the nation's poultry factories where an estimated 125,000 workers do not have legal working status. The Pew Center also estimates that the approximately 1.4 million undocumented workers in agriculture account for about 58 percent of that industry's workforce.[37]

Wages vary for people with no working papers. In New York City, the going rate for restaurant workers is about $4 per hour,[38] while nannies and house cleaners may get a dollar or two more per hour. Construction workers can make as much as $12 per hour,[39] though in most cities the rates are around $5 to $8 per hour.[40] Work in construction is irregular, often requiring a long wait on a street corner for a prospective employer to drive past and solicit workers. Poultry workers in the middle of the country on average make $7.60 per hour, a rate that has dropped over the last few years.[41] Tomato pickers in Florida earn a paltry 40¢ to 50¢ per bucket, which at 125 buckets per twelve-hour workday equals about $7.50 per hour.[42] But when one compares all these wages to what one can earn in Mexico or Central America—in Mexico the Army pays the equivalent of $2 per hour while Wal-Mart pays approximately $1.20 per hour[43]—the lure of working in the United States becomes clearer.

In 2003 the number of U.S. residents of Mexican origin was 25.3 million, or 9 percent of the U.S. population.[44] The majority resides close to Mexico in the border states of California, Arizona, and Texas. Only 12 percent of these 25.3 million hold professional or managerial positions.[45] California and Texas (along with Florida) are also projected to account for nearly one-half (46 percent) of total U.S. population growth between 2000 and 2030.[46] Mexico accounts for the largest source of legal migration to the U.S. each year, but given the difficulties of attaining a U.S. visa, Mexicans also account for half of the population of undocumented immigrants in the U.S.[47]

Maria says that in all her years of being a kitchen hand in New York City, she has never once worked with an American. "Ecuadorians, Bangladeshis,

Egyptians, Guatemalans, and plenty of my people—Mexicans—but never an American."[48] Because the working conditions are so poor and the pay is well below minimum wage, the turnover of kitchen hands is high. Maria is certain that she is not taking a job away from an American, because she says that no American would ever do the work she does for the corresponding pay. With only a second-grade education, Maria has a sophisticated understanding of the U.S. economy. "If they were to send us all back to our countries, *this* country would collapse. Who would cook and clean for them? Who would provide them with cheap food, and who would break their backs under the hot sun in the farms and fields around the country? They need us, because no one else will do this awful and dirty work for so little money."[49]

U.S. elected officials on both sides of the aisle agree with Maria. The need for cheap labor, however, is the U.S.'s big elephant in the room. Many will talk, in hushed voices and behind closed doors, about how Americans would never work under the conditions that undocumented immigrants do for the money they are paid. However, there is little political will to either better regulate the industries that use this labor or legalize the passage of immigrant workers to the U.S.

While certain industries use more undocumented labor than others, corporate America benefits greatly from this cheap labor pool that crosses the border each day. The miserly wages and the money saved because no benefits are paid, as well as undocumented workers' unwillingness to agitate for improvements because of their precarious immigration status ensure that undocumented labor is overwhelmingly subservient and cheap. This low-cost workforce further benefits the corporate bottom line because it maintains a steady downward pressure on wages in general.

In early 2005 Republican Senator Larry Craig authored a bill called Agricultural, Job Opportunities, Benefits and Security Act (AGJOBS) that would grant three-year temporary working visas to agriculture workers. Senator Craig said he was pushing for this legislation because the American agriculture industry needed a consistent labor source. In response to my question as to why there weren't American citizens lining up for these jobs when there are such high national levels of unemployment, Craig was blunt: "It's hard work. It's dirty work . . . in the 100-degree heat, in the mud and the dirt, lifting, hoeing, pushing, working. It's the reality of the work itself," he concluded, that made it too undesirable for American workers.[50] In fact, when I suggested to Craig that it may instead be an issue of extremely low pay and that AGJOBS might just serve to legalize an underclass, his response belied his GOP roots: "It's an entry-level job. And to criticize it would mean that you would deny the right of anybody [to] access. People without skills don't start midway up the rung. They work their way up."[51] The political reality is that AGJOBS has little chance of becoming law.

Almost every time President Bush talks about immigration he proposes a guest-worker program. While the Right is quick to condemn this proposal, aligning it with amnesty (the president is just as quick to assure his critics it is not amnesty), we have barely heard the voices of the immigrant advocates who are also highly critical of such proposals. Although the president has never given much more detail than a sound bite on what his ideas are for guest workers, it is clear that migrants would be legally channeled into very low-paying work for a set period of time and then sent home. There is occasional talk of a path to citizenship, which seems a just reward for such critical work to the U.S. economy. As such, any moves by President Bush to pass a guest-worker proposal would likely be opposed by both the Left and the Right, winning support only from the business lobby that depends on such labor.

Tucson public defender Isabel García sees today's problems at the border as steeped in the history of what she calls a "violently imposed border."[52] García says it was cleaned up when the 1848 Treaty of Guadalupe Hidalgo ceded Texas to the U.S. and the Gadsden Purchase handed over southern New Mexico and Arizona to the U.S. for a mere 10 million dollars. Although the border has come to be clearly defined in the U.S. psyche, in Mexico it remains much more fluid.

I talked to many migrants in both Mexico and the U.S.—those who had crossed or were about to cross the border—and without exception each person did *not* understand that doing so without a visa is considered illegal in the U.S. and that the U.S. government would treat them as criminals if they are caught. In their minds, they are simply coming to work. Migratory patterns in Mexico reflect rural populations migrating to urban areas in massive numbers as work dries up due to an intensification of corporate globalization. The North American Free Trade Agreement (NAFTA), enacted in 1994, corresponds almost directly with the economic crisis in Mexico that forced so many off their land.

The agriculture provisions of NAFTA meant that Mexican farmers had to compete with the more highly productive, highly mechanized, and highly subsidized farms of North America. Almost immediately, imports of Mexican staples like corn, beans, and barley flooded into the country at prices that few Mexican farmers could compete with. Since NAFTA was implemented, the price of corn dropped nearly 50 percent while the price of tortillas—a staple of the daily Mexican diet—*increased* 40 percent.[53] Another particularly illuminating statistic, which appears in a Carnegie Endowment for International Peace study, shows that 1.3 million farmers have abandoned their plots as a direct result of the inundation of NAFTA-driven imports.[54]

NAFTA has not only failed to benefit the majority of Mexicans economically, but, in fact, plunged the country more deeply into poverty. NAFTA was implemented under a Democratic president, and it set the stage for expanding the U.S. economy by entering into unequal trade relations with poor countries. Under the successive Bush administrations, these free-trade policies have been the centerpiece of economic policy. The rhetoric of leaders pushing the trade agreements always aims to convince constituents of affected countries and the American people that the treaties will be beneficial for all involved.

In a 2005 question-answer session, President Bush said that the solution to the growing volume of people trying to cross the border seeking work is for "Mexico to grow a middle class." He continued:

> That's why I'm such a big believer in NAFTA. It's in our interest that wealth be spread out through the hemisphere—the best way to spread wealth is through trade—so that Mexico can grow and become a vibrant place, so people are more likely to be able to find a job closer to home. But the reality is if you make fifty cents in the interior of Mexico and five dollars in Texas, you're going to do five dollars, if you can make it.[55]

In the decade since NAFTA was implemented, Mexico has become the U.S.'s second-largest trading partner, after Canada.[56] In 2004, the U.S. and Mexico traded $266.6 billion worth of goods, a 300 percent increase since 1994. Yet Mexico still ranks as one of the world's poor nations. NAFTA created only half a million jobs in Mexico, the vast majority of which are at low-wage assembly factories, or *maquiladoras*, that U.S. multinational corporations set up in the border regions. And with the extension of free-trade agreements around the world, the last few years have seen a dramatic flight of these factories to even cheaper labor sources, leaving Mexico with a rising unemployment rate.[57]

Writers such as David Bacon and John Ross have chronicled the devastating impact that NAFTA has had on Mexican workers and its failures to lift most Mexicans out of poverty.[58] In 1996, two years after NAFTA's birth, Ross reported that 2.4 million jobs had been lost in Mexico.[59] Some Mexican workers who were employed in maquilas on the border were laid off when the U.S. economy suffered a recession in 2001. The Mexican government estimates that 400,000 border jobs were lost.[60] But many workers who obtained jobs in the NAFTA economy in Mexico saw their real wages decline as there were virtually no labor-protection regulations imposed on employers. According to David Bacon,

> a study by the Center for Reflection, Education and Action, a religious research group, found that at the minimum wage, it took a maquiladora worker in Juarez almost an hour to earn enough money to buy a kilo (2.2 pounds) of rice, and a worker in Tijuana an hour and a half. And yet another study by the Economics Faculty of the National Autonomous University in Mexico City says Mexican wages have lost 81 percent of their buying power in the last two decades.[61]

NAFTA has helped boost the Mexican economy slightly—but the riches have flowed to the upper classes. In the ten years since NAFTA began, the World Bank said that the divide between rich and poor in Mexico has become one of the greatest in the world outside of Africa.[62]

When the U.S. government was attempting to sell NAFTA to the American public, it proclaimed that NAFTA would solve Mexico's poverty problem and would therefore end the influx of immigrants to the U.S. Yet as Tucson public defender Isabel García points out, at the very same time that these claims were being made, the government was building walls along the border for the first time in history. "If they truly expected for the issue of immigration to be solved, why in the world would they need these steel walls?" she asks.[63]

The steel walls that were built on the border were part of a series of operations. One was Operation Gatekeeper, which concentrated resources in the western area of the San Diego border, driving much of the undocumented traffic toward the more isolated eastern area near Otay Mesa where border crossers are more easily detected and caught. In Texas, Operation Hold the Line focused on the El Paso border, while Operation Safeguard assigned more agents to the Tucson sector and constructed a new wall near Nogales.

The year after NAFTA was implemented, Mexico experienced a dire economic crisis. The numbers of Mexicans attempting illegal entry into the U.S. during 1995–96 soared, and for the first time, Arizona began to experience the effects of the increased traffic due to Operation Gatekeeper and the tightening of the San Diego border region. "What they fail to say is that since the beginning of this southern border strategy, *their* policy has really created havoc in our borderlands. Because they have funneled 52 percent of all the traffic here, there are extreme problems for Arizona," García complains. "Those who live in the border region realize that we share everything, that while there may be a wall or a fence that separates us, we share everything. We share land and air, we share language and history and culture, and we share economic dependence."[64]

Despite increased patrolling activities, the number of immigrants attempting to cross did not fall—they were simply funneled into new areas. In June 1996, the Border Patrol union publicly alleged that Border Patrol supervisors were improperly manipulating data to create the false impression that Operation Gatekeeper had successfully deterred illegal crossings at the San Diego border. In addition, union members alleged that they were being instructed not to arrest undocumented crossers so that the level of apprehensions would appear to have dropped. With the implication that fewer migrants were coming across the border illegally, Operation Gatekeeper would seem to be a resounding success.[65]

As the economic realities of NAFTA forced hundreds of thousands off their land, massive internal migration occurred across Mexico. Many sought jobs in tourist destinations and big cities, but there was not enough adequately paying work. The logical next step was to move north of the border. U.S. Border Patrol admits that 99 percent of those attempting to cross are simply seeking work.[66] It is the 1 percent who are smuggling people or drugs or weapons that justifies the intense policing of the border. Kat Rodriguez of the human rights organization Derechos Humanos in Tucson calls this policy shortsighted and politically convenient: "Militarizing certain parts of the border is pointless because it does not address the root cause of why people migrate. It is simply like squeezing a hose in certain parts, which ensures that other areas bulge."[67]

From Nogales, many of the recently deported who have just shared their stories will head sixty miles southwest to the tiny town of Altar. This is one of the bulge areas. The main plaza in Altar is like that of most other small Mexican towns. It includes a church and multiple vendors selling food and cheap plastic goods. But this plaza is also the daily meeting place of hundreds of men, women, and children who aspire to walk into the United States and find work and a new temporary life.

People begin waiting in the plaza as early as six in the morning. Coyotes designate a meeting place from where the journey will begin. In the cool morning, clusters of mostly men huddle together sipping hot coffee, praying, or simply staring vacantly ahead. Most carry one small bag and a gallon of water, a woefully inadequate amount for the long desert hike they are about to undertake. Many are well dressed. Everyone wants to look their best when they arrive in the United States. Tragically, most first-time crossers have little idea what they are in for. Some women are decked out in high-heeled shoes and fancy tops. They actually believe that they will be walking for only half an hour. The desert is littered with women's shoes, discarded along the way because they are completely unsuitable for the journey.

Sadly, bodies are also found decomposing in the desert, often women or children, left to die because they could not keep up with the group. No one knows exactly how many migrants have lost their lives attempting the crossing. Most nongovernmental organizations (NGOs) concur that since 1995, with the implementation of the various operations, about 2,600 people have died on their journey across the border.[68] The majority of the deaths have occurred in the ruthless heat of the summer months. In 2004 in the state of Arizona, U.S. Border Patrol reported 141 deaths. The Mexican consulate puts the figure at two hundred.[69] Humanitarian groups along the border put the number higher still. In July 2005, as temperatures soared, seventy-nine deaths were recorded in Arizona alone.[70] According to government figures for the 2005 fiscal year, the total number of deaths across the entire border region was a staggering 473.[71] This is the highest figure since Border Patrol began recording the numbers in 1999. Children, women, and men perished from heat exhaustion, drowning, vehicle accidents, and exposure to the cold.[72]

One might imagine that such a high number of deaths on the border would spark a national scandal or would, at the very least, be newsworthy. But as a LexisNexis search of the country's leading news sources reveals, the border deaths during 2004 were of minimal interest to the media. The *New York Times* saw fit to report on border deaths twelve times in 2004, and the *San Francisco Chronicle* notched up ten articles. The *Washington Post* didn't think the deaths mattered much since its reporting comprised mostly one- to two-line descriptions under the "National News in Brief" section. No analysis, no context, no investigations.

Since the government has acknowledged that the majority of crossers are coming to the U.S. to work and, moreover, putting their lives in grave danger by attempting the crossing,[73] a lukewarm humanitarian gesture has emerged as part of increased funding to the Arizona sector of border patrol. Out of the 534 border patrol agents who will be assigned to police the Arizona border for 2005–2006, the job description of twenty-six officers includes "search and rescue efforts to save the lives of migrants in peril."[74] Border activists question why so many resources are put toward driving immigrants into dangerous situations from which they then need to be rescued.

As one of the lucky ones who made it through the deadly border crossing and is well settled in New York City, Maria wishes on a daily basis that she could have found these work opportunities back in Mexico. "I miss my hometown so much," Maria sighs. She often contemplates returning to look after her parents who are still in Tlapa. They are very old and sick and have no one to take care of them in their one-bedroom cinder-block home outside of town, far from most basic services. One night her parents' house was broken into, and her father was severely beaten. Maria is helpless to do anything from New York. "If I went back to Mexico to help my poor parents, I would have to do that awful desert crossing again just to come back to my home here in East Harlem where I have my six children to care for."[75]

Maria knows many families who have lost loved ones during the crossing. "I feel so very sorry for those poor people who made the trip from other Central American countries," Maria has told me many times. For them the journey is much longer and more dangerous, depending on how many borders they have to cross. Maria has also worked with men from China and other Asian countries who had been packed into the bottom of large cargo ships, where they lay hidden without food or water for a week or more while they made the trip to Mexico. From there, many were too ill to complete the coyote border crossing.[76]

Catholic-Run Community Center, Altar, Mexico

In Altar there is plenty of evidence of a small-scale, bustling industry that services, and profits from, the border crossers. Local hotels meet every incoming bus from *both* directions, each full of either the recently deported or the fresh faced about to try their luck. They take advantage of workers trying to save their money by cramming many people into one room and charging inflated prices. Small restaurants do a thriving business and even a simple loaf of bread is more expensive in Altar than in neighboring Mexican cities. In the middle of this exploitative environment is a Catholic-run guest house that provides free accommodations, meals, showers, and advice to anyone. The center's director, Francisco Javier García Arten, used to be the mayor of Altar and now hosts a daily news program on a local radio station. He also facilitates regular discussions between migrants who are using the center's facilities and Americans who are visiting to learn about the realities of the border.

During one such encounter, a group of fifteen white, middle-aged Pentecostals from Washington State ate dinner with four migrants who had just been deported to Nogales and had made their way to Altar. The Tucson-based organization Border Links had arranged the Pentecostals' tour, and only one of them spoke Spanish. A young Mexican-American employee of Border Links, Hector Suarez, translated, both culturally and linguistically. As one of the deportees said grace before dinner, there was an audible gasp when the translator relayed that the deportee was giving thanks for his first meal in one week and asking that his children, all four of them, would also find food to eat somewhere.

After dinner, as the group arranged the chairs in a circle and introductions were formally made, there were many questions. The Pentecostals wanted to know why people would risk their lives to come to the United States. What ensued was a heart-wrenching discussion in which the four indigenous men described the poverty that pushed them to leave their families and make the risky crossing. On the part of the indigenous men, yet again, there was a complete lack of understanding as to why they are considered criminals for simply trying to find work. "Aren't we helping America by working for all of you?" one dejected man asked the Pentecostals.

Historians note that for the past hundred years the U.S. government has actively encouraged undocumented migration. "Why?" asked public defender and immigration activist Isabel García, as she went on to answer her own question. "Because it's good for our country, good for the economy. Multinational corporations run immigration policy in this country, always have, and they are motivated mainly out of economic interest."[77] Yet García also points out that everyone has benefited from illegal migration. "We've been able to raise families on cheap vegetables, cheap clothes, cheap services. In other words, there is a great demand for immigrants. Not only by large corporations, but we have all benefited. All of us. Our economy has been sustained in large part due to the undocumented labor force in this country."[78] *Washington Post* reporter Renee Downing sums it up perfectly: "If, by magic . . . the border were sealed and the estimated eleven million people living in this country illegally were deported—America would most likely be unrecognizable, and not in a good way. Crops would rot in the fields, bathrooms would stay dirty, mothers of small children would be stuck at home. America is addicted to cheap labor, and withdrawal is beyond contemplation."[79]

In the Catholic guest house in Altar, the Americans were riveted as they listened to the recently deported migrants. Each man's story was at once devastating and fantastic. For the Pentecostals the stories helped to complete the picture of how NAFTA has impacted both urban and rural Mexico. Maybe the men seemed like characters in a movie—so real that they became unreal.

One man tried four times to cross and was caught and deported each time. Another man walked for four days, and when he did not reach Phoenix, he told his coyote that he was giving himself up to Border Patrol and going back home to his family in Chiapas. He was so close, yet couldn't take another minute of walking. Three other members of his group also gave up, to the anger of the coyote, who, after promising a two-night journey, would now be three people short of the fifteen-hundred-dollar fee per person. Yet another man had been attacked by bandits and then fleeced by a hotel owner in Phoenix. All were there in the Catholic shelter divulging the details of their horrific experiences in monotone voices while they stared vacantly at the floor.

U.S. Customs and Border Patrol (CBP) will receive a budget increase of nearly 4.8 percent, one of the highest in government, under President Bush's proposed 2006 budget. The budget for CBP totals $6.7 billion, which CBP clearly states will be overwhelmingly used to hire more patrol agents and invest in technology to secure the borders against terrorism.[80] Immigrant rights activists like Kat Rodriguez firmly believe that government actions on the border amount to a war against poor, brown-skinned immigrants, who under current immigration laws will never secure a legal visa to enter the U.S. and work. Activists say this CBP offensive has militarized the border. CBP's own chief commissioner, Robert C. Bonner, reiterates the military analogy when he speaks of his agency's work and refers to Border Patrol agents as "boots on the ground,"[81] a highly warlike term used by the Department of Defense to refer to soldiers deployed to action.

Many have accused U.S. Border Patrol of fighting a war on the border against an overwhelmingly unarmed and nonthreatening people. CBP agents are armed at all times with pistols loaded with live ammunition, known as "lethal deterrent." Agents on duty also use collapsible riot-style steel batons and pepper spray.

There are also weapons, lethal and nonlethal, that are available for agent use. One of the agents' more controversial weapons of choice, which has met with outrage from the Mexican government, is the chili-powder gun. This weapon has been in use since 2001, and CBP says it is a nonlethal alternative to a firearm when migrants get violent and resort to, say, "throwing rocks."[82] This is not your traditional pepper spray, however. Fired from a paintball style–gun, a plastic ball filled with a chili powder is released. The powder severely irritates the eyes, nose, and skin, but has also been reported to cause welts and other serious injuries.[83]

In addition, one of the many unofficial border patrol Web sites (usually run by agents or ex-agents) describes how agents "have available for check out shotguns and M-16's or other automatic weapons."[84] And as if that weren't enough, Border Patrol also has special units, like the REACT unit in San Diego, which are more highly armed. Agents assigned to REACT use such weapons as the Colt M-4A1 5.56mm carbines, specially modified Remington 870 shotguns, Beretta pistols, and sniper rifles, among other weapons.[85]

Anti-immigrationists, who promote and enact armed citizen patrols of the border, say that government spending on the border is nowhere near enough. Immigrant rights activists, on the other hand, say that the government is cracking down on the wrong people and spending way too many taxpayer dollars on militarizing the border. The Right has mobilized itself to carry out actions such as armed citizen patrols, while immigrants' rights activists try to provide desperately needed humanitarian aid to the thousands who cross each week. As border crossers continue to die on their northward journeys, immigrants' rights activists point out that the government simply pumps money into new technology to patrol the border, making the workers' journey more dangerous, while it refuses to address the root causes of immigration.

San Diego, California

On a sunny San Diego morning in April, Officer Thomas Jiménez, a six-year veteran of Border Patrol, began a routine surveillance of the westernmost border areas. His eagle eye always searches for hints of human movement. He has been through intense training. Officer Jiménez has done solo night duty in the Arizona desert where he has apprehended groups as large as sixty people trying to cross into the U.S. while his nearest backup was half an hour away. This kind of situation, which he acknowledges is not all that common, is why Officer Jiménez says Border Patrol needs to be armed.[86]

U.S. Border Patrol agents are trained in tracking human trails (Jiménez says with confidence that he can look at a footprint and tell how long ago it was made). They are also taught Spanish and tested every six months in proficiency, given extensive weapons training, and put through extreme physical fitness workouts. Border Patrol officers are rewarded with a starting salary of around $34,000.

Protecting the border (as most Border Patrol officers would describe their job) has given Officer Jiménez, the son of an immigrant Mexican family, a stable job and a secure future. As we drove the few miles back from the border to Patrol headquarters in San Diego, Jiménez pointed out his newly purchased cookie-cutter house in one of the recently developed housing sprawls that has sprung up outside San Diego. Many families are moving closer to the border and into these housing estates, Jiménez explained, "because it is now so much safer with the stepped-up border protection, while still being a short twenty-minute drive to downtown San Diego."[87]

In the days, weeks, and months after 9/11, legal border crossings from Canada and Mexico into the U.S. became bottlenecks where people were forced to wait hours as each vehicle and person was thoroughly checked. It soon became clear that the government needed to implement a system that did not cause a near shutdown at the borders. Motivated mainly by economic concerns over the impact on trade, then Director of the White House Office of Homeland Security Tom Ridge emphasized that the government was "working with Canada and Mexico to institute smart borders that will keep the terrorists out, while letting the flow of commerce in."[88] This so-called smart-border policy involved new kinds of collaboration between the United States and the Canadian and Mexican governments.

Francisco Arten from Altar describes the post- 9/11 national security focus as a "handy smoke screen for the Bush administration." He explains:

> Terrorists are highly funded and thorough in their planning. They would never risk sending their personnel through a highly militarized border. The nineteen hijackers did not come into the U.S. illegally—they all had visas. So why on earth would you fortify only the southern border, when your own government says the overwhelming majority who cross illegally are coming to the U.S. to work, and say it is in the interests of protecting the homeland from another terrorist attack? Are the American people that dumb that they believe they will be safer if thousands of foreign workers are rounded up like cattle and sent back? [89]

Dating back as early as 1850, U.S. employers saw the need to import foreign labor to work the cattle ranches and increase fruit production in the Southwest. In 1848 a large influx of Chinese laborers immigrated to the Pacific Coast, where they were employed in railroad building by Charles Crocker, who owned the Central Pacific Railroad. By 1867 there were 250,000 Chinese in California, the majority of them manual laborers. When Americans began to see the incoming Chinese workers as a threat to their jobs, Congress passed the Chinese Exclusion Act in 1882, restricting immigration to the U.S.

Mexican field workers began coming to the U.S. in the mid-1800s, immigrating to areas that had, until very recently, belonged to Mexico.

Working conditions were exploitative and salaries were extremely poor. Then, a century later, with the onset of World War II, the U.S. realized it desperately needed labor on the home front, and between 1942 and 1964 millions of Mexicans were brought in temporarily under the Bracero Program to work for U.S. growers and ranchers. This influx of Mexicans consisted of impoverished farmers who were promptly sent back to their abandoned fields in Mexico after they ensured that the U.S. was the most abundant agricultural center in the world. Bracero employers were infamous for their appalling treatment of Mexican workers.

U.S. Border Patrol was created in 1924, formally acknowledging for the first time that the U.S. had something to actively protect from its southern neighbor. The law stated that undocumented workers were fugitives. In the years following the introduction of Border Patrol, the notion of an "illegal alien" spread in society. Without a doubt, the prime targets of suspicion were Mexicans living in the U.S. In 1954 the INS conducted Operation Wetback, a heinous sweep through Mexican-American communities in which any Mexican deemed undocumented was arrested and deported. Over one million Mexicans, including U.S. citizens, legal permanent residents, and visa holders, were boxed up and shipped back en masse to Mexico. Isabel García says that with the post-9/11 budget increases for the border, the focus on detention and deportation of many more Mexicans smacks decidedly of Operation Wetback.

In an air-conditioned, white, unmarked SUV, Officer Jiménez drove me through the border areas where the construction of the controversial secondary fence had been begun and was then stalled due to environmental concerns. The purpose of the primary fence, a patchwork of corrugated iron sheets, is to stop vehicles from driving across, Jiménez pointed out. Because the other side of the primary fence faces Mexico, and because there is little cooperation from Mexican officials in policing the border, Jiménez said that most people simply put a ladder up to the fence and then jump it, hence he emphasized the need for this secondary fence on the U.S. side of the border. As we drove along the space between the fences, reminiscent of a no-man's-land, Border Patrol agents on small ATVs sped by. They looked like kids playing on dirt bikes, except they were uniformed and armed. Jiménez said that they were probably on the trail of some recently crossed migrants.

In 1996 the immigration reform bill mandated that a secondary fence be built along the San Diego border. The legislation considered decades-old environmental laws, which the building of the wall might violate, and accorded the power to waive certain laws "to the extent that the attorney general determines necessary to ensure expeditious construction of barriers and roads."[90] The fence would disturb, among other sensitive ecosystems, the Tijuana Estuary. The Sierra Club and five other groups filed suit to stop the fence. The complaint stated that the loss of the lands to the fence "in both ecological and political terms defies quantification."[91] It listed 370 species of migratory and native birds that use the Tijuana Estuary as an essential breeding, feeding, and nesting ground. The area is also home to six species on the brink of extinction, including the San Diego Fairy Shrimp and San Diego Button Celery. In 2003 the California Coastal Commission sided with environmentalists when it decided that the potential environmental damage far outweighed the needs of Border Patrol for a wall,[92] so the building of the wall was halted. In 2005 legislation called the REAL ID Act, the authors went one step further and decreed that not only shall environmental laws not exist in this zone, but as a direct affront to those who brought legal action the first time, no judicial oversight or review would be possible.[93] In other words, construction of the wall was a done deal. No lawsuits, no matter what. Adios Fairy Shrimp and Button Celery.

As the heat of the San Diego day intensified, Officer Jiménez's tour of the border also warmed up. He took pains to explain how much respect San Diego Border Patrol has for the environment: "We're trying to do everything to protect the environment, but when you look at national security and you look at the environment, well, you just have to determine which is more important."[94] All the while, the SUV's CB radio was abuzz with a possible sighting of people on the side of a hill. The ATV officers converged from all around, leaped off their vehicles, and began traversing the hillside. The CB radio voice announced that it was likely a group of six or seven. Officer Jiménez drove quickly to the site, and we stuck our heads out the window to spot the transgressors who were caught a few minutes later.

In 2000 Border Patrol made 1.6 million apprehensions. That's an average of more than 4,380 arrests *per day*. Every year since then, the number has steadily fallen to half that; in 2004 there were 800,000 apprehensions crossing into the United States via the Mexico land border.[95] More than half of the 2004 apprehensions came along the 261-mile Tucson sector of the border, where official figures say 491,771 undocumented entrants were arrested. Ten years ago the number of arrests in the Tucson sector was 139,473, but the numbers were much greater in the San Diego sector.[96] For fiscal year 2004, San Diego CBP apprehended just over 69,000 undocumented migrants.[97] Border Patrol in Tucson says this highlights their increased capacity to detect crossers and make arrests. Critics like Kat Rodriguez say this is the bulge effect in action.

With Operation Gatekeeper putting the squeeze on the San Diego sector, migrants have simply moved further east. The total number of crossers, Rodriguez says, has not decreased, with many reliable estimates showing the overall numbers in fact increasing. The Migration Policy Institute has documented that the population of undocumented immigrants "has been growing robustly during most of the period of 'concentrated border enforcement.'"[98] While no one has exact numbers on those trying to cross into the United States each year, most experts put it at well above one million people.

The five men and two women who the Border Patrol agents have just apprehended sat in single file with their heads bowed and looks of sheer disappointment on their faces. They were caked in dirt and sweat and looked exhausted. The immigrants were not far inside the U.S. border and did not have far to go to make it to a densely populated area when they were caught. "They underestimated the technological powers of border patrol," said Officer Jiménez. Aerial cameras probably spotted them. Border Patrol has used its increasing budget each year to invest in, among other things, ground sensors that send a signal each time they are triggered, massive stadium lights to illuminate border areas, ATVs for greater mobility, constant helicopter patrols, aerial cameras, and even low-flying robotic aircraft.

The increased funding for technology to patrol the borders has been sold to the American people with the guarantee that it will protect against terrorism. The largest DHS contract currently in the works is called the American Shield Initiative (ASI), worth a staggering $2.5 billion. Border Patrol says ASI will "significantly strengthen our ability to detect, intercept, and secure the borders against illegal aliens, potential terrorists, weapons of mass destruction, illegal drugs and other contraband."[99] The contract is sweeping in the services and products it requests. From unmanned drone planes to databases that store the massive numbers of fingerprints currently being compiled, ASI is justified under the guise of protecting the nation against terrorism.

In December 2005 a government audit exposed the uselessness of one of the highly touted devices employed at the border: ground sensors. Audit investigators studied every single alert generated by embedded ground sensors during certain periods of April and May 2005. They found that a sensor was triggered every forty-four seconds and that *less than 1 percent* of the alerts led to arrests.[100] Yet despite its own findings, the government is determined to push ahead with this kind of technology for the border and is expected to award the $2.5 billion ASI contract at some point in 2006.

As Officer Jiménez juggled two cell phones and the CB radio, he proudly rattled off statistics that he said illustrate the success of Operation Gatekeeper.

The numbers of apprehensions in San Diego have dropped dramatically, he told me. This fact belies details that show that numbers have dramatically increased in other areas along the border because fewer people are attempting to cross in San Diego. The success of Operation Gatekeeper has also led those trying to cross the border to have to do so under much more dangerous conditions. Moreover, immigrant advocates are extremely focused on the fact that the government is not doing anything to address poverty and unemployment, two of the root motivations for the massive exodus north.

Jiménez veered a little off message when I asked him if one solution to the problem that consumes 99 percent of CBP resources would be to create jobs that pay a living wage in Mexico, to which he responded, "We don't study what causes migration." His job is simply to apprehend lawbreakers. Immigrant advocates charge that the Bush administration, through an expansion of free-trade policies, has sought to exploit every economic advantage with Central American and Caribbean countries, leading to an intensification of poverty and unemployment in many poor countries. As a result there are even more people who want to come to the U.S. to work. Kat Rodriguez insists that undocumented workers should not be punished for American economic needs. "The bottom line is that legal immigration is not providing for our economic needs here in the U.S., so it is being supplemented by undocumented workers. Until we have policies that will provide the labor that is needed by our economic system, you are going to be pushing would-be migrants into the gauntlet of death."[101]

Officer Jiménez does acknowledge that the overwhelming majority of those the Border Patrol catches are simply coming to the U.S. to work. When pushed about why they are treated as criminals if they are nonviolent and have not hurt anyone with their actions, Jiménez responded by rote: "Crossing the border is a violation of our laws."[102] Jiménez, who represents the U.S. government, imparted a more humanitarian sentiment than the minutemen who have garnered a lot of press for their hard-line, anti-immigrant views. In statements reminiscent of those made by President Bush, Jiménez clearly understands that the people he apprehends every day are fathers, husbands, brothers, and mothers—people who will work for wages that most Americans cannot. Yet just like President Bush, Officer Jiménez believes that the solution is apprehending and jailing individuals who cross the border. He doesn't see the irony in the fact that those migrants that he and his fellow officers do not catch, the ones who make it to their destination and find some low-wage work, are supporting his lifestyle. As Isabel García says bluntly, "If you eat at any fast-food chain, if you shop at any big discount chain store, or if you get your fruit and vegetables from any big supermarket, then you are doing so on the back of undocumented labor."[103]

Those who advocate sealing up the border use the argument that illegal immigration is a drain on the U.S. economy. They say that illegal immigrants use services, like schools and hospitals, and that U.S. cities end up bearing the burden, resulting in lesser services for everyone else. There are many studies, however, showing that undocumented workers *contribute* billions to both local and federal coffers.

On a state level, perhaps one of the most comprehensive and illuminating studies comes from the Thunderbird Business School. It collected data based on numbers from the 2000 Census, which documents that out of the total 464,000 Mexican immigrants currently in Arizona, 61 percent are undocumented. The study calculated sales tax revenues and federal income tax contributions of Mexican immigrants in Arizona, which in 2002 equaled approximately $599 million. The study also evaluated the total costs of services for Mexican immigrants in Arizona to be $250 million, with $31 million in uncompensated health-care costs for undocumented Mexicans. The net figure? A surplus of $318 million for the state of Arizona.[104]

Federal government statistics show that almost $7 billion are contributed by undocumented workers to Social Security each year. Unlike permanent resident and citizen workers, undocumented workers will never see this money when they pass retirement age. It is an unacknowledged payment to the federal retirement fund. As a result of the 1986 Immigration Reform and Control Act, which set penalties for employers who knowingly hire workers who have no work authorization, most undocumented workers simply purchase false identifications or Social Security numbers to get hired. Employers use the excuse that they did not know their worker was using false documents. And while a worker must provide paperwork, the employer must declare and pay payroll taxes for each employee. The Social Security office says that employers pay taxes for three quarters of those working without documentation.[105]

Maria's eldest son, Juan, who she brought from Mexico through a coyote in 2003, is her brightest hope. Juan is now nineteen. He finished tenth grade in Mexico and has a deep desire to study and get a good job. He also likes to dress well and try different hair products that he finds in drug stores. Maria doesn't have the money to satisfy any of his desires, so Juan put aside his dream of continuing his education and found work in a restaurant in downtown Manhattan. When he was hired, the boss did not ask Juan for any paperwork. After two weeks, working six days a week, Juan inquired when he would be paid, and only then did his employer ask for a Social Security number. When

Juan told him that he did not have one, his boss told him simply to "find one," or he would not get paid. Juan was very mad. He had worked hard, and his boss never said he had to show paperwork to get paid. Juan's employer was unmoved by his pleas for payment, and eventually, at the prompting of his employer, Juan tapped into the underground market for fake Social Security numbers. For a seventy-dollar expenditure, Juan can now get any job he wants and is contributing to a system from which he will garner no benefits.

Back in the SUV with Officer Jiménez, I watched as the border crossers were taken into custody. Jiménez asked me if I brought a camera along for the ride so I could photograph the seven people that his fellow agents had just apprehended. I hadn't brought a camera, and Officer Jiménez seemed disappointed. When I asked what would happen to the seven migrants, he ran through the options. If they are Mexican citizens and have no prior criminal record or no previous formal order of deportation, they are given the option of voluntarily returning to Mexico. A person can be returned multiple times without incurring any jail time. Each immigrant, Jiménez said, may also chose to go before an immigration judge and either plead a case to stay (for example, if they have U.S. residency documentation that has been lost) or make a claim for asylum. Most accept voluntary return, and after being fingerprinted, they are put on a bus back to the Mexican side of the border.

Mandatory fingerprinting of all apprehended persons is necessary, according to Border Patrol, in order to quickly ascertain whether the person has a criminal record, an outstanding warrant, or a prior deportation order. All fingerprints are immediately compared against those in the FBI's National Crime Information Center (NCIC) database. If a match is made, the person is immediately detained and prosecuted. Before biometrics information was captured digitally, agents were not so quickly and easily able to run someone's prints. Civil libertarians have registered deep concerns with these practices on two fronts. First, as the Electronic Privacy Information Center (EPIC) has charged, the NCIC is known to have many "record inaccuracies" that rarely get corrected. EPIC finds it problematic that CBP would rely on an inaccurate system as it checks for criminals.[106] Moreover, the Department of Justice recently ruled to exempt such records and databases from the data quality requirements of the Privacy Act. In making its case, EPIC cites a 1995 Supreme Court opinion that raised serious concerns about law enforcement's reliance on faulty data systems.[107]

Second, civil libertarians are concerned that the fingerprints are stored in what is becoming one of the largest data banks ever to be compiled of very personal information. And CBP is constantly pushing for more funds to invest in emerging data capture and collection technologies. The ACLU says that DHS's problems stem from "a surplus of information, not insufficient investigatory powers."[108] They charge that while DHS collects reams of data, only a tiny percentage of it might be useful in catching terrorists.

As the Border Patrol officers began loading the apprehended migrants into what activists call "dog-catcher" vans, Officer Jiménez mentioned that any undocumented person caught in the United States can technically be prosecuted for illegal entry, a federal offense. It carries a sentence of up to six months in federal prison if the person has never been convicted of a crime or deported before, but up to twenty years depending on their prior deportations or criminal record. While not all of those apprehended are prosecuted, lawyers like Isabel García in Tucson argue that the government is still prosecuting way too many.

Tucson Federal Court is a hive of activity. Every day, 85 percent of the business transacted in this palm-tree fringed desert courthouse is the processing of migrants.[109] García says that the amount of money the federal government is spending on capturing and trying people is unprecedented.

> You see these desperately poor people, all brown, mainly indigenous men who come in chained, escorted by very expensive personnel from the U.S. Marshall's Office. You have CBP with all of their staff that has grown dramatically and all their equipment to firstly capture and then collect data on the offenders. They come in to federal court to testify at the expense of taxpayers. The cases are prosecuted by U.S. attorneys, defended by federal public defenders, then you have all the court staff of the magistrates, the U.S. district court judges, who get the felony convictions, and all of this business is every single day in Tucson Federal Court and other courts along the border. From there, the offenders are sentenced to federal prison. And we have seen a dramatic growth in the prison industry. It is one of the fastest growing industries in this country, and more and more, it is to incarcerate migrants.[110]

García calls this whole process the government's "deportation arsenal," which the government itself boasts about. On DHS's Web site, listed under its successes for 2004 in Arizona, it reports a 309 percent increase from 2003 in the number of "criminal aliens" passed through the judicial process and deported, and a 30 percent increase in the number of "aliens" detained and removed.[111]

The most compelling evidence that CBP oftentimes provides to the U.S.

attorney is the migrants' own admission that they crossed illegally, according to García. She says that for all the expenditure on technology and personnel, very few cases can actually provide evidence that the migrant crossed illegally into the United States. Those that get prosecuted, for the most part, are the migrants who fess up to CBP on their capture. "It's all an arbitrary system," García adds. "The individuals they try come from the pool of people that they catch. And on a daily basis, they know they have all these prosecutions to make, so they pick out people who they know will be the easiest to convict."[112]

Back in the San Diego Border Patrol SUV, Officer Jiménez went on to tell me that if the apprehended immigrant is not Mexican, they are immediately detained until they can appear before an immigration judge. The wait to see a judge often takes weeks, during which time the person sits in a jail cell under the jurisdiction of DHS. Most will then be ordered deported to their country of citizenship. The consequences of this formal deportation order are more serious than the voluntary return option offered to Mexicans since it makes any reentry attempt without proper documentation a felony crime with up to two years in federal prison, known in legal terms as "1326."

While San Diego is home to a burgeoning Border Patrol population, there is also a small yet vibrant community of people who are dedicated to defending the growing numbers of those being prosecuted under 1326 and facing serious jail time for illegal entry or illegal reentry. On any given Sunday, between putting in extra hours to prepare for one of their many cases and visiting clients in jail, trial attorneys Marisa Dersey and Heather Rogers can be found atop one of the many swells that attract so many surfers to San Diego. Both describe their weekend surfing as necessary to their courtroom battles. Oftentimes the best Dersey and Rogers can do is reduce their clients' sentences. Yet both are passionate about their clients' rights inside a system that leaves them little leeway.

Community defenders have to be creative as they try to show why their clients did not reenter the United States illegally or why there were no grounds for stopping and questioning their clients in the first place. In one case that Rogers was defending, she loaded up a car with the equivalent weight of two people and sacks of soil corresponding to the weight of the drugs that had been seized, and videotaped it being driven down the street. Rogers was attempting to convince a federal judge that the car did not look abnormally weighted down, as CBP claimed when they stopped the vehicle. If Rogers could convince the judge that CBP did not have reasonable suspicion for stopping the car, the case against her client would look a whole lot different. The judge ruled against Rogers.

"Many who we get on 1326 have lived their whole lives in the U.S., but were born in other countries," says Dersey. She continues:

> They have committed some crime for which they are deported after serving their time, and because most have never lived in the country they are being deported to, have no family there, and often do not speak the language, they just come right back across the border. And for this crime of illegal entry they are looking at five to ten years in prison, simply for crossing the border. Very rarely do we have clients who do not have any family in the United States.[113]

Prosecutions under 1326 have dramatically increased in recent years. It is up to the government to determine how many people are prosecuted using 1326, and in recent years the numbers have escalated. Dersey says,

> I think one of the most heinous things you can do is prosecute an individual for returning to see their family or coming to an economic opportunity. Yes, they have been convicted of an offense, but they have served their time. Let them move forward. By continuing to prosecute them for offenses in their past, you're not moving forward. The law needs to be changed, plain and simple.[114]

San Diego Federal Court is one of the courts with the largest number of prosecutions in the country. Many of the cases are notched up as victories for the assistant United States attorney (AUSA) because so many defendants accept a plea offer in exchange for an admission of guilt. Federal Defenders of San Diego, Inc., says that the U.S. attorney's office almost always offers a plea agreement, and until recently, the offer stood capped between a sixty day and thirty month jail sentence. Post-9/11, the plea offer was raised to forty-eight months. But as Marisa Dersey points out, people with a prior record who were previously deported and are facing the charge of illegal entry have little chance of winning in court. This is true no matter how minimal their prior charge or sentence may have been. "In other words," says Dersey, "if an individual is extended a 48-month offer and he knows that if he goes to trial he is looking at 100 to 125 months, there is a high likelihood he's going to plead guilty."[115] Rogers, Dersey, and other trial attorneys could easily filibuster the AUSA plea offers and take every case to court, which would slow down and logjam the entire system. This is why, according to Dersey, the government makes the offers harsh, yet attractive enough to ensure a quick conviction.

Dersey, Rogers, and a host of other hardworking defenders are on the front lines day after day as they attempt to stem the flow of prosecutions. Dersey tells me a personal story that aptly illustrates how little the general public knows about the government's pursuit of noncitizens:

> So I called my Mom one day very upset after a client of mine was sentenced for illegal entry. He received eighty-six months. And I didn't tell her what he was charged with. I said, "Mom, I had a client get eighty-six months today." And in my mind, you know, I do the math, you know, where will I be in eighty-six months? And how will my life have changed? And here is this person sitting in a cell for eighty-six months. So I asked her, "Guess what he did?" and she said, "Oh, did he rape someone, did he kill someone?" And I said, "No, no, no. He crossed over without papers to see his family." She was shocked. I mean, that's sick. It's wrong.[116]

High prosecution rates equal more federal dollars to the assistant United States attorney's office, more funding for prison beds to house the growing criminal population, and additional resources toward border patrol to increase their apprehensions. These increased prosecutions of illegal entry and illegal reentry are keeping southwestern prisons populated and growing. Writer Judith Greene has been on the case of the boom in private prisons for the last decade. She notes that in the years since the enactment of the harsh immigration reform in 1996, when Congress greatly expanded the number of crimes for which a noncitizen would be deported after serving his or her sentence, there was "an explosion in the number of non-U.S. citizens in federal prison."[117] After 9/11 that explosion has become an all-out assault. Isabel García sees this phenomenon as much more than just a ploy to fill up prison beds—she sees it as the criminalization of migrant workers. "Protecting against terrorism and criminalizing migrant workers have become synonymous," says García.[118]

In the aftermath of 9/11, a twenty-two-point pact called the U.S-Mexico Border Partnership Agreement was signed on March 22, 2002, between the two neighbors. It includes such items as sharing information on passengers arriving by air into Mexican airports, identifying and hastening the border crossing for frequent "low-risk" travelers (most of whom are conducting commerce between the two countries), and regular consultation on visa policies. One of the criticisms of this agreement is that while it has attempted to systematize and secure the process of crossing the border legally, it has made life extremely difficult for those who live on both sides of the border—

for example students who go to school in the other country, families who have relatives on the other side of the border, and even tourists who used to shop across the border. Perhaps more worrisome to migration experts is that this agreement has shifted the focus onto security and has emphatically derailed the years of planning toward a broader and more comprehensive migration agreement between Mexico and the United States. Attempts at constructive policy that took into account the reasons so many people move northward have been squashed.

Meanwhile, if one looks for possible connections between the 9/11 terrorist attacks and security lapses at the Mexican border, it's clear that there aren't any. The government's own commission investigating the terrorist attacks found that the hijackers did not attempt to cross into the U.S. by land, nor did they enter without valid visas. The opening statement of the first chapter of the 9/11 Commission's report declares that "The success of the September 11 plot depended on the ability of the hijackers to obtain visas and pass an immigration and customs inspection in order to enter the United States."[119]

Interestingly, the same 9/11 Commission report painted a clear picture of just how easy it was for the nineteen hijackers, most from Saudi Arabia, to take advantage of the virtual red carpet successive U.S. governments have rolled out to Saudi citizens to obtain tourist, student, or business visas to enter the United States.[120] In fact, the 9/11 hijackers could not have had an easier time getting into the country, despite the false information given on visa applications, their incomplete applications, and their ability to enter the country without a visa simply by smooth-talking airport immigration officials.[121] Therefore, if the goal is to use technology to root out terrorists, why not militarize the Saudi consular offices? Why not have unmanned drone planes flying over Riyadh or Jeddah spotting those who might be potential terrorists? The simple answer is because these actions would not make the U.S. any safer from another potential terrorist attack and they would likely only sour relations with one of the only pro-U.S., Arab allies in the Middle East—which the United States depends on for oil.

Furthermore, in its own press release entitled "Border Agency Reports First Year Successes," CBP runs through the amount of drugs it seized, the number of individuals apprehended and deported, and even the amount of revenue it brought in (second only to the IRS). Yet interestingly, in the section that highlights the successes of CBP's antiterrorism efforts, there is not a single case of a terrorism suspect apprehended on or around the U.S.-Mexico border region.[122]

Meanwhile, with so much attention and so many resources focused on patrolling and policing the southern border, the northern border with Canada seems almost naked. Over 90 percent of the Canadian population lives within one hundred miles of the U.S. border and about 100 million people cross the U.S.-Canada border each year.[123] The northern border has not been forgotten by the Bush administration, it just hasn't been militarized in the same way the southern border has. There are vast stretches that are not policed at all. No fences, no stadium lights, no border patrol officers. Critics say the Bush administration's claim of protecting against terrorists crossing the Mexican border is easily exposed as a smoke screen simply by looking at the reality of the barren northern border. "If terrorists wanted to enter the U.S. illegally, they would absolutely go in via the Canadian border," says Isabel García.[124]

In early 2005, the *New York Times* reported that "Border Patrol agents interviewed in February in the Nogales region said privately that the get-tough policy was an all-but-impossible expansion of a nearly hopeless mission." The *Times* went on to quote an anonymous Border Patrol officer: "Anyone with any determination can still make it into the United States," said the agent, who refused to give his name because he feared being fired. "It is all nonsense, all smoke and mirrors."[125] So if the militarized border is not actually protecting against terrorists, it is also too simplistic to conclude that the beefing up of border security is to stop illegal immigration.

The Bush administration's pandering to big business and its cronyism in handing out government contracts has come to define the two-term presidency.[126] Studying the most recent focus on increased border security suggests that there is a strong case to be made for wasted taxpayer dollars as companies big and small cash in—all at the expense of noncitizens' human rights and civil liberties.

Consider the expenditure on robotic aircraft. In June 2004, Border Patrol units began using Israeli-made unmanned aerial vehicles leased from the Defense Department for the Arizona Border Control Initiative. According to an agency statement, two Hermes 450 unmanned aerial vehicles (UAVs) were used to assist Patrol officers in surveillance. "The development of the UAVs in protecting the borders of the U.S. demonstrates the commitment this [Bush] Administration has to testing new technologies and systems to better secure America," said Asa Hutchinson, Undersecretary for Border and Transportation Security.[127] The purpose of these UAVs is to relay digital pictures of people and vehicle movements to Border Patrol officers who monitor the incoming images from a ground station. The four-month trial cost $4 million and the eight-month trial cost $6 million.[128] Not a single terrorist was identified or caught. And in the eight months that the unmanned drones patrolled the skies over Arizona, they accounted for less than 0.5 percent of the sector's total apprehensions of undocumented entrants for the last fiscal year.[129] This can hardly be counted a success.

There is an even more overt border scandal that calls into question the need for expensive technology. In 1996 a $239 million contract was awarded to the International Microwave Corporation (IMC) to install cameras and ground sensors along the northern and southern borders. IMC was later bought by L-3 Communications, one of the largest defense contractors in the United States.

In 2002 reports started to emerge that the cameras were not working. Along the northern border, east of Blaine in Washington State, the cameras were malfunctioning 95 percent of the time due to an inability to endure rain, fog, or temperatures below sixty-eight degrees fahrenheit. An investigation by a local TV station, KIRO Team 7, exposed shoddy work by IMC, which led to the equipment failure. The investigation also exposed that only one of the thirty-two cameras was actually recording to a VHS; the rest required constant human surveillance to spot illegal entrants.[130] The situation on the southern border was similarly bad. Not only were cameras malfunctioning, but there was extensive evidence that they had not even been installed. Investigators found many lying in the desert. Border Patrol officials said this showed how vulnerable the country was. Yet it can also be argued that no more harm came to the United States from a terrorist crossing into the country via a land border when this equipment was malfunctioning or lying idle, illustrating that some of these great expenditures on technology are indeed immaterial to stopping terrorism.

Among the proponents in Congress of a militarized border is Texas Democrat Sylvestre Reyes, who arrived in the House of Representatives in 1996 when immigration was a hot topic. A former Border Patrol chief, Reyes wasted no time in pushing for a tightening of the borders, loudly advocating the use of technology such as cameras and ground sensors. When the contract went to IMC, no one seemed to notice that Reyes's own daughter, Rebecca Reyes, worked at the company. And as the shoddy work was carried out on the taxpayer's dime, IMC and then L-3 Communications made regular campaign contributions to Representative Reyes, totaling about $17,000 over the past five years. Reyes claims he had no part at all in the contract going to his daughter's company.[131] L-3 also has a high powered and well-connected lobbying team, including Linda Daschle, former deputy federal aviation administrator and wife of the former Senate majority leader.[132] A General Services Administration (GSA) report in December 2004 found that the contract was awarded as a sole-source contract with no other bids entertained. The GSA also found that the government paid up to 300 percent more than it should have for equipment like cameras and that the work was extremely shoddy.[133] Further contracts that have been awarded for use both along the land ports of entry and in airports have shown little or no proof that they have captured any terrorists, instead picking up countless immigrants for old convictions, visa overstays, or undocumented status. The Homeland Security Information Network (HSIN) is one such contract, awarded to ManTech by DHS in January 2004 and worth $33.1 million.[134] As discussed in chapter five, this expensive program has thus far rounded up only immigrants and not a single terrorist.

Yet another technological tool that has aided the government in arresting undocumented immigrants is its collection of digital biometrics as part of the US-VISIT program. This called for another slew of contracts to companies that make the appropriate technology. Consider Cross Match Technologies, Inc., which has the contract to supply DHS with digital fingerprinting machines. It is a relatively small contract at $2 million, but significant nonetheless in the role it plays in helping the government collect and store fingerprints of noncitizens and foreign nationals. Again, while DHS trumpets the success of this technology, it is critical to note that DHS has conveniently stopped touting the fingerprint database as necessary for rooting out terrorists—the initial justification for implementing the expensive technology and policies.[135]

In March 2004 Asa Hutchinson, Undersecretary for Border and Transportation Security in the Department of Homeland Security, spoke before the House Committee on Government Reform about US-VISIT. He began by lauding the success of the program, and his statements, notably, did not include any mention of terrorists. "Since the US-VISIT entry procedures were implemented, we have caught a fugitive who escaped from prison twenty years ago. We have caught and extradited a felon wanted for manslaughter. We stopped a drug dealer who had entered our country more than sixty times in the past four years using different names and dates of birth."[136] Given that this program was sold to the public as an antiterrorism program and not a single terrorist has been picked up, and that the overwhelming majority of those fingerprinted are noncitizens, it becomes clear that this program is targeting immigrants.

The Rainbow Bridge, Niagara Falls

One of the most popular routes between the United States and Canada is the spectacular Rainbow Bridge that crosses Niagara Falls. While the falls themselves make an obvious natural barrier between the two countries, for much of the long border between Canada and the U.S. there is nowhere near the level of patrolling or militarization that the southern border experiences. If the Bush administration was truly concerned that terrorists would use a land border to illegally enter the country, there is no reason why the Canadian border should not look like the Mexican border. But it doesn't.

Yet as one high-profile case illustrates, the differential treatment at the northern and southern borders is not simply about differences in the migration patterns from Canada and Mexico to the United States. The case of the so-called Wilson 4 highlights that there is clearly racial profiling behind those who are stopped and apprehended, even on the Canadian border. In fact, a federal immigration judge found in July 2005 that four Latino students were targeted by immigration officials at the Canadian border for inspection simply because of their race. Judge John Richardson threw out the government's deportation order for the four undocumented students because he found that the immigration officials had violated the students' constitutional rights against illegal search and seizure. In other words, the judge found that officials only asked the students for proof of status because they were Latino.[137]

In the aftermath of 9/11, bilateral relations with Canada have focused on immigration, commerce, and the shared border. The Canadian government immediately undertook measures that tightened screening processes of incoming passengers at airports, increased its detention and deportation capacities, hired extra staff to screen incomers at the land borders, and began a process to upgrade the technology of all the equipment that is used in these efforts. On December 12, 2001, Canada and the United States signed the Smart Border Declaration. The thirty-point plan includes the sharing of information and the development of joint technology to monitor, track, and store information on passengers entering both countries via international airports as well as those using the land ports of entry.

Led by its stronger southern neighbor, Canada has complied with U.S. efforts to turn the borders into so-called safe zones for commerce. People traffic is highly monitored, but nothing like it is on the southern border. This makes it hard to avoid the racial implications of the disparate treatment between the northern and southern borders. As the evidence in this chapter indicates, the militarization of the southern border over the last decade must be seen as low-intensity warfare against an unarmed, nonthreatening, brown-skinned people. War has always been profitable for industry in the U.S. and the current low-intensity war against undocumented immigrants is no different. From the unmanned drones to the private prisons that detain undocumented immigrants, from the ground sensors and stadium lights to the nonlethal Border Patrol weapons, corporations are cashing in and the taxpayer is footing the bill.

If the militarized border actually stopped immigrants from crossing, the U.S. economy *and* American quality of life would be devastated. Elected officials understand this, and successive presidents have done little to change the economic conditions that propel the northward migration. In fact, the neoliberal economic model[138] that Washington and the U.S.-led World Bank and International Monetary Fund impose on countries such as Mexico has only made the economic conditions harsher for the masses, ensuring a steady northward flow. This is good for the U.S. economy because it guarantees cheap labor for U.S. corporations as well as profitable contracts to police the borders.

The Peace Bridge is another entry point into the United States from Canada, a little further down the Niagara River from the Rainbow Bridge. Border politics in the post-9/11 world are startlingly represented with these contrasting images: to the north, it is rainbows and peace, and to the south, it is walls, unmanned drones, and death.

Chapter II

ROUNDUPS AND REGISTRATION, DETENTION AND DEPORTATION

In a particularly gripping Spring 2005 episode of *Law & Order SVU*, a young Eastern-European woman had been raped, and the detectives were on the case. The young woman was too scared and humiliated to testify, though her testimony would surely have put the assailant behind bars. As the detectives built their case and tried to convince the young woman to testify, the plot took a surprising turn. The defendant's lawyer called immigration authorities and turned in the young woman in order to prevent her from putting his client behind bars. The rape victim was an undocumented immigrant, and she was thrown in jail to await deportation. Outraged by the defense lawyer's tactic, the detectives pulled some slick moves to save the young undocumented immigrant from ruining their case and got her out of jail. She testified, the rapist went to jail, and the young woman was granted a green card in return for her testimony.

If only it were that simple.[139]

Miami, Florida, Summer 2005

"I'm no relation of Saddam," Iraqi citizen Samir Hussain told me.[140] He had just been released after nine months of incarceration in Miami's Krome Detention Center during 2004–2005. Hussain certainly looks nothing like Saddam Hussein. He is energetic and always laughing—a well-built young man with sweet eyes. Hussain came to the U.S. in 1996 on a visitor's visa. He had escaped Iraq years before and had been living in Egypt trying to secure legal status because he was afraid of returning to Iraq. Hussain had been drafted into Saddam's army and could not bring himself to carry out the atrocities that he says were demanded of him. So he fled. Neither Saddam, nor the Iraqi army had any sympathy for deserters, and his life was in danger every moment he was in Iraq. On coming to the U.S., Hussain applied for asylum protection. He was given a work permit and led a productive life as his asylum case wound its way through the system.

Unfortunately for Hussain, on his allotted day in court to decide his asylum petition, the government attorney said Hussain's paperwork had been lost. This automatically dismissed the case and left Hussain in legal limbo. Although he was not deported because he had not lost his case, he had just had his day in court with no resolution. Hussain tried repeatedly over the following years to have his case heard or at least have his status regularized. He sought congressional support and legal support, but no one succeeded in having his case reopened. So Hussain continued to work at a hotel in Miami using his government-issued work permit, but he had no permission to stay in the U.S. permanently. Because of a bureaucratic bungle beyond his control, Hussain had no ability to regularize his status in the United States.

Within days of the 9/11 attacks, Hussain lost his job. "The manager told me that he couldn't have an employee with such direct connections to Saddam Hussein."[141] Hussain had no such connection except for a similar last name. For the next two years no one would give this talented young man a job. Hussain decided to use the time to focus on having his immigration case resolved. So he bought a Greyhound bus ticket to Los Angeles (where his case had previously been heard in court) and decided to go back to the judge and plead his case.

Hussain never made it out of Florida. He was picked up on the Greyhound bus very early into the journey when Border Patrol stopped the bus in Fort Lauderdale and demanded to know each person's country of citizenship. "Everyone on the bus was an immigrant," Hussain said. When he stated that he was Iraqi, Hussain was ordered off the bus. Despite having the paperwork to prove that his case was still pending, Hussain was taken to Miami's Krome Detention Center and placed among the prisoners who had served time for criminal convictions and were awaiting deportation. Hussain had no prior record, neither a criminal conviction nor an immigration violation. Yet the U.S. government's tough-on-immigration arsenal had kicked in, and if the government succeeded, Samir Hussain would be sent back to Iraq, a country that the U.S. was occupying and that was roiling with violence.

The government finally released Hussain and later granted him a green card. They had nothing on him, and he had done nothing wrong. But it could so easily have gone the other way. As the stories in this chapter illustrate, most immigrants are not as lucky as Hussain and end up deported, with little chance to stop their deportation or undo it once it has occurred.

Hussain believes that he was as much a victim of U.S. government incompetence as he was a victim of U.S. narrow-mindedness and discrimination. In many ways, Hussain's case illustrates how the current practices of arresting noncitizens under the guise of the War on Terror—jailing and then deporting the majority—have combined to target immigrants. This detention-deportation arm of immigration enforcement is not a post-9/11 phenomenon, but in the current post-9/11 era, the scope and methods of arresting immigrants have vastly increased, the length of detention and conditions inside the jails have worsened, and the number of people who are permanently removed from the country has escalated.

Manhattan, Winter 2005

On a bitterly cold Saturday morning in Manhattan's West Village, the New York University lecture hall was full. The workshop was called Detention 101: Detention, Deportation, and the Criminal Justice System. Local community groups Families for Freedom and the Immigrant Defense Project had commandeered the space and sent out mass e-mails, inviting individuals from the public policy and legal communities, the media, and concerned community members to come and learn about the phenomenon of immigrant detention and removal. Using the advanced technology of the NYU classroom and the simplicity of age-old role-play techniques, Aarti Shahani, Subhash Kateel, and Benita Jain, directors of Families for Freedom and the Immigrant Defense Project, drove home their grave concerns about what is happening to noncitizens in today's America.

In the aftermath of the attacks on the World Trade Center and the Pentagon, Subhash Kateel had confided his fear to me that the government would use the tragedy to more deeply divide immigrants from citizens. Almost four years later, his worst fears have come to pass. Since the passage of the 1996 immigration legislation that made a wider range of criminal convictions grounds for permanent removal from the United States, many noncitizens have come to learn firsthand that their life in this country is never guaranteed.

Perhaps the point was made most emphatically when Deportation 101 dramatized a case study called *Jorge v. George*. "On the same day in two different parts of the city, the police picked up two men, Jorge and George, for the same exact offense," Kateel told the packed room. "George is an American citizen, and Jorge is a green-card holder who has lived in New York since age three. Jorge's entire family is in New York, and he has been through the public school system and now has a job as a cell phone salesman. He is happily married to a U.S. citizen. George, also happily married, sells cell phones as well. Both men were caught one day for separate shoplifting offenses. Both were arrested, prosecuted, and found guilty. Both received a jail sentence of one year.

"But!" Kateel paused dramatically. "When both have served their time, George walks out of prison and back to his life, his family, his wife. He will go on to become a successful cell phone salesman. Jorge, however, is not allowed to walk free and pursue his cell phone salesman dreams. He is transferred to immigration custody and put into deportation proceedings because he is now considered removable from the country for his crime—the *exact same* crime that George has now put behind him and gone back to his life. Jorge sits in prison for another eight months as he appeals, and then he gets put on a plane and sent to the Dominican Republic, the country where he was born but has never lived. Worse still, Jorge can never come back to the U.S. because his crime is considered by immigration to be an aggravated felony which comes with a permanent bar to reentry." As people in the lecture hall gasped in horror, Kateel concluded his energetic performance. "Jorges are getting deported every single day across America. *Every single day*. And that is why we all have to care about what is happening."[142]

The use of detention and deportation as tools of immigration policy was greatly enhanced in the 1996 immigration legislation. The government says that over 1 million legal permanent residents and undocumented immigrants have been deported since 1996.[143] By 2005 the total was nearing 1.5 million.

In the years after the laws took effect mandating both jail time and deportation for immigrants found guilty of an aggravated felony after they had fully served their time, many "Jorges" learned firsthand that the system has no sympathy for them. Of the hundreds of thousands who were imprisoned prior to 9/11, many were in immigration detention after completing a criminal sentence. After 9/11 the government sanctioned sweeps through immigrant communities under the guise of the War on Terror, and an untold number were snatched from their lives and thrown into jail. They had committed no terrorist or criminal offense, but the prison system was now being used as a tool for dealing with those who simply did not have legal status or who had overstayed a visa in the past.[144]

In the weeks after 9/11, U.S. lawmakers approved a vast piece of legislation called the USA PATRIOT Act. Signed into law in October 2001, the new law gave the government unprecedented powers to detain noncitizens who the attorney general determines should be interrogated for connections to terrorism. In further regulatory changes after 9/11, U.S. Attorney General John

Ashcroft empowered immigration prosecutors to suspend a judge's release order in cases involving immigrants. The mandate was broad and the immigration authorities (then the INS) did not have to prove any links to terrorism or crime to supercede an immigration judge's order.[145]

In June 2006 a Brooklyn federal judge ruled that the government could use immigration laws to detain noncitizens purely because of religion, race, or national origin. The ruling, which stunned the immigrant rights community, yet barely rated any sustained national attention or dialogue, also said noncitizens could be held indefinitely and without explanation. The ruling came in direct rebuttal to a class-action lawsuit filed by Muslim immigrants swept up, detained, and deported after 9/11 when no links to terrorism could be found.[146]

A systematic campaign swept through immigrant neighborhoods of New York City's outer boroughs and resulted in the arrest of thousands of noncitizens.[147] The government said that only those with links to terrorism were being picked up. Numbers were impossible to ascertain from the government, so community organizers became the frontline for information gathering and legal assistance.

As I collected people's stories in the months after 9/11, familiar themes emerged. Of the fifty or so people I interviewed extensively—all Muslims of Arab or South Asian descent—it became hard to classify any one story as random bad luck or inappropriate treatment by a single bad-apple officer. FBI and INS officers were making most of the arrests, sometimes assisted by the New York City Police Department. In each case that I documented it was obvious that officers took advantage of the fact that people did not know their rights. The overwhelming majority of cases saw people arrested without any due process.

Adem Carroll, an organizer in New York City with the Islamic Circle of North America, has fielded hundreds of calls since 9/11 from people arrested and detained. In early 2002 he told me that he was receiving reports of many arrests where "no warrant is produced, no proper ID is produced, the INS or FBI walk right in without identifying themselves and demand to see people's ID." Carroll said it was happening all over the country.

> They think that because these folks don't know their rights that it is OK. I would say that in 90 percent of these cases, there is no proper process, there are no Miranda Rights read, and whether there's pounding at the door at 5:00 a.m. with threats and curses, or whether they are nice and polite, in almost all cases these families are put under real pressure to show ID in their own homes,

> which they do not have to do, and then unfortunately, when they cannot provide adequate documentation, they are taken in.[148]

One man I met in early 2002 was visiting the Brooklyn offices of the Coney Island Avenue Project (CIAP), a detention-watch program after 9/11. His name was Allah Dita. Dita was a short, stocky man with a desperation that exuded from every limb of his body. Dita was extremely frightened. He had come from Pakistan some years ago and had made Brooklyn his home. Dita was a green-card holder with three U.S.-born children. He was at the CIAP offices because he wanted to learn his legal rights and because he was very afraid that if he returned home he would be arrested. Dita's story about the unidentified law enforcement officers who came to his home, which poured into my microphone with passion and desperation, embodied the experience of a growing number of immigrants.

> The first time he come to my house, and then he come again after two days. He ask, "Who are you, what your name?" I tell, "My name is Allah Dita." He ask, "How you spell?" and I tell him, "A-L-L-A-H D-I-T-A." He write it down. He tell me, "Who is the woman?" and I tell, "She is my wife," and he say, "What is her name?" and I say, "Anur Fadma," and he say, "Who is the baby?" and I say, "It is my baby. I have three babies. They born here." Afterward he show me picture and say, "You know this guy?" I say, "I don't know." He keep asking. And then he go. Then after two days he come at 5:30 a.m., he almost break my window yelling "OPEN DOOR! OPEN DOOR! POLICE!" I say, "OK. I open." He say, "POLICE." I say, "OK, I know you are police." He say, "Who is Allah Dita?" I say, "Me, why what is the problem?" He say, "I have your picture, come with me." I say, "Why I go with you?" He say, "Who is Anur Fadma?" I say, "She is my wife here." He say, "OK, come on everyone, come with me." I say, "Why we come with you? What paper you got to say we come with you? Show me paper, show me court letter to say why we come with you. If you have paper, I go with you." He says, "Here, sir," and he shows me paper with my name and says, "This you?" I say, "Yes, but before you coming to my house, another policeman come, I give my name, this I gave him." He tells, "I have picture of you." I say, "This my picture? Check up, this NOT my picture. Look." Picture is of another guy. He says, "You come with me." I say, "Why I go with you? This NOT my

> picture, this is other guy. LOOK." After he told me, "Give me your green card or passport or what ever you have."[149]

Allah Dita managed to fend off the officer. But the FBI came back weeks later and arrested him. It took CIAP weeks to locate him, in which time his wife and three children were in desperate straits. Dita was the wage earner. Anur Fadma was left with nothing.

Community organizers began to receive daily calls complaining of another round of arrests. Bobby Khan of CIAP used to call me on a weekly basis with a breakdown of where and how many men had been arrested during the week. I would call government offices to follow up, and on the few occasions that my call was answered, I was routinely told that no such arrests were occurring or that there was no information regarding the people I was calling about. With such firm government denials in the early days, the mass arrests garnered no media scrutiny.

The Justice Department, then responsible for all immigration matters and under the leadership of John Ashcroft, had indeed authorized the mass arrests of thousands of Arabs, Muslims, and South Asian men. One week after the 9/11 attacks, Ashcroft ordered the FBI and all law enforcement to use "every available law enforcement tool" to arrest those who "participate in, or lend support to, terrorist activities."[150]

Once someone was in custody, ostensibly on suspicion of terrorism, the government could prosecute him or her for immigration violations. As I collected stories from individuals who had been arrested, or their family members, the overwhelming majority fell into this category. They had been picked up jointly by the FBI and INS, questioned extensively by the FBI about terrorist activities, and then passed on to the INS for immigration status prosecution when no terrorism connections could be substantiated. "Ashcroft is interested in defending his dragnet—the higher the number that he can charge with crimes, the greater his ability to say, 'See? We told you they were criminals,'" attorney Claudia Slovinsky, a member of the National Lawyers Guild, said of the mass arrests.[151] The sweeps were decried by immigrants and their advocates, and were also scathingly rebuked by the government's own internal investigations.[152]

The mandate for all noncitizens from certain Arab and Muslim countries to register with the government was another highly questionable policy inflicted on immigrant men in the months after 9/11, one that sent many straight to jail. Young men from Bangladesh, Indonesia, Egypt, Bahrain, Iran, Iraq, Syria, Algeria, Morocco, North Korea, Oman, Jordan, Kuwait, Pakistan, Libya,

Sudan, Saudi Arabia, Afghanistan, Algeria, Eritrea, Lebanon, Qatar, Somalia, Tunisia, United Arab Emirates, and Yemen were all mandated to register. On November 9, 2001, in one of the first incarnations of this program, known as "special registration," the FBI sought interviews with some five thousand visitors or foreign national men between the ages of eighteen and thirty-three who had entered the United States after January 2000 and were from countries "where there have been strong al-Qaeda presences."[153] The interviews were initially said to be voluntary, yet it quickly became apparent that if the desired Arab, Muslim, and South Asian men did not show up for an interview, it could be considered an immigration violation.

The new policy began to wreak havoc on the lives of many across the country. Kamal Essaheb came to the United States from his native Morocco with his parents and siblings on a tourist visa when he was eleven years old. His parents applied to change their status to legal residency, enrolled Kamal and his siblings in school, and made Queens, NY, their home. Kamal was a model student and breezed through high school. He never thought about his right to be in the country, his immigration status, or that he was anything but "American." Kamal first learned that he was not a U.S. citizen when he tried to apply for financial aid, had to produce his Social Security number, and for the first time was told by his parents that he did not have one. Kamal persevered and paid his way through Queens Community College, where he was studying when the attacks occurred on September 11, 2001.

In 2003 Kamal was a law student at Fordham University as a prestigious Stein Scholar in Public Interest Law and Ethics. There had been a buzz in the community and the media about a registration program that involved the country of Morocco. Kamal did not think he and his family were included, but a quick Google search proved him wrong. In January 2003, with a year of studies ahead of him, Kamal and his younger twin brothers and father went to register. Immigration authorities instantly realized that the men had overstayed their original tourist visas from over a decade ago, and all the men of the Essaheb family were put into removal proceedings.

Immigrant communities around the country began to report horror stories of mass arrests of men who went to register as per government regulations. Families were ripped apart, and entire communities devastated by the jailing of their men. Take, for example, the Iranian community in Los Angeles. In December 2002, as boys and men between the ages of sixteen and eighty-five hurried to comply with a December 16 registration date, hundreds were accused of being out of status and thrown straight into a dungeon jail at the registration offices. It seemed almost impossible to the many wives and mothers left behind that their male relative could go to a simple immigration appointment and not return. The boys and men were hardly fed and were kept in deplorable conditions. Some reported being repeatedly strip-searched. In the end, all but twenty were released. The majority were in application process for a green card or had some other form of legal status in the United States. Yet they spent from a few days to many weeks behind bars while the INS figured out its mistake. These men were lucky that they had good legal representation, but many other men around the country who complied with the registration rules spent *months* locked up with little hope of rapid release or avoiding deportation. Many were deported during these registration processes without any real ability to contest.

Immigrant jails also began to fill up with those unable to prove legal status during the course of a routine police stop. Since 9/11, due to intense federal pressure, cities around the country have, to varying degrees, empowered their state and local law enforcement officials to increasingly serve as immigration cops. In Florida, local police now have access to immigration records through their patrol car computers. In 2004 thirty-five state law and local enforcement officers were deputized to act as Immigration and Customs Enforcement (ICE) agents, with another thirty-five federally approved for 2005.[154]

Immigrant advocates are outraged by this trend. The Florida Immigrant Advocacy Center (FIAC) has been at the forefront of the fight to prevent local police from questioning about an individual's immigration status. Many immigrants do not go to the police when they are in trouble because they fear that they will be forced to provide proof of status or simply be turned over to the INS. FIAC and immigrant rights groups countrywide have documented that this problem is rampant in immigrant communities and getting worse. Immigration law is extremely complex, and FIAC points out that local law enforcement officers do not have the extensive training in this complicated field that DHS officers receive, increasing the chances that they will unjustly arrest individuals.[155]

Law enforcement agencies themselves are opposed to their being made responsible for policing people's immigration status. "You are asking for big trouble when you ask police to start acting like immigration agents," says former police chief in San José, CA, John D. McNamara. "I didn't let the police check for immigration or citizenship status. That wasn't my job—my job was to protect people. We couldn't do our jobs if people who saw a crime or are a victim of crime don't want to report it."[156] This has been a major concern in cities like New York and Los Angeles, where there are high numbers of immigrants. In fact, there have been large mobilizing efforts on the part of rights groups to draw attention to the fact that immigrants, documented or not, are being driven underground out of fear of authorities. Because immigrants are not reporting crimes or evidence they may have about a crime, advocates argue that communities as a whole are less safe.

Immigration legislation that passed the House in December 2005 gives all state law enforcement the power to "investigate, identify, apprehend, arrest, detain, or transfer to Federal custody aliens in the United States . . . for the purposes of assisting in the enforcement of the immigration laws of the United States in the course of carrying out routine duties" (Section 220). To aid in the complex business of determining a noncitizen's immigration status, the bill provides for federally funded "pocket guides" to assist police officers (Section 221).[157] If the bill becomes law, immigration enforcement will be the duty of every law enforcement officer in the country.

Some noncitizens ended up in immigration custody after 9/11 because they were the victims of neighborhood snitches. Across the country, as authorities encouraged citizens to report suspicious behavior, local and state police often wound up making immigration arrests. St. Louis immigration attorney Dorothy Harper says she and fellow attorneys experienced an immediate increase in the numbers of clients who had been reported by coworkers, neighbors, or ex-girlfriends. As the government asked for citizens to be on alert and report suspicious persons, Harper says many undocumented individuals with no connections to crime or terrorism were turned in to authorities.[158] While the media eventually picked up the story that major cities like New York, Miami, and Los Angeles were conducting widespread arrests based on anonymous tips, small cities like St. Louis were also rocked by unaccountable neighborhood patrolling and profiling.

Encouraged by government- and media-instilled fear, people took it upon themselves to report what they deemed to be suspicious behavior. Campaigns sprung up everywhere, from New York City subway ads ("If you see something, say something")[159] to an official Department of Justice program called "Operation TIPS," which aimed to turn one in twenty-four Americans into citizen spies. The spies would be those with access to people's homes and businesses: letter carriers, utility employees, truck drivers, and train conductors.[160] Civil liberties groups were outraged and very quickly the cases of regular people being arrested or questioned by authorities began to grow. Most were Arabs and Muslims. Some cases were extremely alarming.[161]

One of Dorothy Harper's clients, who she represented in October 2001, was an Egyptian man named Osama who worked at St. Louis airport as a mechanic for a freight company. He had overstayed his student visa, acquired false working documents, and practiced his trade for many years. After the 9/11 attacks Osama was reported to law enforcement by a coworker. Yet all the authorities could accuse Osama of was that he did not have legal status. He was arrested and jailed, making him an immigration detainee. During his bond hearing the government presented secret evidence that neither Harper nor Osama were allowed to see. Harper is certain that Osama was in no way connected with terrorism and was a simple overstay case. After months in jail, Osama was deported to Egypt with no evidence shown that he had committed a criminal act.[162] Harper, a midcareer attorney at a St. Louis law firm, says she had never before seen a case where the government withheld evidence and claimed it was secret. Harper was learning firsthand how the government was fighting its War on Terror.

In fact, this encouragement to "say something" was even used as a convenient tool of retribution. U.S. Marine Philippe Louis Jean returned from active duty in Iraq and clashed with superiors back in Camp Pendleton, CA, when they refused to give him the promotion he had earned on the battlefield. Haitian-born Louis Jean was threatened by his superiors that if he persisted in trying to obtain the higher rank, they would report him to the INS for a previous conviction that made him deportable—despite the fact that Louis Jean had served his full sentence of thirty-seven days for that conviction. Louis Jean, a green-card holder, assumed that military service for the country automatically made him a citizen. He was wrong, and for his past conviction of thirty-seven days, Louis Jean spent an additional ten months in a San Diego jail as he appealed his deportation order—almost ten times his original sentence.

Louis Jean told me that when the first sergeant who reported him to Immigration saw how easy it was to have him imprisoned, he began reporting all the noncitizens in his unit. Louis Jean knows this because he began to see his fellow immigrant Marines in jail with him.[163]

What has become clear in the years after 9/11 is that noncitizens are the fastest-growing population in the prison system. Whether picked up as part of government-sanctioned sweeps to root out supposed terrorists from the community; whether detained after complying with the government's registration mandate; whether arrested in the course of a routine police stop for a nonimmigration-related matter; whether victims of an anonymous tip and arrested; or whether legal permanent residents with a past criminal record for which they have fully served their time, immigrants have become the target of a fear-ridden, revenge-seeking society and a government in need of an enemy on the homefront against which to fight its War on Terror. There is little sympathy for the many innocent immigrants getting caught in the middle who have found themselves part of an expanding noncitizen prison population.

ICE Offices, Federal Building, St. Louis, Missouri

On a warm spring morning in 2005, Suzanne Brown sat in the lobby of the Federal Building in downtown St. Louis going through information regarding the clients she was hoping to visit in the detention holding area of Immigration and Customs Enforcement (ICE). Brown has short curly hair and a soft, warm smile. She has been defending immigrants ever since she went to law school at age forty. Over the years, Brown has seen a lot of changes to the way noncitizens are treated. When her Peruvian-born U.S.-citizen husband was arrested in 2004 as he waited in the ICE offices to post bond for a client, Brown was frustrated, though not surprised. Brown's husband works in her law offices and regularly conducts business for the firm at the ICE offices. On that particular day an officer decided to ask him for his citizenship papers, which he was not carrying—enough to get this U.S. citizen arrested. On the day I met Brown, she was hoping to meet with a young woman who was picked up by police a few days earlier and handed over to immigration authorities when she couldn't provide proof of status.

When immigration authorities arrest individuals in St. Louis, they are held in the ICE offices of the Federal Building until they can be transferred to the county jail that is a three-hour drive from the city. Most often ICE will transport inmates back to their St. Louis offices for attorney visits, but not always. Under immigration law, guidelines say that authorities have to facilitate an attorney visit, but the guidelines are not enforceable, so it frequently doesn't happen.

Bill Goodman, legal director of the New York City–based Center For Constitutional Rights, explained the differences between the criminal justice system and the immigration justice system:

> If you think of the criminal justice system as a pipeline, you start with the arrest, after which, under normal circumstances in this country, the defendant gets brought before a judge and charged with a crime. And then they have a trial in which they say either I am guilty or not guilty, and a judge or jury decides if that is true. Evidence is presented, and the government has to prove beyond a reasonable doubt whether the person violated the law. And if they

> are convicted, then they get sentenced and go to jail. That's the other end of the pipeline. In the case of people who are arrested for violations of the immigration law, that's where it stops. The pipeline gets plugged up at that point. Except they get held in jail for months, sometimes indefinitely.[164]

Noncitizens generally do have immigration hearings with a judge and are supposed to be notified of the charges against them before they can be deported. They also have the right to counsel, but the government will *not* provide an attorney if they cannot afford one. Benita Jain, attorney with the Immigrant Defense Project of the New York State Defenders Association, says that while noncitizens do have some rights, "many of these 'rights' have become meaningless—the laws have changed to make deportation a 'mandatory minimum' for many people, where the judge has no discretion to prevent deportation."[165]

In the St. Louis ICE offices, Suzanne Brown was skeptical about whether her request to visit with her new client would be honored, lamenting that "it is very time consuming to drive six hours round-trip just to conduct one simple attorney visit."[166]

Before the Department of Homeland Security was created in 2003—effectively separating the branches of immigration enforcement—the Immigration and Naturalization Service (INS) offices in the Federal Building of St. Louis were a one-stop shop for all immigration matters. The same physical offices still exist, but now different agencies occupy each one. Suzanne Brown sees her detained clients in an attorney visiting room of the ICE administrative center, a regular-looking office but for the two gray holding cells in the corner. That day, Brown's client Veronica was locked inside one of those cells, and much to Brown's relief, she was able to see her client immediately. Many times Brown has waited hours only to be told her client was not brought down from the jail.

Veronica is a chubby and sweet-looking young woman. Her bright orange prison jump suit and plastic flip-flops make her look childish, like she is at a pajama party. Veronica is twenty-two years old and was picked up by St. Louis police when, during a parallel-parking effort at a local mall, she rammed into the car behind her. When the local police asked for her driver's license, Veronica showed a fake permit. She was then asked if she was a citizen or if she had a green card. Brown's radar was immediately triggered on hearing this detail. She said she needed to check local laws, which were changing too often to keep up with, to see if local police had the right to ask for proof of immigration status.

A growing number of immigrants have come to the midwestern city of St. Louis over the previous decade.[167] Bosnian and Albanian refugees have been resettled in St. Louis, while Mexican and Central American immigrants have been in St. Louis for many years, taking advantage of seasonal work visas and a previous amnesty that allowed long-term working individuals to regularize their status.[168]

Veronica was first brought to St. Louis from her home in Mexico when she was sixteen. Her father was a seasonal worker, but he did not want to leave his wife and young daughter in Mexico. They crossed coyote-style into the United States and joined Veronica's father in St. Louis. Veronica's three older brothers and one older sister are all legal permanent residents and have been in St. Louis for over ten years. In 2001 Veronica was picked up by immigration authorities for being out of status and signed a voluntary departure order. She was given one month to leave the U.S. In that time, Veronica married her sweetheart and then filed for an adjustment of status before going back to Michoacán in Mexico to wait for her paperwork to be processed. During the two years that she waited, her husband committed a crime and was arrested and jailed in Illinois. All by herself in Mexico, Veronica finally got fed up of waiting and paid a coyote to bring her back to her parents and four siblings in St. Louis. She found a job as a waitress and decided to wait until her husband was released from jail to regularize her status. Being young, Veronica picked up English quickly and dreamed about taking classes to earn a high school equivalency diploma. Although she was not able to complete her studies in Mexico, Veronica is smart and believes she will make it far if she can finish school. When I met her, Veronica was sitting in a local county jail with twenty other women detainees and was facing serious federal time because she already had a previous deportation order.[169]

In the ICE offices and holding cells in St. Louis, a large framed photo of the first President Bush peered over Suzanne Brown as she and Veronica met in a locked (from the outside) office. As she fumbled with a Spanish phrase here and there, Brown continued to solicit details regarding her new client's case. In the office next door, an ICE official questioned a man in Spanish.

The agents in the ICE office, dressed in casual civilian clothes, are the ones who decide whether Veronica can be released on bond pending her court date. When Brown requested Veronica's previous case details from one of the baseball-capped ICE officers, he told her in a soft voice that a bond decision would be made soon but that he doubted she would be successful. Brown responded in a similarly soft-spoken manner that her client had complied with a previous deportation order and that she has extensive family ties in St. Louis, making her a very good candidate for bond. The officer shrugged, smiled sympathetically, and closed the door. "They are all numbers," Brown said, referring to the way ICE officers treat detainees. "Sometimes we get lucky, but when the cases for bond get denied, they have to go before an immigration judge."[170]

While lawyers and immigrant advocates struggled with making bail for those detained in the aftermath of 9/11, a 2003 Department of Justice internal investigation has revealed that there was indeed a policy of blanket denial of bail. A 2003 Office of the Inspector General (OIG) report harshly criticizes the Justice Department's efforts to oppose bail for all immigration detainees through its use of a "no bond" policy that overrode judicial orders to release detainees on bond while their immigration cases were pending. The report, in criticizing its own department procedures, documented that when INS attorneys raised questions about the lawfulness of denying bail, the Justice Department did not address these issues in a timely manner.[171]

Back in the St. Louis Federal Building, as Brown and I waited right outside the door of the ICE office for the official to provide Brown with Veronica's Alien Number, people filed in and out, taking care of routine immigration business. Brown explained how there have been many cases of people coming in to file various immigration papers—adjustment of status, work permission, travel permission—who are deemed to be out of status by the administrative CIS officials and reported to the ICE officers next door. Brown says this is extremely problematic because the CIS clerks who staff the desks at the St. Louis office are hired for administration purposes and have no training in immigration enforcement. When reported to ICE officials, these oftentimes perfectly legal immigrants are arrested on the spot and held in jail until their adjustment-of-status case is completed. "This pisses me off," says Brown, "not just as an attorney when I see how trivial the case for jailing someone is, but as a taxpaying citizen who is outraged that my money is being spent this way as so many resources are wasted on locking up harmless people until their case winds it way through the system."[172]

With noncitizens being denied bail and sitting in jail on immigration violations for extended periods, the process is costing the federal government upward of $600 million per year. According to the Office of the Federal Detention Trustee, in 2002 the majority of federal detainees were held in state and local prisons.[173] There were simply not enough immigration beds to cope with the massive numbers arrested in the post-9/11 period. In the last few years, the government, encouraged strongly by the corrections industry, has been signaling its intent to move away from this responsibility by contracting out more detention services. Each year there is more money for new immigrant jails and detention beds. This has been welcome news for private prison companies, which had been experiencing a slump.[174] In the post-9/11 years, the private-prison landscape across the country has boomed.

Meanwhile, as the number of immigrant detention centers increase,[175] and immigrant advocates and community organizers struggle to win bonds for detained immigrants, many wait for months—sometimes years—to see a judge or as their case is being appealed. As you read these words, untold thousands languish in county jails and immigration detention centers around the country.

The individual stories, when heard together, tell a tragic tale.[176] One element of the tragedy that got lost in the rush to arrest and detain was that the INS, and later DHS, did not have enough beds in immigration facilities to house the thousands who were being picked up. Many got placed in county or state jails in the middle of criminal populations. One particular man's story highlights not only this practice, but also the abuses and neglect of the entire detention system.

In April 2002 the FBI arrested Farouk Abdel-Muhti at his home in Brooklyn. Farouk was Palestinian, out of status, and a volunteer producer of Pacifica Radio's New York station, WBAI, where he regularly produced radio programs that criticized U.S. and Israeli foreign policies. In the summer of 2002, when he managed to get a call out of the jail, he told me he was currently in New Jersey's Passaic County Jail. "Passaic is a criminal facility with the criminals like murderers and rapists and the INS detainees together. They put me for one month with those criminals."[177]

Passaic County Jail was built to house eight hundred inmates, but in the period following 9/11 there were up to twenty-one hundred inmates, with a peak of five hundred immigration detainees. Passaic County Jail has been called one of the worst immigrant jails in the country. It was exposed for its use of dogs to attack detainees[178] and its abusive treatment (like turning off the heat and confiscating blankets in the middle of winter)[179] that led to inmate hunger strikes. All the detainees I interviewed who had been in various New Jersey facilities classified Passaic as the harshest. In fact, just one month shy of the release of an OIG investigation into the conditions at Passaic in early 2006, Passaic County Sheriff Jerry Speziale announced that the jail would stop housing immigrant detainees. His reasons included the safety threat that he said immigrant detainees posed,[180] as well as the fact that his staff was pitted against the demands of immigrant rights activists, which distracted them from doing their job.[181]

Farouk was jailed in various facilities around the country over a two-year period. He was never charged with a crime. It seemed nearly impossible to believe that for merely being out of status, Farouk was plucked from his life and indefinitely detained with convicted murderers and rapists. Authorities also transferred Farouk multiple times without informing his lawyers or family.

Prisoner transfer has been a tool of the detention system that the INS and later DHS have both used at will, with little information provided when a detainee is transferred. According to the Legal Aid Society, New York–area detainees are increasingly sent to a federal detention center in Oakdale, Louisiana. The Oakdale Federal Detention Facility is situated in a very remote region of the state and houses over eight hundred detainees at any given time. The reason most often given for the transfer is that there is not enough space for them at their local centers. Advocates complain that no consideration is given to the fact that relatives, as well as any evidence that a detainee might need to defend his or her case, remain in New York. And unlike in New York, there are no pro bono lawyers in Oakdale.[182]

Nancy Morawetz is a professor of clinical law at the New York University School of Law who has studied the impact of remote imprisonment on the only legal remedy available to detainees once a deportation order has been issued—their *habeas* actions. Morawetz examined the docket of the courts in the western district of Louisiana, and her conclusion was startling: "Little doubt exists that when the government chooses to transfer a detainee to Oakdale, it greatly increases the chances that the individual will be deported prior to any substantive review of the case."[183]

During his two-year detention, Farouk spent eight straight months in solitary confinement in a tiny York County jail cell with no light for twenty-three hours and fifteen minutes per day. He was subject to extensive interrogation and was often denied food. He stated publicly that he was repeatedly abused, physically and verbally. On the rare occasions he was allowed to visit a health clinic, Farouk was handcuffed and shackled. After two years and extensive pro-bono support from the Center for Constitutional Rights, a federal judge ordered that Farouk be deported, charged, or released. As with so many other cases, all the government could accuse Farouk of was being out of status—for which he was treated like a criminal of the worst order.

Because DHS could not deport him—Israel refuses to accept Palestinians, and Israel exists on what was his homeland, relegating him stateless—and they lacked evidence to bring charges against him, they were forced to release him. While Farouk's family, friends, and comrades celebrated, DHS silently transferred Farouk to Atlanta. He was supposed to be free, but not even his lawyers were informed of his whereabouts. He was finally freed on April 12,

2004. Sadly, Farouk died of a heart attack two months later. His family says the extreme stress he was subjected to, coupled with the unhealthy conditions and lack of medical attention during his two-year ordeal, led to his early death.

Farouk's case exposes the government's disingenuous claim that by rounding up suspect immigrants it is fighting terrorism. Being close to the case, I came to know the particular details well. Farouk was not charged with a single crime in the two years he was held. Yet the 2001 Supreme Court decision of *Zadvydas v. Davis* mandated that an immigrant awaiting deportation cannot be held for more than six months.[184] The Supreme Court, however, was generous to the government, as section 241(a) of the Immigration and Nationality Act states that authorities have only ninety days to carry out an order of deportation. In 2003 the Justice Department's own internal review found it unacceptable that so many detainees were being held longer than ninety days and that immigration authorities were not attempting to remedy this.[185]

If the government had evidence that Farouk was involved with or connected to terrorism, which could have justified holding him longer than ninety days, they had ample time to charge him. He would have been accorded a government-appointed attorney and faced charges in a criminal court. But the government had nothing, raising the question of how many other undocumented immigrants are being held for inhumane periods under inhumane conditions.

Farouk's case is, in fact, far from unique. The detention and deportation arm of immigration enforcement is routinely accused of abusing detainees, and these abuses are documented by human rights groups such as Amnesty International[186] and Human Rights Watch.[187] Some detention centers were worse than others. Consider the Metropolitan Detention Center in Brooklyn, New York. Community organizers who were receiving frequent and shocking reports of abuse and mistreatment began to hold weekly vigils outside the prison. In 2003, a government investigation confirmed these abuses, documenting that prison guards "slammed detainees against the wall, twisted their arms and hands in painful ways, stepped on their leg restraint chains, and punished them by keeping them restrained for long periods."[188] The report also documented patterns of denying legal phone calls to inmates, keeping detainees in cells that were brightly lit twenty-four hours a day, and secretly recording attorney visits (a violation of federal regulations).[189] For the multitude of people who had been systematically swept up, randomly apprehended, or transferred into immigration custody on the termination of a criminal sentence, life was very hard inside America's immigration jails.

Immigrant Jails, Miami

Many of the trees that line the road for miles around the Krome Detention Center are an ashen gray color. Each tree stands alone, like a Christmas tree lot the year someone decided there would be no Christmas. The trees are a fitting welcome to, and an eerily appropriate metaphor for, one of the most active immigrant jails in the country.

Krome is what is known in the immigration world as an SPC, a Special Processing Center—a kind of a supercenter for the detention and deportation arsenal of the government. Each facility contains all the usual elements of a jail: pods (cells where noncitizens are detained), recreation areas, attorney-visiting cells, and even a law library. SPCs also house immigration courts where detainee cases are tried. There are currently nine SPCs across the U.S. and Puerto Rico, with the newest one in Buffalo, New York.

Ten men have filed into the indoor gym at Krome where an attorney waits to give them a know-your-rights educational talk. Under immigration law, there is no mandate for the government to provide noncitizens facing deportation with legal representation. In fact, 90 percent of all immigrant detainees go to trial unrepresented by lawyers. For this reason, small, proimmigrant lawyer groups around the country, finding themselves unable to cope with the tens of thousands who need legal representation, attempt to work with groups of detained people to teach them how to represent themselves. Immigration law is not only extremely complicated, it is also constantly changing and is interpreted in different ways by different judges around the country. Lawyers are themselves often pressed to understand how best to argue a client's case to avoid deportation.

At Krome, all the inmates are noncitizens and are incarcerated because the government believes they should be deported from the United States. Krome inmates are divided into three color-coded groups: Blues, Oranges, and Reds. The Blues are the noncriminal offenders: asylum seekers, visa overstays, and undocumented immigrants. The Oranges and Reds are criminal offenders, the Reds apparently having committed more serious crimes than Oranges, hence the more dramatically colored prison jumpsuits. Both groups have either been convicted of a crime in the past, for which the Department of Homeland Security considers them to be deportable, or have been transferred after serving time for a criminal conviction to face an additional—and often very harsh—punishment from immigration.

When I visited Krome I was struck by how the majority of the inmates are black- and brown-skinned. One of the inmates I met was branded with a Red jumpsuit because his crime—for which he had already served his time—was selling stolen merchandise "off the back of a truck," which immigration authorities had classified as an aggravated felony. He had just arrived at Krome and was in a disoriented and confused state. As he asked questions, other inmates jumped in with answers. The Deportation 101 workshop came flooding back as I realized this Red-coded detainee was a Jorge.

Hamza Zakir is a Krome veteran. As if to really pound home the lessons of Deportation 101, each of the Krome detainees I met that was coded Orange or Red was some version of a Jorge. Zakir is from Jordan and has been detained as an Orange at Krome since June 2004. His case had already been decided, and he had a deportation order to Jordan, but the U.S. government does not have an agreement with the government of Jordan to carry out the removal.

Zakir says he made one big mistake when he smoked a joint of marijuana—"getting caught." He did time in a local county facility and was then immediately transferred to Krome because he is not a citizen. Zakir is a green-card holder and was leading an upstanding life with a good job and a large and supportive family. Like so many other Americans, Zakir enjoyed an occasional joint, and inside Krome he was paying dearly for it.[190] Zakir says he had never really thought about becoming a U.S. citizen; he didn't care about voting, which was the only benefit he thought citizenship would bring him. Despite having lived most of his life in the U.S., at all times with legal status, Zakir now deeply regretted not becoming a citizen.

Human rights advocates say that the government cannot detain a person indefinitely just because a country that will accept them cannot be found. In 2001, the Supreme Court ruled against the government, saying that the law mandated that a person cannot be detained indefinitely. The highest court gave the government six months to find a solution—such as a third country willing to take the deportee—or mandated the detainee be released from jail. Nationals of countries like Cuba, Vietnam, Iran, and Jordan have all faced the double jeopardy of being caught in a system that is unwilling to release them because it would highlight the unnecessary nature of detaining them in the first place. Each case seems to get treated with little respect for the law. With cases mounting where DHS is unable to secure arrival consent from certain countries to which they are trying to deport individuals, in January 2005 the Supreme Court ruled in favor of DHS, stating that prior consent of the receiving country is not required. The practical application of this means that the U.S. will now be able to deport individuals to, say, Somalia, a country with no recognized functioning government. When Somali authorities have refused to accept arriving individuals—after an expensive taxpayer-funded jet has flown the shackled deportee there and then brought them back—the Department of Homeland Security has just let them languish in a U.S. jail.[191]

There is no independent oversight of the government to make sure it is in compliance with the law. A Government Accountability Office (GAO) report in May 2004 documented how immigration authorities have been using legal technicalities to exploit the law and keep people detained, making it difficult to track whether immigration is actually in compliance.[192]

Realizing there is growing public scrutiny of its practice of detaining some noncitizens beyond the legal limits, the government went on the offensive. Encouraging the American people to fear those who are detained, President Bush completely misrepresented in a November 2005 speech on immigration those detainees with deportation orders but no country to accept them. "Under current law, the federal government is required to release people . . . if their home countries do not take them back in a set period of time. . . . Those we [*sic*] we're forced to release have included murderers, rapists, child molesters, and other violent criminals."[193]

In fact, Bush's comments tell only a very small part of the truth. While there may be some serious offenders among those who are being released because there is no country that will accept them, every one of those offenders has completely served their time, be it for illegal entry, smoking a joint, shoplifting, or murder. The equivalent of what the Bush administration is attempting to pursue for these Jorges would ensure that not a single convicted citizen-criminal would ever be released from jail because they would constitute a threat to society for the rest of their lives. It contradicts one of the basic ideas behind the criminal justice system—the societal consensus that the individual's time served constitutes their punishment and reform, prerequisites to being reaccepted into the social fabric. Why should it be any different for a noncitizen? Moreover, the danger of mentioning only serious criminals when talking about noncitizen offenders is that it leads the public to believe that all immigrants being released because no country will accept them are murderers and rapists, rather than the petty offenders that comprise the actual majority.

On the heels of the Bush speech, in legislation that passed the House of Representatives in late 2005, there was a clause that dealt directly with governments that either refused to receive their nationals or that delayed responding to a DHS request to accept a noncitizen with a deportation order. Should it become law, this clause would give the Secretary of the Department of Homeland Security the power, after consulting with the Secretary of State, to deny admission into the United States to nationals of countries that refuse to take back a deportee.[194] Therefore, if a country denies reentry to one deportee, all subsequent nationals from that country could be refused access to the United States.

With very little media scrutiny of the assertions made by public officials about immigration, the country remains woefully misinformed about who is being rounded up, jailed, and deported. As exemplified by Bush's comments, all immigrant detainees have been portrayed as persons with terrorist connections or as dangerous criminals, and one has only to scratch the surface to discover how far from the truth this is.

Like most other inmates in the country's detention facilities, Iraqi citizen Samir Hussain had no idea why he was in jail, how long he would be there, or what he could do about it. Immigration advocates have harshly criticized the Department of Homeland Security for placing people in such information strangleholds. Most detained immigrants learn their rights and learn how the system of detention works from fellow cellmates who have been locked up longer than they have.

When Hussain arrived at Krome, he was immediately put into deportation proceedings. While he waited for resolution to his case, Hussain worked two jobs. He began the day at 4:00 a.m. in the kitchen preparing breakfast for other inmates. When his shift finished around 10:00 a.m., he had earned fifty cents. Hussain then went directly to the prison laundry for another shift, where he washed inmates' clothes. For this he also earned fifty cents, bringing his daily earnings to Krome's maximum allowance of one dollar per day, per prisoner. Hussain said he needed the money to buy basics like telephone cards and toothpaste. Krome management has the best defense possible for their offensively low wage-scale: they are mandated to pay that amount, and not a cent more, by the U.S. Department of Homeland Security.[195]

As prison services and correctional facilities have become increasingly privatized over the years, the main argument given by both the government and the corrections industry is that private business can operate detention facilities much more cheaply than the government. The extremely low wages undoubtedly allow for lower overheads and bigger profits.

Samir Hussain paints a bleak picture of life inside Krome. Like many immigrant detainees, he had never been in prison before. He had never been forced to eat what he was given, nor forced to shower and sleep when he was told to do so. Most officials go to great lengths to explain how "administrative detention" is not jail, but when one is inside these facilities, it is hard to describe it any other way.

Krome SPC is currently expanding its capacity to hold immigrant detainees. Sometimes it gets so full that guards have to set up cots for new arrivals. To keep an immigrant behind bars, DHS pays an average of sixty to ninety dollars per person per day.[196] And when DHS has no beds in its own facilities, it sends detainees to a jail that it has contracted to hold immigrants. One of the newer facilities in Miami's Broward County is the Broward Transitional Center (BTC). This jail appears to be a tropical hotel from the outside and a public high school on the inside, yet the sleeping quarters and the mess halls are quintessentially jail-like.

BTC, which is owned and run by a company called the GEO Group, Inc., won their contract from ICE on August 8, 2002. The GEO Group was formerly called Wackenhut—a prison corporation with a shocking record of abuses against inmates and of mismanagement. Yet with a simple name change, this leading corrections company has managed to continue reeling in government contracts.[197]

Inside BTC, I met a very distraught woman, Suzette Fertil, who said she was at her wit's end.[198] Suzette is from Haiti, as are many of the detainees at BTC. So many Haitians are detained there that this Florida jail has come to be known as "little Port-au-Prince," like suburbs in Miami are known as little Havana.

Suzette had been in BTC for nine days when I met her. She had been moved to three other jails in Florida before finally being brought there, and of the four jails she had been in, this one was the closest to her family who live in Miami.

Suzette came to the U.S. from Haiti on a boat in 1996, after organizing on behalf of the Aristide government put her life in danger. Thugs had burned down her mother's house and had brutally assaulted Suzette. She arrived in Miami and applied for asylum. As she waited for her case to be heard, Suzette used the work permit the INS had granted her to begin working for the Florida Department of Children and Families as a support worker for children in need. She loved her work, and those she worked with loved her. Suzette made only $22,000 per year, but she was happy. For the first time she was living in peace.

The INS says it mailed Suzette a letter in late 1997 saying that her asylum application had been denied and instructing her to leave the United States. Suzette says she never received the letter. This lost notification changed her life.

It is very likely that Suzette never received this letter. It has been well documented for years by the Justice Department's own watchdog, the Government

Accountability Office, that the INS keeps inaccurate and incomplete records. In 2002, the INS let hundreds of thousands of change-of-address notifications sit unread in a warehouse.[199] In December 2003 a federal jury in Santa Ana, CA, found an employee of the INS guilty of shredding ninety thousand visa applications, complete with applicants' correct contact information.[200]

Inside the Broward detention center Suzette's mood visibly changed as she continued her story. Her face glowed with enthusiasm as she talked about her job or about her four-year-old daughter's antics or about how her husband had wooed her. But then her slight lisp would become more pronounced and her face would tighten as she remembered the reality of where she was and what was ahead of her.

Suzette was detained in Tampa after she and her husband were interviewed for Suzette's green-card application based on her marriage to a U.S. citizen. At first, the interview was successful, according to Suzette. The interviewing officer told the couple that there was no reason they would be denied as they had all the proof required to show that they were indeed married. Suzette and her husband were overjoyed and sitting in the INS offices waiting for the final seal of approval, when another officer came out and told Suzette she was under arrest for a previously ignored order of deportation. Then and there, the officer slapped handcuffs on her and took her away from her husband, her daughter, her job, and the life she had come to know in the United States. Suzette told the officers she had not received any notice that her asylum case had been denied, and despite the fact that she had been minutes away from being granted a green card, Suzette was placed in a jail in Tampa. "In Tampa I never saw daylight. They yelled at us like we were pigs, like we were no better than a bunch of dogs," Suzette said tersely.[201]

One of the harshest criticisms of privately run jails is that the prison guards who staff them are very poorly trained. The guards do not receive formal training in immigration law nor in cultural sensitivity. Complaints from inmates range from those like Suzette's—poor treatment—to utterly traumatizing experiences. One case involves inmates who had been forced to eat worms in the country from which they had escaped; prison guards forced these inmates to eat spaghetti even after they had told the guards they thought the pasta was worms. The Department of Homeland Security outsources detention services, and there is little oversight or accountability of the contractors.[202]

Former Marine Philippe Louis Jean—who was detained for ten months in the San Diego Correctional Facility, a prison run by the Corrections Corporation of America—described the treatment by the prison guards as "humiliating and degrading."[203] Louis Jean was surprised to see that many of the prison guards were ex-military; he had even trained and served with some of them in the Marines. "The pay and conditions are much better," one of the prison guards, an ex-platoon mate, told Louis Jean.[204] This same ex-marine also gave Louis Jean a dramatic insight into the way the prison guards are trained. "He told me that they were taught to treat us all like garbage. That we were all just a bunch of complainers who were going to be deported anyway and that they did not have to put up with anything we said or did."[205] Around the country there are many documented cases of guard abuse of detainees such as rape and routine beatings.

Suzette was transferred to three different jails over a three-week period before ending up at BTC. Her husband had to take care of their daughter and fight for his wife's release, leaving little time for work. In order to survive, he put their recently purchased house on the market. Suzette's bosses spoke up on her behalf, as did her fellow church members and neighbors. Their message was that Suzette is an upstanding woman who pays her taxes and contributes enormously to her community.

The paralegal visiting BTC from the Florida Immigrant Advocacy Center (FIAC) advised Suzette to accept deportation to Haiti. Once there, Suzette would have a ten-year ban against reentry. She could apply for a waiver of deportation, and, if successful, continue her green-card application based on her marriage. When I asked the paralegal what chances Suzette had of coming back to the U.S. if deported, he dropped his head and whispered, "Not good." He went on to tell me that while the government continues to deny it, there *is* special treatment meted out to Haitians. As the years go by, he says, it only gets worse.[206]

For her part, Suzette was clear about what she wants. "Just deport me," she exclaimed loudly enough for nearby guards to hear. "Please, I am pissed off. I am wasting my life in here. My daughter is growing up and she needs me. Just deport me so I can try and get my family back together again. Being in here is a waste of time. I am not a criminal."[207] Even if she wanted to be flown back that moment, Suzette still had a long way ahead of her.

The Center for Constitutional Rights' Bill Goodman says that the government has successfully worn people down by putting them in jail.

> What you have is a situation where people got sick of being in detention and said, "We're willing to go, we want to get out of here. We don't like being held under these extreme and inhumane conditions," so the judge says, "OK, I'll enter an order of deportation." Now how much time does it take the Justice Department to

> buy a plane ticket and get them out of the country? These people were held for months longer. At that point, legally, those detentions became violative of the Bill of Rights because they changed from being immigration violators to being criminal suspects. And as such, they had a right to be charged with a crime, they had a right to have an attorney appointed for them, they had a right to be brought before an independent magistrate. And these rights were violated on a wholesale basis over and over and over again, hundreds, perhaps thousands of times.[208]

Suzette's case is almost impossible to win, typical in the post-1996 period when a judge's discretion is limited. Suzette did have an order of deportation that, arguably, she never knew about. However, since she was about to receive a green-card and had multiple witnesses from the community testify on her behalf, she could have put forward a defense that asked the judge to consider the mitigating circumstances. However, due to the 1996 legislation, judges no longer have the flexibility to consider these factors. Suzette understands that she stands very little chance of remaining in the U.S. and hence *wants* to be deported. Before that can happen she must first wait to go before an immigration judge.

Lawyers and human rights groups have extensively documented that most people who go before an immigration judge have very little understanding of what is occurring. One illustration of this came in a poignant letter I received via community organizer Adem Carroll. It was from an inmate detained in a New Jersey facility. After inquiring if his family in Egypt had been informed of his circumstances, the man who wrote the letter describes his bewilderment after a recent court appearance:

> I am still very confused as to what happened at my last session with the judge, why did the judge postpone my trial until Feb 2002? Did the lawyer ask for that? Only Allah knows what I am going through. They put me in solitary—if it wasn't for Allah I might lose my mind or have a nervous breakdown. May Allah safe guard everyone. All I wonder is why I am in this situation? Why the maximum security? Why solitary confinement? Many questions and no answers. Well what is my charge? No one knows. Please send me a letter to tell me what the next session requires.[209]

Immigration detainees are technically afforded access to the federal courts to prove their right to stay in the U.S. once a deportation order has been issued and an immigration court has denied an appeal. However, few have the resources or legal counsel to pursue their case in federal court. And even at the lower level, immigration court proceedings are difficult to understand, making it extremely challenging and risky for detainees to defend themselves.

Newark Immigration Court, New Jersey

Despite the fact that I was the host of a national daily news program and had been regularly covering the post-9/11 political climate in New York, I had been unsuccessful in gaining press access to any New York or New Jersey detention facility or courtroom. Then, on a hot and sticky morning in August 2002, I witnessed my first immigration court trial. I went with a local lawyer to New Jersey, and I must have appeared to be one of the defendant's relatives because nobody asked me why I was there. I kept my press credential well out of sight.

On the drive to the courthouse, I was briefed on the client's case. I was also able to talk to the detained man's brother, Ali, who had himself been detained and accused of connections to terrorism, only to accept a voluntary departure months later when the government could pin nothing more on him than a visa violation. Ali and his brother, Majid, were from Pakistan. Ali was hoping that Majid would be lucky enough to convince the judge that while he had been out of status at one point, he currently had a pending adjustment-of-status application that should be allowed to run its course. On this morning, however, Ali wasn't too hopeful.

The New Jersey courthouse was like any other sterile government building. The trials were held in one small room where five rows of wooden benches facing the judge's desk were packed in. Majid's lawyer and brother were almost barred from his trial. U.S. Marshals guarded the closed door and many ladies in brightly colored *salwar khameez* waited nervously for their chance to enter. One lady told us that a group of detainees had been taken in, but the Marshals were not allowing family members inside. The attorney who brought me to the court was frantically trying to ascertain if her client was inside, if he had already had his trial, or if he had even been brought from the prison to attend his own trial, but the U.S. Marshals were unmoved. We got a quick peek inside every time the door opened, and finally when a U.S. Marshal turned his back we were able to sneak in.

We were extremely lucky, because as we entered Majid was being unshackled from the other seven men he was chained to, hand and foot. It was a shocking sight: eight men, all in bright orange prison jumpsuits, all South Asian, all shackled to each other. They were crammed together on one bench. Their faces looked drawn and desperate. Their crime: being out of status.

As Majid was hauled into the tiny space between the wooden benches and the judge, the lawyer sprang to her feet only to be barked at by the judge to sit down. Majid's lawyer tried to explain that she was the defendant's counsel, but the judge was not listening. Instead, in pure Judge Judy–style, Ali's brother was yelled at: "YOU HAVEN'T PROVIDED ANY PAPERWORK TO PROVE YOUR RIGHT TO BE IN THE U.S." At this point Majid's lawyer managed to assert that she was entitled to represent the defendant, and the judge then turned her wrath onto the attorney. In a matter of minutes the case was over, and neither Majid nor his lawyer had gotten in a single word. The judge ruled that Majid had one month to come up with the paperwork. "AND STOP WASTING MY PRECIOUS TIME, BECAUSE IF YOU COME BACK HERE AGAIN WITHOUT THE PAPERS, I WILL ORDER YOU DEPORTED IMMEDIATELY. CONSIDER YOURSELF WARNED."

With that, Majid was hauled back to his seat, and the next man was yanked out of the shackled bunch. We were promptly ejected from the tiny courtroom. The lawyer was distraught. She had every piece of necessary paperwork with her. The judge had not given her a second to present it. And there was nothing she could do. She had no idea how to proceed and felt like she had failed Majid. But we were told by the U.S. Marshal to leave the area, and that was that.

Ali was crying as we left the federal building. He was incredibly pained to see his brother treated like a criminal of the worst order. Ali had been through the system, and he knew firsthand that treatment in the county jails was humiliating and demoralizing. And he wondered what he would tell Ali's wife. "His family is suffering very very miserable circumstances. Nobody can really understand what his family is going through. He is the one earning hand of his family, and now his family is really suffering."[210] Majid's family, likes scores of others, was living on charity because their breadwinner was in jail.

In many places around the country, defendants are not even afforded the chance to go before a judge who is in the same room. Telephonic and video trials are increasingly being used. Suzanne Brown tells me that because there are no immigration judges in St. Louis, bail-appeal hearings are always telephonic, making it much harder for a judge to accurately gauge the merits of the case.

Telephonic hearings are problematic for much the same reason that the more commonly used video trials are problematic, according to Benita Jain of the New York State Defenders Association.[211] Eighteen facilities that house immigrant detainees say they use video conferencing equipment to conduct critical immigration hearings.[212] Increasingly, a video trial is all detainees get before they are ordered to be deported.

In a video trial, a television and camera are set up with the immigration judge in the courtroom; and the defendant, inside his or her prison, is placed in a room with a video camera; and the lawyer, if the defendant is lucky enough to have one, must choose between being with the defendant or with the judge. Often they are miles apart. Critics charge that video trials deny detainees a fair hearing. The detainee is often unable to consult with the lawyer during the hearing, nor can the detainee review any evidence submitted by DHS in the courtroom. There are translation issues and frequently there are technological failures as well. Traci Hong of the Asian American Justice Center has warned that video hearings could violate some basic rights. "As more merits hearings are held by video conferencing, an increasing number of respondents in removal proceedings are in danger of losing their constitutional and statutory rights to a full and fair hearing."[213] In fact, the U.S. Court of Appeals for the Fourth Circuit stated in 2002 that "video conferencing may render it difficult for a factfinder in [an] adjudicative proceeding to make credibility determinations and to gauge demeanor." The court also acknowledged that for an immigration judge, a "petitioner's credibility and demeanor plays a pivotal role in an asylum determination."[214]

Yet, even if a detainee were to get a judge who allowed the defendant a fair chance to plead his or her case, the law does not allow the judge any discretion. While the 1996 changes broadened the class of offenses that would make a noncitizen deportable, they also narrowly restricted the discretion that an immigration judge had to grant relief. As San Diego trial attorney Marisa Dersey explains, "Pre-'96, if someone is convicted of some offense and is a green-card holder but had lived here a number of years, the judge had discretion to conduct a hearing and see if the merits of the person's case outweighed the negatives that had happened. And if the judge agreed, they could allow that person to remain in the U.S. Now there is very, very little discretion."[215] In other words, before 1996, a judge had the power to accord Jorge the same treatment as George, once Jorge had served his time. Now this rarely happens.

So while many detainees languish inside U.S. jails, there is also a steady traffic *out* of BTC, Krome, and the many detention centers around the country. Inmates, however, are not being released to freedom. Most are awakened in the early hours of the morning, shackled, and taken to a nearby airport, where they are put onto a plane and deported. Immigration authorities do not inform family members or lawyers as to when a deportation will occur.

Keeping track of Suzette's case from New York became all but impossible. On one of my routine calls to the Department of Homeland Security office inside BTC, an officer, Diane, told me that they are mandated not to disclose any information regarding a pending deportation for issues of "national security."[216] When I badgered Diane about why family members could not be informed, asking what possible national security risk it could pose, she told me that "if we were to inform people when we were about to deport someone, everyone would show up at the airport, including the media." Diane concluded, "And that, Ma'am, would pose a huge national security risk." Frustrated, I retorted, "So a mother cannot even know when her own child is about to be taken away from her for good?" To which Diane responded, "Ma'am, we don't even tell the alien when they are about to be deported."[217]

What happens to a deportee once they arrive in their native country is largely unknown and depends greatly on the country they are deported to. Some are able to walk out of the airport and begin to make a life for themselves. Others are subject to harassment or are reincarcerated because the accepting government views a deportee as a danger to its people.

Deportations of nationals from Mexico and the Caribbean make up the bulk of those being removed from the United States. From 1996–2003 close to one million were found removable to this region alone.[218] Caribbean countries have found it difficult to deal with the increasing flow of deportees from the U.S.[219] When a final deportation order is issued for an individual, DHS contacts the consulate of the country to which they intend to deport the person. Most embassies then verify that the person is indeed a national of their country before issuing travel documents. The Barbadian embassy told me that all deportees are flown out of New York's JFK International Airport on American Airlines and are always accompanied by a government escort. The U.S. government pays all the costs.[220] For Haitian criminal deportees, most are dropped off in Port-au-Prince by specially chartered U.S. Marshals planes, though the government has also sent many a detainee on regular American Airlines passenger flights. Yet whichever way they arrive and despite the fact that each one has fully served his or her sentence in a U.S. prison, nearly every criminal deportee is taken straight to a Haitian jail cell.

There has yet to be an investigation by the U.S. government into what happens to deportees once they arrive in the recipient country. Journalists and academics have exposed how deportees' lives are in danger when they are deported to the Democratic Republic of the Congo or to the Dominican Republic.[221] On a trip to Haiti in 2004 to cover the removal of the Aristide government, I began to learn about the situation facing Haitian-American deportees. One particular man's story seemed almost unbelievable.

Wilber is a Haitian-American man who had lived in the U.S. since he was eight years old. He was a green-card holder and is married to a U.S. citizen with three children who are also U.S. citizens. He served eighteen months in a local county jail in New Jersey for domestic violence. Once his sentence was up, he was promptly transferred into DHS custody and five months later deported to Haiti. After he walked off the American Airlines flight, his handcuffs hidden under his shirt, Wilber was put straight onto a National Penitentiary (NP) bus and taken through the streets of Port-au-Prince to Haiti's notorious jail. In the NP, he went without food for weeks. He got desperately ill and received no medical treatment. He also became an easy target for the guards, as his wife would send him money from the U.S. He was routinely brutalized if he didn't hand over enough to satisfy the guards. For beating his wife, this man served a criminal jail term in the U.S., an immigration jail term in the U.S., and then served a jail term in Haiti. He finally managed to get out after his wife came up with enough money to bribe the Haitian prison guards. Wilber now lives in Canada because under his deportation order he is permanently barred from returning to the United States. His wife and children continue to live in the States.[222]

On my return to the U.S., as I told friends the stories from my reporting trip to Haiti, what seemed most shocking to them were my descriptions of the Haitian-American deportees. Few thought it conscionable for the U.S. to deport individuals into such abusive situations. I decided to keep investigating.

National Penitentiary, Port-au-Prince, Haiti

A constant stream of women, arms laden with bags of food, flows through the gates of Haiti's main prison each day. The National Penitentiary is a few blocks from Haiti's National Palace and central government buildings, right in the heart of downtown Port-au-Prince. The women are not visiting their incarcerated relatives; they are performing the daily duty of bringing food to their loved ones. The women are allowed to enter the prison and hand over their Styrofoam containers, Tupperware, or bags of food to a guard. Then they just hope it actually reaches the man for whom no means were spared to scrape together the meal. Feeding an incarcerated relative amounts to a full-time job in Haiti. And it probably means the rest of the family will go without, or live on scraps, to allow the bulk of the food to keep their relative inside alive.

Haitian jails fail every standard of human decency. If your relative does not bring you food, chances are you will go hungry. There is no drinking water, just whatever your relative brings you. Inmates are packed like sardines into cells. There are no beds, just a few filthy mattresses in each cell. Inmates either sleep on the hard floor or share the mattresses. Each cell has one bucket in the corner that is used by all the cellmates as the toilet. Often the bucket overflows and days pass before it is emptied and cleaned. Health problems will only be treated if your family can find a nurse to visit you. Needless to say, the cells stink and the inmates are in extremely poor condition.

The women that come to the prison to bring food and water have to pass an armed UN patrol, barricades of the Haitian police, and finally the prison guards themselves. Their entrance is steeped in deep humiliation, as the women are forced to smile, flirt even, with each layer of armed security. These are the people oftentimes responsible for the arbitrary jailing of their relative, and they also hold the power to reject the women's food deliveries altogether.

Haiti's criminal justice system is ruled by the gun. The Red Cross in Haiti says that 95 percent of inmates have not seen a judge or lawyer and do not have sentences.[223] Human rights groups have routinely reported the beating of inmates by the guards, sometimes to the point of death. Massacres of inmates in the National Penitentiary (NP), sadly, have occurred too frequently to be dismissed as rare events. Treatable diseases kill inmates regularly. On one of my visits, five inmates had died the previous week from beriberi. According to Father Jean Juste, a Haitian priest detained twice at the NP on trumped-up charges, "You can consider yourself lucky to make it out alive."[224]

In the middle of this prison is a relatively foreign population: U.S. criminal deportees. When I visited the jail in May 2005, I was told there were about sixty deportees currently locked up there. During my December 2005 visit, there were between 130 and 180. No one, not even the warden, had an exact figure. These inmates, along with the many who came before them and those who are detained in other prisons around Port-au-Prince, were deported from the U.S. for a range of reasons, but all shared one thing in common—they were not U.S. citizens. When I visited, the deportee population included a few who had committed serious criminal offences, such as kidnapping, but the majority had lesser U.S. criminal records such as shoplifting, theft, or minor drug possession. Yet no matter what crime they had committed while in the U.S., they had all fully served their time. If these deportees had naturalized, making them a George instead of a noncitizen Jorge, they would be freely living and rebuilding their lives in the United States. And there were even some deportees inside the National Penitentiary whose only crime had been an immigration violation, like arriving in the U.S. without proper documents or overstaying a visa.

For all the deportees, landing inside Haiti's National Penitentiary is a fate much worse than any imagined. It also raises serious questions about the U.S. policy of deporting people to a situation where human rights abuses, which could be tantamount to torture, are the norm.

U.S. federal and immigration courts have acknowledged that Haitian deportees with a criminal record—be it for minor drug possession, domestic violence, or armed robbery—will face indefinite and preventative detention with the horrid conditions I witnessed. These U.S. courts have even acknowledged that deportees have faced police beatings, been burned with cigarettes, and even been choked, hooded, and given electric shocks.[225] Before 9/11, these kinds of acts would have been considered tantamount to torture. But in the days of the War on Terror, White House legal counsel is producing documents that tremendously narrow the definition of torture.[226] While the Abu Ghraib photos exposed what most deemed outrageous behavior, it was not classified as torture. One then wonders what chance a Haitian deportee has in making the case.

Since 2002 none of these conditions, however horrific, amounts to the rapidly narrowing government definition of torture. In the landmark "Matter of J-E" case decided on March 22, 2002, the Board of Immigration Appeals ruled that "indefinite detention," "substandard prison conditions," and "isolated instances of mistreatment that may rise to the level of torture" for Haitian deportees did *not* constitute torture as defined in the case's decision.[227]

In what has been a largely unnoticed mass expulsion of noncitizens since 1996, the threat of facing severe human rights abuses after deportation is not enough to halt a removal. David Brotherton is a sociologist who has been studying the rise of deportations among the legal resident immigrant population of New York City. As part of his research, Brotherton lived in the Dominican Republic for one year documenting what happened to U.S. deportees. Because of his focus on this issue, he was recently called to testify as an expert witness about what a defendant would face if deported back to the Dominican Republic. The defendant was facing removal because of a conviction for a fight in a bakery when he was drunk. No one was hurt and nothing was damaged or stolen. His lawyer told him that he should plead guilty because he would get three years instead of fifteen if found guilty at trial. The defendant, Mr. Delgado, believed his lawyer and took the plea. What Delgado didn't know was that on completion of his three-year sentence, he would be put into immigration removal proceedings because he was only a green-card holder and not a citizen. Brotherton writes about the immigration trial that ensued to attempt to halt the deportation:

> The lawyer for Mr. Delgado looks at me, smiles, and begins his cross-examination. He first asks me to describe who I am and what I do. He then asks a series of questions that revolve around whether or not deportees are likely to be tortured by the Dominican government or whether the police will torture them with the complicity of the government. I did my best to paint a picture that fitted this scenario but I couldn't honestly say that torture is something deportees should expect. Rather, I said that in the present climate where deportees are being scapegoated then it follows that the police who are often authoritarian and out-of-control will abuse them. It also follows that many will land back in prison, after being put in preventive custody. Given the nature of the Dominican prison system, its appalling lack of resources and the normalization of brutality that goes on inside, it is likely that such deportees will suffer physical and psychological harm. The judge then countered that this was not the same as torture. Physical abuse and beatings by the police do not meet the criteria, he said. What was torture? It was the government-sanctioned use of extreme pain to extract information from a subject. It was the pulling out of people's fingernails, the attachment of electrodes to people's testicles, and the extraction of teeth without anesthetic. That was torture.[228]

Brotherton continues his powerful account with a quotation from the judge:

> "As I have said, time and time again, Mr. Crichter (Mr. Delgado's lawyer), you fail to make the case that deportees will be tortured at the behest of the Dominican government. Rather, you assert repeatedly that, in general, harm will come to these deportees. I have no doubt that the country we are sending them to is a bad place. I have no doubt that the deportees do not wish to go there and that life will be difficult for them. I have no doubt that for some of them it will lead to serious harm. But that, according to the law of the United States, is not the same as torture. If I were to allow such evidence, if I were to agree with you that that is torture,

> this appeal will simply be turned down at the next level, which is the Board of Appeals in Washington. They have done this to me already. I had a gentleman here who was going to be sent back to Barbados with full-blown AIDS. The man desperately needed his daily cocktails. His lawyer argued that if he were sent back there would be no chance that he would continue to be treated and therefore be kept alive. I agreed with him and I ruled that in such a case we would be sending this man to his death. The Board of Appeals disagreed with me and sent him to what I am almost certain was his death. That, Mr. Crichter, is the law of this land."[229]

In December 2005, after expert testimony from Professor Irwin Stotzky, internationally recognized expert on Haiti and director of the Center for Human Rights at the University of Miami School of Law, an immigration judge ruled that prison conditions in Haiti are "so deplorable as to rise to the level of constituting torture in their own right."[230] While Judge Kandler's ruling may have helped one immigration detainee avoid deportation, another expert on Haitian prison conditions, Michelle Karshan—Executive Director of Alternative Chance, an organization that works with criminal deportees in Haiti—was not optimistic that the decision would affect all Haitians with pending deportation orders. Each case has to be fought before an immigration judge, and Karshan is constantly called on as an expert to testify or to submit affidavits regarding the Haitian prisons. Success in halting deportations is rare.

According to the 1996 changes to immigration law, non-U.S. citizens face virtually mandatory deportation to their country of citizenship or country of birth if they are convicted of an aggravated felony.[231] Immigration law lists more than two dozen categories of offenses that are deemed aggravated felonies.[232] Furthermore, immigration courts and federal courts have issued varying opinions about whether specific offenses fit within these categories. When classifying a crime as an aggravated felony, the federal government and many judges insist that immigration law is not concerned with whether criminal law classifies a crime as a misdemeanor.[233]

The process for defining whether a crime is an aggravated felony under the Immigration and Nationality Act (INA) is complicated. According to an opinion of a Sixth Circuit Court of Appeals that overturned a sentence based on the immigration authorities' claim that a drug possession offense was a "drug trafficking" aggravated felony, "deciphering what the term 'aggravated felony' means in the INA requires us to navigate a rather confusing maze of statutory cross-references."[234] Some offenses are deemed aggravated felonies whether or not a criminal court sentenced the immigrant to any time in jail, while other offenses turn on the sentence imposed. For example, for theft offenses such as shoplifting, if two men are convicted and one is sentenced to one year in prison and the other is sentenced to 364 days in prison, the latter is not an aggravated felon under immigration law because his sentence was less than one year. For the extra day of time served, the former faces mandatory detention and mandatory deportation under immigration law. The complicated question of whether an offense should be classified as an aggravated felony is perhaps best summed up by Richard Posner, a conservative federal judge on the seventh Circuit: "The only consistency that we can see in the government's treatment of the meaning of 'aggravated felony' is that the alien always loses."[235]

The word on the street in Haiti is that the U.S. pays the Haitian government per deportee.[236] Exhaustive searches and calls to the Department of Homeland Security came up with no corroboration of this from U.S. authorities. Ira Kurzban, who was the Miami-based attorney for the Aristide government, told me that in late 2003, when the Aristide government was increasingly refusing to accept deportees, the U.S. government began offering to pay the Haitian government per deportee. Kurzban says that he was a party to the negotiations but did not see the final agreement that stated how much would be paid per deportee. "The U.S. was getting angrier and angrier," Kurzban told me, "and putting more and more pressure, and then Alex Baptiste stepped up to the plate and said, 'Well, we can make an agreement about this and get some funds that hopefully will be used to help people once they come back to Haiti to transition back into Haitian society.'" Alex Baptiste was then a midlevel official in Aristide's foreign ministry. Baptiste later became part of the government that took power after deposing Aristide, and Kurzban is certain that no U.S. funds are being used to resettle the deportees. In fact, every single one of the deportees I met in Port-au-Prince said they had not received a penny from the Haitian government, nor any kind of repatriation services. "I guess they use the money paid by the U.S. government to lock us up," one recently released deportee told me. Kurzban is also just as certain that the U.S. government knows that its money is not repatriating deportees, but is happy to turn a blind eye so long as Haiti continues to accept the deportees.

Harlem and Washington Heights, New York City

Since coming to New York I have lived in West Harlem, home to many African Americans, Dominicans, and, increasingly, Mexicans. While the War on Drugs, which has impacted New York State through the punitive Rockefeller Drug Laws, has incarcerated a steady flow of my neighbors over the years, those sentences are now turning into ones for permanent removal from the country. I was shocked to learn that some twenty-five thousand Dominicans have been deported from New York—mostly men from Washington Heights—since 1996.[237] Families are being torn apart, breadwinners taken away, communities devastated. Many of the people being picked up for misdemeanor crimes are from low-income families and subject to representation by the city's overtaxed legal aid lawyers. However, regardless of whether they receive free legal counsel or have an expensive private attorney, quite often a defendant is pushed to accept a plea bargain, without understanding that a conviction will make them deportable. The effects of the deportation arsenal that kicks in once individuals complete their criminal sentences are being felt in my neighborhood, as well as in Brooklyn and Queens, home to many Caribbean, Arab, Latin American, South Asian, African, and Russian communities. It is no exaggeration to say that immigrants—legal permanent residents, visa holders, and undocumented workers—are being steadily removed from the country. Close to 1.5 million people have been deported over the last ten years (2004 saw over 200,000 formal removals from the country),[238] and the numbers continue to grow each year. The deported leave behind dependents: spouses, children, parents, and other loved ones. Many of these family members have no choice but to leave the U.S. as well to be able to live with their deported family member, a forced exodus that receives little, if any attention.

Chapter III

THE END OF ASYLUM AS WE KNOW IT?

Vimral, a beautician in New York, is an attractive young woman with long jet-black hair, piercing eyes and a slim figure. She was born in Guyana and raised in a family of practicing Hindus. Vimral was born male and always thought she was a gay man. She was born with male genitals but stronger female hormones, a fact that has caused her many problems.

"I suffered so much when I was a kid," Vimral told me with sadness. She was tormented not only by other kids, but, worse still, by most of the adults in her life.[239] "My parents just wished for a normal boy, and my father beat me often." Vimral tried to commit suicide three times before she reached eighteen. At a young age her parents separated, and her mother went to Venezuela to work and send money home. Some of the few pleasant times Vimral experienced were while she lived with her grandparents during her school years. But as she got older, she suffered more and more, and reached a point where she said she would rather that the men who constantly harassed and persecuted her "kill [her] than keep going through what [she] was going through."[240]

Incidents of harassment were so common in Vimral's life that she found it difficult to distinguish the ones that could be life threatening from the ones that were not. She soon began to wonder how she could escape. One evening a group of men started calling her "gay," and telling her, "We'll show you how we treat gays here." They proceeded to pin her down and inflict serious burns on her body with wood from their barbeque. "I was badly burned and very afraid," Vimral explained, "but I still had to go to work each day and earn my living. Was I supposed to just hide at home?"

The final straw for Vimral came when she was on her way home from work one evening. A group of men wanted to see if she was a man or a woman so they attempted to strip her naked. "But when they got my pants down, I had another pair of pants on. I always wore two pairs of tight pants for exactly this reason." When they couldn't get her pants off, one pulled out a knife and slashed her badly across the thighs, and then the group proceeded to beat her so badly that she was left for dead on the side of the road. Vimral decided that if she survived, she had to get out.

Luckily, Vimral had enough money to go to the Bahamas. There she tried desperately to secure legal working papers. After renewing her tourist visa as many times as she could, Vimral realized she had no option but to go back to Guyana, whatever the consequences. Her nightmare began when she went to the airline office in the Bahamas to buy her ticket back to Guyana. After making the purchase, Vimral went and sat in a park under a big, motherly tree and cried bitterly. "I knew what would happen to me if I went back . . . I was just hoping they would actually kill me and not just hurt me so bad that I would be left a cripple."[241]

As she sobbed, an older woman came to her and consoled her. The lady listened as Vimral expressed her deep fears of returning to Guyana. It was this woman, "an angel" Vimral calls her, who informed Vimral that she was what the United Nations called a refugee and that she could seek asylum in another country. It so happened that Vimral's flight back to Guyana stopped in Miami for a layover. Not knowing what seeking asylum truly meant, Vimral sat in transit in Miami International Airport weighing her options. Then, as her flight to Guyana was being called, Vimral did it. She went forward and told a U.S. immigration officer she was afraid of returning to Guyana.

After all she had been through, her confession at the Miami airport began a new nightmare. For telling immigration authorities that she was afraid of returning to Guyana, Vimral was arrested and put in jail. That was after the immigration officers tried to tell her that she had to return to her country because she would be deported anyway. Vimral knew she couldn't return to Guyana. In the ten hours she was left by the officers to sit in the airport, she became only more certain of this. Vimral had joined a growing population of asylum seekers who, on arriving on U.S. shores, are quietly shuffled into prison as their cases wind their way through the system.

With the passage of the various immigration reform acts of 1996, Congress distinguished itself among developed nations as it became second only to Australia in allowing for the detention of any arriving asylum seeker. The policy was justified as necessary based largely on statistics that most people with deportation orders, issued when asylum claims were denied, had never left the United States. Lawmakers deemed it necessary, therefore, to keep all arriving asylum seekers under close scrutiny. In the days of the expanding private-prison industry, that meant inside a jail cell.

Broward Transitional Center, Miami, Florida

As described earlier, the Broward Transitional Center is a friendly looking establishment in Miami's Broward County, the facility where I first met Suzette. BTC's outer façade, however, is deceiving. Its warm pink exterior, ringed by tropical palm trees, appears to be anything but one of Miami's largest immigrant detention centers. Yet to enter this GEO Group–run jail, one must have prior clearance from the Department of Homeland Security and leave photo identification with the security agents at the front reception.

Inside BTC, as I observed a pro bono paralegal advising inmates on their cases, I had the chance to talk with some of those detained. On that day, legal advice was being offered in Creole-Spanish. Because very few inmates speak English, and DHS does not provide multilingual legal assistance, legal help is very hard to come by for detainees.

As detainees came in seeking advice, I was particularly struck by one middle-aged man. His face looked drawn and tired, and I guessed that he was in his seventies. He was clearly desperate and extremely confused. José Inez Rodriguez Cruz had arrived from Nicaragua, and for three days he sat in BTC without being told why he was there or what was in store for him.

"I left my wife and my small beautiful daughter in Managua because they would have killed us all," Rodriguez Cruz blurted out before he even sat down at the table. "I had to get out, to save all our lives."[242] When he was younger he was forced to join the Sandinistas. "I could never justify their violent tactics, which I, as a guerilla soldier, was forced to participate in," he told me in well-enunciated Spanish. Rodriguez Cruz deserted the Sandinistas as soon as he could. He fled with his wife to Costa Rica, where he lived for five years and where his daughter was born. Then the government in Nicaragua changed, and Rodriguez Cruz thought it was a new day. He felt confident that he could return with his family to Managua, to his home, and live in peace. He learned very quickly that he was wrong. When Sandinista members found out that he was back they continuously pressured him to rejoin. His life was threatened repeatedly. To make matters worse, he could not find work because employers were afraid of hiring ex-Sandinistas. Fearing for his life, and with a family to feed, Rodriguez Cruz decided to come to the U.S. and seek asylum. He still had some months remaining on an existing multiple-entry tourist visa, and he decided to leave Nicaragua.[243]

If Rodriguez Cruz had tried to apply for asylum a couple of decades earlier based solely on his claim of persecution by a communist-leaning political party like the Sandinistas, he would have fit the bill perfectly. At the height of the Central American civil wars, many Nicaraguan immigrants were given refugee status in the U.S. because they were fleeing communism. Immigrants from Guatemala and El Salvador, on the other hand, were considered economic migrants who couldn't possibly be refugees because they were coming from "friendly" regimes that the U.S. government supported.

"Historically, U.S. refugee policy has been ad hoc and very much an arm of foreign policy," according to U.S. asylum officer and union organizer Michael Knowles.[244] "Throughout the years of the cold war there was a simple equation with regards to determining bona fide refugees; people fleeing from communist countries were automatically refugees." This application of refugee protection by the world's richest country was not necessarily in compliance with the United Nations Refugee Convention of 1951, of which the U.S. was one of the initial architects. In theory, the U.S. was bound by the convention, but it didn't have any laws or regulations for implementing it. From year to year, Congress, in consultation with the State Department and the INS, would determine a quota for refugees that would be allowed entry. And for those arriving in the U.S. claiming the need for asylum, there was indeed an "ad hoc" process applied, as Michael Knowles called it—unless the asylum seeker was from Cuba, Hungary, Nicaragua, or other countries that had communist leaderships. Then in 1980, the U.S. implemented an asylum policy formalizing criteria and a process by which bona fide refugees could be determined. The Refugee Act finally brought the U.S. into compliance with the 1951 UN Convention. So if he had wanted an easy road to refugee status in the U.S., Rodriguez Cruz was about twenty years too late with his claim.

When his plane touched down in mid-May 2005, Rodriguez Cruz did not know that he had to express a "credible fear of persecution" at the airport itself. He planned on entering and then filing an application for asylum. As he presented an immigration official his passport with his tourist visa in Miami International Airport, the official asked him to open his fanny pack. The pack contained business cards of Rodriguez Cruz's friends in Miami—a gardener and a painter. The immigration officer immediately sent Rodriguez Cruz to secondary inspection for further scrutiny as he deemed that the business cards meant that Rodriguez Cruz had entered the U.S. to work illegally.

Such further questioning is carried out in an area of the airport known as Secondary Inspection, found in every U.S. port of entry. The primary immigration officer—the first point of contact for foreign nationals who attempt to enter the U.S.—decides which cases merit further scrutiny. Those most often called to Secondary Inspection include individuals who rouse suspicion or whose documents seem suspicious, an individual who needs a higher level of clearance, someone who is being "paroled"[245] into the country, or generally any person who does not appear to be a bona fide entrant. Since 9/11, Secondary Inspection around the country has markedly changed.

Having been paroled into the United States myself many times because of my previous visa status, I have had a level of access to Secondary Inspection rooms over the past few years that no amount of press requests would ever have gotten me. Secondary Inspection rooms vary from airport to airport, from hi-tech and open at Miami International Airport, to small, drab, gray and low-tech at Los Angeles International Airport (LAX). I have witnessed officers interrogating both adults and children, fingerprinting men who are in handcuffs, and generally using the power vested in them to determine whether people will or will not be permitted to enter the country.

In Secondary at LAX, an officer called my Mexican friend's sister-in-law to verify that my friend was really married to whom she said she was. My friend held for three hours because the officer suspected that she was lying to him. In Secondary at Newark International Airport, my sister witnessed an officer scream at a three-year-old girl who was hiding behind her father's legs to see whether the father was telling the truth about his immigration status. Secondary Inspection has been little scrutinized as a part of the U.S.'s immigration system, but as Rodriguez Cruz and many other immigrants discover, Secondary is often the closest that would-be immigrants ever get to the U.S.

In Secondary, one of the first statements made to Rodriguez Cruz by the Customs and Border Control officer, Hector Maxwell, was the warning that "this may be your *only* opportunity to present information to me and the Immigration and Naturalization Service to make a decision."[246] Refugee advocates argue that this requirement is inherently flawed as it ignores the fact that many asylum seekers are frightened of people in uniform (oftentimes the persecutors that they are escaping are government officials in uniform), while many may not know to disclose, or even be able to disclose, the harrowing details of their case on this first questioning at the airport.

Furthermore, as Miami Federal Defender Marc Seitles points out, when CBP is about to conduct what it calls an Administrative Interview that will elicit information that could be used in an immigration trial or even a federal criminal trial, the foreign national is not read any Miranda rights. "The questions that are asked at Secondary are not administrative at all," says Seitles. "They are questions that go to the heart of their case, and their answers will be used against them if and when they are prosecuted." Accordingly, Seitles believes that not reading Miranda rights is simply "ludicrous."[247]

Rodriguez Cruz told the immigration officer who was processing him that he was coming to the U.S. to work and that he had done so four times in the past, but that he was afraid of returning to Nicaragua. This disclosure immediately put Rodriguez Cruz into an asylum track, rather than a simple tourist entry. It also made him potentially deportable because he admitted to having worked without authorization in the past. Rodriguez Cruz offered the name and address of his previous employer. When asked, "Do you understand that by working without CBP authorization, you violated the terms of your visa?" Rodriguez Cruz responded, "No."[248]

In response to the officer's continued questioning, Rodriguez Cruz gave him an account of his life, a very brief one, as the Administrative Interview allowed only two paragraphs for Rodriguez Cruz to sum up his fear of returning.

Rodriguez Cruz passed stage one in the asylum track: convincing the airport officer that he had a "credible fear" of returning and that he deserved to go before an immigration judge to establish his "well-founded fear" of returning. Had he failed this Administrative Interview, he would have been put into "expedited removal" proceedings.

The 1996 immigration law gave INS inspectors at U.S. airports the power to order the immediate deportation of arriving persons under a process known as "expedited removal." An arriving foreigner is expected either to present valid travel documents on entry or state clearly their fear of returning to their country. Under the 1996 law, if either of these is unclear to the adjudicating immigration officer, the arriving foreigner can be immediately put into removal proceedings. In November 2002 the powers of expedited removal were expanded to include all non-Cubans arriving by sea, and then in August 2004 the Department of Homeland Security passed these powers on to all Border Patrol officers. They could now summarily deport any undocumented individual who is caught within one hundred miles of the Tucson and Laredo Border Patrol sectors and who had been in the U.S. less than fourteen days.[249] Using the powers of expedited removal, immigration officers may chose to deny asylum seekers a hearing before an immigration judge; if this is the case, then asylum seekers face a five-year bar to legal reentry.

The government's own review of the expedited removal procedure, conducted with unlimited access to various ports of entry, including airports and land border ports, found that the policy was implemented with little consistency. It states that "most procedures lacked effective quality assurance measures to ensure that they were consistently followed. Consequently, the outcome . . . appears to depend not only on the strength of the claim, but also on which officials consider the claim, and whether or not the alien has an attorney."[250] Furthermore, in all the cases that the study monitored, 15 percent were not referred for an Administrative or Credible Fear Interview, and in half these cases the officer incorrectly noted that the individual had stated no fear of returning to their country.[251]

Although Rodriguez Cruz beat the expedited removal stage, he will likely be denied asylum because anyone who participates in "persecution" cannot be granted asylum, even if they were forced to do it. After interviewing Rodriguez Cruz, Officer Maxwell noted on his record that when the Sandinistas were in power they committed offences like executing political opponents. The sources the officer cited were a *Wall Street Journal* article from 1990[252] and a Human Rights Watch report from 1989. Officer Maxwell, while sympathizing with Rodriguez Cruz's claim that he escaped from the Sandinista army, states, "The applicant did not attempt to prevent the commander from giving the orders or attempt to prevent the execution of the orders."[253] Rodriguez Cruz haltingly initialed each page of the Credible Fear Interview document that will no doubt be used to deport him. Now Rodriguez Cruz sits in BTC, dazed, confused, and no less afraid for his family's life.

When I met Rodriguez Cruz inside BTC, three days after the airport interview, I was the first person to look at a copy of his Credible Fear Interview. I asked him in Spanish if he understood that the document, written in English, stated that he participated in persecution, concluding, therefore, that he should be denied asylum. He did not. He kept saying that he simply answered the officer's questions and that he abhorred what the Sandinistas did. "I did what I could to help people escape the Sandinistas until I could finally escape myself," Rodriguez Cruz told me, as if I had the power to grant him asylum. He said that he would be even more aggressively targeted if he was sent back because the Sandinistas would be even "more angry" with him for bringing further disrepute to their political party. The level of detail Rodriguez Cruz gave me in twenty-five minutes was not represented in the written Credible Fear Interview. I began to feel truly awful that I was the one having to explain the ins and outs of the system to this desperate man. It made me wonder how advocate lawyers manage to do this on a daily basis, especially when they know they will lose most of their cases.

The paralegal at BTC told me, as if to offer the silver lining in the otherwise very hopeless cloud that hangs over Rodriguez Cruz, that he was lucky that he entered on an authentic and valid passport. Under a new measure, which the government deems necessary to protect the borders, those who present fake or doctored documents are being prosecuted. Nearly all of these prosecutions take place in Miami, where the federal defender's office has been flooded with cases based on the use of false documents. This new policy began in Miami in late 2002. It is justified in the context of 9/11, with the U.S. attorney in Miami, Marcos Jiménez, citing the hijacker's use of false information to get visas and get into the country. For Jiménez, false documents equal potential terrorists, and he has been unequivocal in his move to prosecute. The Assistant U.S. Attorney, Carlos B. Castillo, reinforced his superior's tough stance: "It is illegal to use false documents in an attempt to sneak into the United States, and it is a crime our office will prosecute."[254]

However, for people fleeing persecution, false documents are often the only way out of a life-threatening situation. The United Nations has clearly stated this,[255] as have any number of refugee protection and human rights organizations. If an individual is escaping government-sanctioned persecution, logically, that individual cannot go to the persecutor and request a travel document. Furthermore, advocates are deeply concerned that "a felony charge is a kiss of death to those seeking legal entry into the United States. Courts have repeatedly upheld immigration officials' right to deny access to aliens with a criminal record."[256]

Consider, for example, the case of Colombian national José A. Builes-Medina. A farmer in his native country, Builes-Medina came to the U.S. after having been shot and left for dead by guerrillas for refusing to pay extortion money. This peasant farmer had police reports and medical records to back up his claims. To make it out of Colombia, he traveled with a fake passport. When Builes-Medina arrived at Miami International Airport, he immediately told authorities his real name and asked for asylum.[257] The U.S. attorney's office prosecuted Builes-Medina for using false documents to enter the country, and he was convicted. Luckily, he was sentenced to time served but then was passed on to DHS custody to pursue his asylum claim. Although his federal conviction does not prevent him from pursuing an asylum claim, it is extremely damaging to his case for legal status.

As with much of immigration law, the impact of the false-document policy can vary depending on the zeal with which it is implemented. The policy of prosecuting asylum seekers for using false documents to enter the U.S. appears to be unique to Miami. From 2002 to 2003 there was a 48 percent increase in the number of defendants being prosecuted by the southern district of Florida.[258] The Florida Immigrant Advocacy Center (FIAC) has been one of the few groups challenging the government on these increased prosecutions. FIAC has written several times to the U.S. attorney's office and has met with U.S. Attorney Jiménez to object to the prosecutions. FIAC bases its concern on article 31 of the 1951 Refugee Convention, which states that "the Contracting

States shall not impose penalties, on account of their illegal entry or presence, on refugees who, coming directly from a territory where their life or freedom was threatened in the sense of Article 1, enter or present in their territory without authorization, provided they present themselves without delay to authorities and show good cause for their illegal entry or presence."[259]

Because of the pressure from FIAC, Federal Defender Marc Seitles says that the government promised that anyone claiming asylum would be allowed to have their case heard before an immigration judge. If the individual is found to have a well-founded fear of persecution, the U.S. attorney would not seek to prosecute the individual for entering with false documentation. But if the individual is denied asylum, instead of being deported, she or he would be transferred to federal custody to stand trial for the use of false documentation to enter the country. Seitles points out that this promise is often not honored.[260]

These federal prosecutions, which appear contrary to international conventions, are a huge resource drain, according to Seitles. When he first started as a Miami federal defender, his were overwhelmingly drug cases. But overnight, in November 2002, Seitles and all his colleagues' cases became mostly immigration-related. Suddenly Seitles was defending the growing numbers who were being arraigned on charges of using a false passport or false visa, or using false documents to attain a passport or visa. Seitles says it was a dramatic shift. Many immigration agents have told him that they have no choice but to focus more on immigration-related cases because the budget for narcotics enforcement has been drastically cut, while the budget for border enforcement has been greatly increased.

Seitles believes that there is merit to FIAC's claim that U.S. Attorney Jiménez has been able to greatly increase the numbers of convictions by allowing most of the defendants to accept a guilty plea in return for time served. And time served usually means one day, which a defendant is ready to accept in return for a guilty plea, because to take the case to court would mean more time spent in a federal detention center.

The U.S. attorney's secret weapon in ensuring that most cases will be hard for the defense to win is the pretrial motion. In this phase, judges have repeatedly refused to have potentially damning and heart-wrenching evidence of the "necessity" for the person's escape—that is, the horrific situation endured in the home country—presented in front of a jury. The prosecutor posits that the defense cannot prove why the only place the individual could escape to was the United States. Why, a judge will always ask, could the individual not go to another country for asylum? Seitles gave me an example of a case where it was argued that the person had HIV-AIDS, and the only place to get the cocktail of medicines needed was the United States. Yet the presiding judge still ruled that this was not enough of a reason to compel the individual to come only to the United States.[261] Given the federal defender's inability to win most pretrial motions, any trace of why the person escaped and used false documents to come to the United States has not been permissible in court.

Faced with not being able to present the details of the case, Miami's federal defender can then only prove that the person did not know they were using a false passport or false visa. Success, however, is minimal. Most of those arrested and indicted for the use of false documentation in Miami will usually be convicted or plead guilty. This in turn encourages very high levels of prosecution. And with rising prosecution levels, the government justifies its increased spending on the detention-deportation arsenal. In 2005 legislation passed the House of Representatives adding a minimum mandatory sentence of six months for the criminal possession of false documents.[262]

David is lucky that he made his entry with false documents to the United States through JFK Airport in New York and that he did it prior to 9/11. David's was a pretty clear case of well-founded fear of persecution. And as his case illustrates well, people fleeing persecution, especially if it is persecution by their own government, will be utterly unable to go to that government and apply for a travel document, forcing many to knowingly or unknowingly use false documents to travel.

When David was nine years old, he fled his home of Sierra Leone after his mother and brother were killed by rebels during the civil war. As David was young, the rebels wanted him to join their ranks and take up arms and do to other families what he had witnessed done to his. David fled to the capital of Freetown.

Seven years later, the war came to Freetown, and David fled again, this time to neighboring Guinea. There, along with thousands of other fellow Sierra Leoneans, David lived for three months, sleeping on a mattress outside his consulate in the capital city. Later he found a place to live with friends. Then the government of Guinea decided that all Sierra Leonean refugees had to leave. David could not bear the thought of what would happen to him if he returned, so he fled to another West African country, The Gambia. In The Gambia, David could neither find work nor gain admittance to school. He kept traveling through Africa, searching for a country where he could live in peace. Eventually, he moved to Senegal, where he met an American lady—a businesswoman—who, on hearing his story, immediately sought to help him. "She told me she would help me leave," he explained. "Everyone in America cannot believe it when I tell them that the business lady never told me where she was taking me and I never asked her. That is the truth."[263] David had come to trust this kind lady. She bought a ticket and a fake passport for David. He never had an inkling that he was about to commit a U.S. federal offense. Actually, he didn't even know he was going to the United States.

The American businesswoman and David traveled from Dakar, via Paris, to JFK. On the Paris-JFK leg, David was surprised that he and the kind lady were not sitting together, but he thought he would meet her after the plane landed. The Paris airport was the last place David saw the lady. On arriving in New York, David was processed through immigration with his fake passport, and when he told immigration officials that he feared for his life if he was to return to Sierra Leone, David was classified as an asylum seeker and taken to jail. Luckily, he wasn't charged with a federal offense. Much later, David won his asylum case. However, if New York authorities had chosen to prosecute him for using false documents, David would have a federal conviction and would likely have lost his asylum case because of it.

In Florida, too many people with cases just as compelling as David's are doing federal time and emerging with a federal criminal conviction for using false documents to enter the United States. A federal conviction is not an automatic ban to asylum but it makes asylum much more difficult to secure. As federal defender Seitles laments, "The irony is that a person could have a federal conviction for using false documents to get out of the situation and still get asylum—it's absurd."[264]

"I was at least lucky that I used my own passport because I heard that they treat you even worse if you use a fake [one]," Vimral tells a tightly packed room at Columbia University one evening in New York in Winter 2005. Vimral remains extremely poised as she tells her story, and with each detail she manages to make another student squirm in horror. Vimral did not need to use false documents to make her escape from Guyana and enter the United States as she was in transit on her way back to Guyana. Her situation highlights the contradictions of the system. At the same time that Vimral was in Miami International Airport, there were likely other bona fide asylum seekers arriving on direct flights who had no choice but to use false documents to get out of their native country and into the United States.

Vimral was jailed immediately on confiding her fear of returning to an immigration officer. She was placed in the men's quarters of the Krome detention facility. For a transgender person like Vimral, this lack of judgment on DHS's part caused great fear and anxiety. She was forced to share a cell, bathe, and use the restroom with unknown men. Lawyers argued that Vimral should have been released on parole pending her case adjudication. But

DHS, in its dual role as both judge and jailer with sole discretionary power with respect to parole decisions, denies asylum seekers the right to appeal a negative parole decision to an immigration judge. And after 9/11, very few cases win parole.[265]

Vimral's case illustrates perfectly that a one-size-fits-all policy for asylum seekers, with little possibility for individualized assessment, is dangerous. Vimral was transferred from Florida to the Elizabeth Detention Center in New Jersey, where she was again placed with men. When she asked for protection, Vimral was placed in solitary confinement. After another two months housed with men on her release from solitary, she was finally granted parole. Lawyers say Vimral is one of the lucky few who make it out on parole.

When asked how she would advise others who are in a situation similar to her own, Vimral does not hesitate. "If they have to come to go through what I have been through, I wouldn't encourage anyone to do that, because what I have been through, I don't think I can face that again. And I don't want even my enemy to face what everyone is going through in there while they are locked up."[266]

A further illustration of the dangers of a system that applies blanket procedures to all cases without considering individual situations is the tragic story of an elderly Haitian minister. Joseph Dantica fled Haiti in 2004 after UN peacekeeping troops took over his church to launch attacks on gangs. The gangs retaliated by attacking Dantica's church and threatening the minister's life. The aging Dantica managed to get together his documents, including a valid U.S. tourist visa, and with his son, came to meet his family in Miami. Dantica was afraid for his life and hoped that while he visited with his family in the United States, the trouble at his church would pass so that he could return home. Dantica is from an area that has been described as the "Fallujah" of Port-au-Prince.[267]

On arriving at Miami International Airport, the elderly Dantica confided to the immigration officer who was processing him that things were not safe for him in Haiti and that he did not know when it would be safe to return. Despite having a tourist visa, Dantica and his son were placed into an asylum track. They were left at the Miami airport for sixteen hours and then taken to jail. Five days later, on November 3, 2004, Dantica died chained to his jail-hospital bed.

While the official cause of death was pancreatitis, the eighty-one-year old man had complained to Krome officials from the first days of his detention that he was not feeling well. According to Dantica's son, who was with him during the ordeal, officials dismissed the elderly man's complaints as a bluff. When it finally became clear that Dantica needed medical attention, he was taken to the hospital. The whole time he was prevented from seeing his family who lived in Miami. It still remains unclear why Krome officials denied Dantica visitation rights with his family and why they delayed medical treatment for so long. DHS officials called Dantica's death "horribly unfortunate and tragic."[268] Yet immigration advocates have blasted the government for hastening Dantica's death. Their underlying question, is who could DHS possibly be protecting from an elderly Baptist minister? Dantica's family sees no contradiction in the dual purpose of his visit. He was fleeing Haiti out of a fear of death, but he was also visiting his family, thus fulfilling the stated reason on his visa. Instead he met his death while in U.S. immigration custody.

There is mounting evidence that the incarceration that led to Dantica's death had less to do with DHS viewing him as a threat to society than with his being Haitian. Since Haitians began fleeing political violence and repression fifty years ago, there has always been a second tier of justice to deal with those who made it to the United States. During the past five years, only 5 percent of the more than twenty-one thousand Haitian asylum applications have been granted by immigration courts.[269] This does not include the thousands who are simply returned to Haiti without even a chance to plead their case.

Haitians not only have a stunningly low rate of asylum approval, especially for a country steeped in deadly government- and gang-sanctioned violence, they also populate Florida immigration jails at alarming levels. Early on, the Bush administration signaled its zero tolerance policy toward arriving Haitians and its policy to keep Haitians detained for lengthy periods. In late October 2001, the then INS sought to prolong the detention of more than two hundred Haitian asylum seekers who arrived by boat off the coast of south Florida using the PATRIOT Act. The government used the events of 9/11 to argue that the boat people were a threat to national security. The INS invoked a controversial regulation issued October 31, days after the Haitian rafters arrived, allowing the INS to detain individuals who had been ordered released by an immigration judge if the individual was a threat to national security. With little individual screening, the Bush administration used the October regulation to continue to detain the Haitians even after a judge had ordered them released. Humans Rights First called the act a "flagrant extension of the discriminatory treatment this minority group has traditionally received in the U.S."[270]

Haitians have also been disproportionately targeted with federal prosecution for using false documents. Fifty human rights organizations wrote Florida U.S. Attorney Jiménez and Attorney General John Ashcroft to protest what the groups called an "inhumane" policy toward Haitians. The letter stated bluntly that the groups believed the U.S. government was targeting desperate and frightened refugees who have no other choice than to use false travel documents to avoid torture or murder at home. Immigration officials said Haitians were not unfairly targeted and were simply detained for longer periods because if they were released, there was a danger that a mass migration to the United States would be triggered. Immigrant rights activists say there is no evidence that there has ever been a rush to the United States by Haitians, despite the critical conditions in that country for the last fifty years.

Yet despite the pressure, Haitians are still being deported for using false documents, even those who arrived ten to fifteen years ago. One particular group of Miami-based Haitians who fled via airplane is currently being targeted for deportation based on their use of false documents over a decade ago. When the refugees arrived in Miami, they told authorities who they really were and asked for political asylum. They were paroled into the United States, given work documents, and built a life for themselves as they waited for their case adjudication. A decade later, the government is deporting these upstanding community members for using false documents on arrival. To highlight how absurd the policy is, if the refugees had flushed their fake passports down the airplane lavatory midflight and simply claimed asylum on arrival in Miami while showing no documentation, they would not be facing deportation today.

In 1998 Congress passed a bill granting fifty thousand Haitians who were about to be deported the right to apply for legal permanent residency. Yet the act did not cover those who arrived by air and presented false documents at the airport when claiming asylum. The end result is that there are now between two and three thousand Haitian nationals in Miami likely to be deported. These are mothers and fathers with U.S.-citizen children for whom Miami has been their only home. Some have already been deported, other deportations are imminent. Steven Forester, of Haitian Women of Miami, Inc., who has worked extensively on trying to get a fix-it bill passed to stop these deportations, calls this policy extremely "short-sighted."[271] He cites the deep community roots that the targeted Haitians have in Miami and the fact that they will leave behind U.S.-citizen children, houses they own, and jobs they prosper at, as reasons the deportations are "not just immoral, but also nuts and hypocritical."[272] Forester is baffled at the logic behind the deportations because he says that sending back these few thousand Haitians will halt substantial remittances that each one sends regularly to family in Haiti, further impoverishing Haiti and continuing the cycle of devastation in that country.

The cruelty of removing a person from the life that they have worked diligently to build is astounding. Refugee rights advocates also argue that it is just as cruel to jail an arriving asylum seeker, in many ways prolonging the suffering they are likely escaping.

The policy of detaining arriving asylum seekers has led many to ask what threat these refugees pose to the United States. It has been well documented that jailing those fleeing life-threatening situations only compounds their trauma. Without exception, of the dozens of asylum seekers I interviewed extensively over the past years, each one was adamant that their detention was the worst possible thing that could have happened to them. Some were so desperate they even considered risking their lives by asking for a voluntary deportation because it was the only way out of jail. Anti-immigration proponents argue that harsh measures are necessary to ensure that asylum seekers comply with court dates and deportation orders. Asylum seekers and their advocates, on the other hand, say that the United States is acting like a despotic regime by taking away the liberty of people fleeing for their lives.

Edward Neepaye, a Pentecostal pastor, fled to the United States after security forces in Liberia threatened his life because he condemned the use of child soldiers and was considered a threat to the ruling regime. Neepaye spent months in a U.S. jail, and after his fear was ruled to be well founded, he was released. Neepaye was constantly told that he was being held as a security precaution, a concept he rejects. "There are certain values that we simply cannot cast aside in the name of national security. We cannot, on the one hand, support freedom and, on the other hand, take away the civil liberties of people who come to this country seeking freedom and justice."[273]

And then there are the thousands of children who are also jailed every year when they arrive in the United States seeking asylum. Asylum-seeking children have been detained in youth detention centers, shelters, motels, and even adult jails. On arrival, children who cannot decisively prove their age are subject to a dental exam that the government claims is the most accurate way to gauge age. However, many scientists and dentists disagree that the bone structure of the jaw is an accurate indicator of age. After age is determined, too often children are nevertheless treated like adults: shackled, handcuffed, jailed, and even at times placed in solitary confinement.[274]

Children who arrive with parents are often separated from them and, at times, even from their siblings. The prospects are even grimmer for unaccompanied children as they are not provided with an adult to help them navigate the legal system with their best interests in mind. Subsequently, many fail to take advantage of relief that is available to them, losing their cases because they simply do not know any better. Furthermore, children often languish in detention for much longer periods with no one to advocate for them and none of the basics that children require like education, physical activity, or a nutritious diet.

Yet, in the years since the detention policy has been in effect, successful alternatives to incarceration have been offered. The advocacy group Human Rights First (HRF) has documented the policies of other developed nations dealing with asylum seekers, noting that Australia is the only country that shares the U.S. policy of detention. HRF highlights Denmark, Germany, Canada, Ireland, and even poorer countries like Lithuania and Poland, describing how each deals with asylum seekers without incarcerating them.[275]

When the 1996 law was passed allowing for the detention of all persons arriving without visas or valid documentation which overwhelmingly impacted asylum seekers, the then INS, under Democratic leadership, immediately set up a program to test community release programs as an alternative to incarceration. The main concern of the INS was that people show up for their court hearings and comply with deportation orders. There seemed to be some political will—despite the harsh laws that immediately sent all undocumented arrivals to jail—to see how quickly individuals could be released after it was determined that they were not a threat to society. They could then live relatively freely as their cases wound their way through the system. Beyond the humanitarian aspect of this approach, it was also thought that it would cost a lot less than lengthy detention.

The Vera Institute for Justice, a nonprofit organization that works on fair practices in government, was asked to conduct an extensive pilot program. Participants needed a U.S.-citizen relative to accept moral—not legal or financial—responsibility for them. They were asked to report to the supervising offices once every two weeks, check in by phone twice a week, and participate in a home visit once a month. If participants complied fully for two months, their requirements were dropped to a check-in only once a month.

Vera's conclusions, delivered in 2000 after three years of work, showed a very high success rate in ensuring individuals showed up to court and proved markedly cheaper than detention. Asylum seekers were present at court dates in 84 percent of the cases, 22 percent more than asylum seekers who were not detained but not in a supervised program. Stunningly, this community-based monitoring project cost 55 percent less than incarceration would have. Immigrants' rights advocates praised the Vera experiment and urged the government to implement similar programs around the country.[276]

But with the new conservative administration taking power in 2001, followed by the 9/11 attacks, hopes of more liberal treatment for asylum seekers quickly faded. The success of the Vera project fell off the radar altogether. The government was now paying more to detain asylum seekers, and the system slowed to a crawl ensuring that individuals spent a much longer period incarcerated. Parole was rarely granted.

Smaller projects popped up in the post-9/11 years that often became the only options for the detained to be released. ICE began an alternative-to-detention program in 2002. It was allocated a budget of $3 million for 2003, of which $2.5 was spent on a one-year pilot at a privately run Wackenhut facility in Florida called the Broward County Work Release Center (BCWRC). This program, which used seventy-two beds for immigration parolees, met with much criticism. The Florida Immigrant Advocacy Center stated that "full-time detention in the Broward facility was clearly not an alternative to detention, as the women housed there were in fact, still in detention."[277] Additionally, around the time that Wackenhut got the contract, it was under fire from Broward County for a high level of escapes and many incidents of improper sexual conduct by BCWRC guards toward residents.[278]

One of the more controversial alternatives was the electronic ankle bracelet. Placing a much greater burden on the participant than the Vera project, the bulky ankle bracelet requires a dedicated phone line at the place of residence and requires that the bracelet function perfectly at all times. If, for example, the device is malfunctioning or gets unplugged and the participant does not notice or does not reset it or call for help within on hour, it is considered a violation. In trials in Florida, participants can be out of the house only during certain hours, which some have complained makes finding and maintaining a job very difficult. Getting caught in traffic and arriving home minutes late is a violation. This program also requires a much greater commitment from the person's sponsor, not to mention the stigma—reported by almost all of the participants—of having a three to four inch wide monitoring device attached to the leg, the likes of which have previously only been used for released sex offenders and other criminals.

Perhaps most astonishing is that as part of ICE's alternative-to-detention program, it contracted a for-profit company to conduct a trial program similar to the extremely successful Vera Institute pilot. Called the Intensive Supervision Assistance Program (ISPA), the contract went to a company called Behavioral Interventions Inc. (BI) of Boulder, Colorado. This supervision program is dramatically more restrictive and invasive than Vera's program. In the first phase, known as the intensive phase, participants are required to wear ankle bracelets, report several times a week to the offices of BI, obey strict curfews that allow minimal time outside of the home, and be subject to unannounced visits by BI specialists. The second and third phases are less restrictive, and the ankle bracelet is removed if there are no violations in phase one. This program usually lasts until the person's case is decided.

Digging into the history of BI is very revealing. BI sued, and won at the district court level, over the fact that it had lost a contract to a company whose staff was more diverse. Of BI's management and staff, 80.4 percent are white and male.[279] Furthermore, around the time of BI's federal DHS contract, the California Department of Corrections was deeply concerned over a contract it was about to enter into with BI because the company BI partnered with had yet to produce a single working device.[280]

In 2000 business was bad for BI, with stocks falling 42 percent.[281] So, as businesses often do, when controversy arrives at their doorstep, BI spun off a subsidiary to secure the next contract: CorrLogic Inc.

Release into a program like the one BI runs, until an asylum decision is made, is currently one of the only alternative-to-detention programs available. And, as is the case in Florida, when a cumbersome, intrusive, and embarrassing ankle bracelet is the only way out of prison, many are signing up. But not everyone with a pending asylum application in the U.S. is subject to incarceration or an ankle bracelet. For those who arrived in the U.S. with a visa and, once in the country, made their application for political asylum, they are treated like any other immigrant who is applying for a change of status: they are given a work permit and allowed to live in the community. At some point they will be called on to make their case to an immigration officer and will need to prove a well-founded fear of persecution to win permanent residence in the U.S. For many of these asylum seekers, their fate rests in the hands of an immigration officer—a man like Michael Knowles.

Washington, DC

Michael Knowles asked me to meet him two blocks from his union office, in a bookstore in Washington's Union Station, "so neither of us wastes our time if the other is running late." As it turned out, Knowles, with his Parisian hat, wispy hair, and tartan scarf, arrived late.

Knowles and I went to lunch at a grill in Union Station. As we sat ourselves at the table, he immediately picked up on my non-American accent and asked where the "British" came from. Knowles is an asylum officer whose regular duty station is at the Arlington, Virginia, asylum office. He is also a union organizer with the American Federation of Government Employees (AFGE). I told him my accent is Australian, and he immediately asked if I was still a citizen there. Then he caught himself, laughed, and said that ten years of being an asylum officer meant that he always questioned people about their background. I told him that journalists do the same.

Knowles worked for many years in Asia doing refugee advocacy work. As he tells it, he was forced to return to the U.S. because his own wife needed asylum status. She had fled Vietnam, making her way into Thailand on a tiny fishing boat. After reuniting with his wife in Thailand, Knowles brought her to the U.S., where he worked briefly in refugee policy and advocacy. Knowles later became an INS asylum officer, and in the time he has been with the INS, has adjudicated thousands of cases.

Knowles's office in the AFGE building is a tiny, fluorescently lit room in the basement. His desk was neatly organized with a large desktop calendar in the center. It was turned to May 2004, nine months behind the current month. When I commented that I liked his drawing of a bald eagle, patriotically colored in red, white, and blue, soaring among clouds that Knowles had sketched, he told me, "that's where I always want to be, high up in the mountains."

After our first meeting, as we waited in the snow for the Chinatown bus that I was catching back to New York, story after story spilled out. One was about Salvadoran former paramilitaries who have been in the U.S. for years awaiting an adjustment of status or asylum under a 1985 class-action lawsuit. Knowles cannot approve legal status as they openly talked about torture they had performed on guerillas. "They thought there was nothing wrong with what they had done because after all the U.S. government was totally supporting them."[282] U.S. law forbids asylum or adjustment of status to former human rights abusers.

Then there was the case of the Somali woman who wept quietly behind her veil as Knowles asked about her claim of being raped, testimony that her male relative translated for her male attorney and Knowles. Although the woman didn't provide any details about the rape, the rest of her story was consistent. Her attorney feared the worst, thinking that Knowles had not performed his duty properly by not forcing her to answer questions about the rape, but Knowles was sincere when he told me that he didn't need to hear the details. "I did not want to compound her humiliation. I granted asylum." After we parted and I was on my way back to New York City, Knowles called my cell phone. He wanted to check that I was on the bus okay, and still more stories tumbled out.

In the crudest sense, the job of adjudicating whether or not a person truly has a credible fear of persecution if they return to their country is almost like tossing a coin. Yet asylum decisions come with life-threatening consequences. Knowles has the power to grant asylum, but he does not have the power to deny. If he doubts a person's claim, he refers them to an immigration judge.

In his office, Knowles will screen only those asylum applicants who are living in the community—those lucky enough to be out on parole or those who made it into the U.S. under another pretext and then later filed for asylum. In Knowles's office, asylum officers are given a four-day turnaround per case. During that time, they review the case materials, independently research the conditions of the country that the applicant has fled, interview the applicant, and come to a determination on the case. Knowing the conditions or having firsthand experience of a particular political regime can save immense amounts of time and research. Knowles notes that with the pressure to process cases so quickly, the easiest thing for an officer to do is consult the State Department logs on a particular country. Obviously this kind of research leads to a very U.S.-biased version of the situation.

Knowles was recruited to the INS in the days when liberal minds thought it necessary to have human rights workers, immigration attorneys, Peace Corp volunteers, and people with extensive international experience make asylum decisions. The ethos Knowles brought to the work back then, and still tries to practice today, is that he is part of a "refugee protection operation." Back when he was hired and trained, he was explicitly told that his purpose was "not to find people ineligible, to bar them, or catch them." According to Knowles, his "purpose is to interview applicants and identify bona fide refugees who meet the International Convention definition." While Knowles has always been clear that this mandate includes a high level of vigilance to "be sure we are not being abused by fraud rings or criminal elements or terrorists," he does add that he is aware of what he calls the "culture of no" that exists in many offices around the country, where there is pressure on asylum officers to deny claims. Knowles, however, has never questioned that his primary function is to identify refugees that the U.S., by treaty convention, is obliged to protect and to not return to a place where their lives would be in danger.

Port-au-Prince, Haiti

On Avenue Jean Jacques Dessalines, one of Port-au-Prince's main drags for all transport going to the south of Haiti, one wonders at what point in Haitian history this oceanfront boulevard was a jewel in the capital's crown. It is lined with bars, restaurants, and hotels that all hint at more carefree times. Today, however, it is caked in dirt, surrounded by trash and sewage, and lined with vendors selling everything from old rusted car parts to hunks of meat swarming with flies. Traffic moves at a snail's pace as the brightly colored tap-taps stop every few meters to load more people into the carved-out rear. People, immaculately dressed with beads of sweat on their foreheads, use these pickup truck like buses and have little other option if they are to move around the city. Toward the southernmost point of the rancid-smelling avenue is UN headquarters. It is staffed by a team of Sri Lankan peacekeepers decked out in signature baby-blue UN helmets. Inside the gates it is another world, completely void of the chaos, odor, and rot of the street immediately adjacent.

"We do not deal with refugees, madam." The UN chief, a Sri Lankan, was quick to inform me that the international body is in no way active in any refugee issues in Haiti. That is the job of the Haitian Coast Guard (HCG), which is situated in the even more tranquil adjoining compound. I was told to wait in a nondescript, cream-colored building with blue trim that was sparsely furnished. There were a few typed memos stuck to the walls, and the only color came from a poster with thirty men's faces on it. Called the "List of Dangerous Individuals," it was an almost-comical wanted poster as many of the photos depict the men in regular clothing, enjoying themselves. It could have been a teenage girl's poster of the most popular heartthrobs.

Joseph Club, a HCG Level 4 Officer, one level short of the highest, soon joined me. This U.S.-trained officer offered precise answers to my questions about the policies and practices pertaining to returned Haitians who had been caught on the high seas by the U.S. Coast Guard. Just a few days earlier 132 people, mostly men, had been handed over to the HCG. They were on their way to the Bahamas. Haitian rafters often try to reach Jamaica, Cuba, and the Bahamas. Only a small percentage have historically aimed for U.S. soil.[283]

In 2003 there were an estimated 11.9 million people around the world in need of protection because they were fleeing persecution of one sort or another.[284] Between 1995 and 2003 the average figure of worldwide refugees was 13.9 million per year. In 2003, the U.S. granted asylum to 244,700 people, about 2 percent of the world's total refugees. There were ten countries that accepted more refugees in 2003 than the U.S. did. All ten are developing countries. When one examines the ratio of refugees in a particular country to the general population, the U.S. ranks twenty-sixth, well behind many developing countries. In terms of dollars contributed toward international refugee aid agencies per capita, the U.S. ranks eleventh, behind many Scandinavian countries and Australia.[285] Many in the human rights community have called on the world's richest country to do more, in raising both the numbers of those resettled in the U.S. and the amount of money contributed toward global work to aid refugees.

The 132 Haitian rafters were four days into their journey to the Bahamas when they were caught by the U.S. Coast Guard. Their journey, like others before them, was in all ways extreme. The rickety fifty-foot sail freighter had a broken rudder and broken mast, was filled with excrement, and provided little protection for the passengers and little room to move about. The U.S. Coast Guard destroyed and sunk the boat because they said it was a navigation hazard.[286]

The number of people who die undertaking such boat trips as they flee Haiti is unknown, but advocates fear that refugees' determination to avoid the U.S. Coast Guard has forced rafters to lessen safety precautions to avoid detection. Among the few documented cases is a 1999 drowning of forty Haitians off the coast of Miami. Two years later, in 2001, the government of the Bahamas reported that eleven Haitians drowned in shark-infested waters as their overcrowded boat tried to reach the U.S.[287] The Migration Policy Institute fears the numbers could be much higher, stating that "unknown numbers of Cubans and Haitians have died trying to reach the United States in rickety boats and rafts."[288]

In a rare recorded firsthand account, a perspective rarely heard in the media, a young Haitian refugee survivor told of another kind of exploitation that has emerged. Because it is virtually impossible to reach Miami, due to the U.S. Coast Guard's relentless patrolling of the waters, unscrupulous guides take advantage of people's desperation, raise their prices for a ride to Miami, and then don't bother to go anywhere near the U.S. In this testimony, a young man describes how he and a family of four were forced to jump and swim for their lives:

> The man on the boat say, "We are here, this Miami! Jump, jump you have to swim." Everything dark but I see lights on the beach so I think we reach Miami. The husband start screaming at the man to take us closer. His children cannot swim. The man on the boat pull out a gun and say no! We have to jump, so I jump. The family jump too, but everyone screaming and the children cannot swim. Soon they drown. The mother drown too. I see them go under, screaming with water in their mouths. The husband try to save them but they dead. The husband can swim, but he don't want to. Everything is sad and soon the husband, he go under too. What else could he do? Me, I just swim and swim until I reach the beach.[289]

This lucky young man had reached Nassau.

"Extreme desperation and fear is what pushes people to risk their lives on the high seas," the International Red Cross representative in Port-au-Prince tells me.[290] In his two-year posting in Haiti's capital, Filipe Denoso has seen and interviewed many who are in desperate circumstances. "People's lives are threatened for political reasons or simply because they have stepped on the wrong side of one of Haiti's powerful gangs." Denoso is convinced that those who take to the seas (as opposed to the many thousands more who flee over land to the Dominican Republic) are truly escaping for their lives. But none of this matters when Haitians are interdicted at sea by the U.S. Coast Guard. All they are entitled to is a safe trip in a U.S.-government boat back to Haiti.

In the tranquil oceanfront setting of the Haitian Coast Guard office, I was thrust a logbook of all those who were interdicted and sent back in 2004. It was surprisingly easy to access. The Haitian authorities were, in fact, proud to show it off to a journalist from the United States. Perhaps I was surprised because I was expecting U.S.-style state secrecy, where answers to simple questions like the numbers interdicted for a particular year are virtually impossible to get, and here I had the Coast Guard showing me the raw data. The list contained dozens of sheets with carefully handwritten entries for each person, listing their name, village, and age. It tells a tragic tale. Mostly men in their twenties and thirties seem to be fleeing by boat, but there are also women and children. As I looked at the manila folder for 2004, I was surprised that the total for the year was only 1,559. It took me back to Denoso's comments that only people who are desperate with fear will risk their lives on the seas. This relatively small number does not constitute a rush to the U.S. And according to U.S. Coast Guard (USCG) statistics, the average number of those interdicted and returned since 1993 hovers around 1,000 per year.[291] In fact, USCG figures show that in the years 2000, 2001, and 2002, there were substantially more Ecuadorians interdicted on the open seas than Haitians.

Advocates' claims of discriminatory treatment toward Haitians are evidenced by the U.S.' policy of interdiction. The U.S. Coast Guard returns only one other group—nationals of the Dominican Republic—and yet Dominicans have in many instances been allowed to proceed to the United States. Cubans, too, are almost always allowed to proceed when found adrift and, in many cases, even receive assistance from the Coast Guard in reaching the U.S.[292] Only Haitians are returned to their native country when found on the open seas.

Returned rafters are all brought ashore to HCG headquarters, where Officer

Joseph Club and I stood amid a shady grove lined with well-manicured shrubs and the emerald green ocean lapping softly at the shore below us. It was hard to imagine the hundreds of Haitians who are processed there every month. HCG sets up a table and records the name and address of each deportee. Then each person is passed on to the Haitian immigration authorities who set up a table alongside the Coast Guard. They say they give each person fifty Haitian dollars (approximately eight U.S. dollars) before opening the gate to Avenue Jean Jacques Dessalines and wash their hands of the rafters. Immigrant advocates who have interviewed returned rafters say many claim to have been given nothing at all.[293]

According to Filipe Denoso of the Red Cross, those who have tried to flee Haiti by boat are targeted by the Haitian police or gang members when they return.[294] In early 2004 an Associated Press reporter who traveled with the U.S. Coast Guard witnessed the interdiction and return of 233 Haitians who were caught in a wooden boat at sea. On their return, as the gates of the HCG compound were opened and the repatriates forced out, the Haitian Coast Guard had "their rifles trained on the taunting crowd to force a passage through for the refugees." The AP article went on to describe how the group walked very uncertainly, most of them barefoot, toward the city of Port-au-Prince, where none of them lived or had even visited before.[295] The 1993 Inter-American Commission on Human Rights special report on Haiti cited cases of repatriated Haitians who had been arrested in their homes and later found dead, others who were beaten by soldiers, and still more who were arrested and tortured inside Haiti's infamous National Penitentiary.[296]

According to Officer Joseph Club, it is when the Haitians are aboard the U.S. Coast Guard ship that they have their chance to ask for asylum. The Haitian side merely accepts their citizens back from the U.S. or French Navy. Immigrant advocates say the State Department calls this the "shout test,"[297] saying that refugees must literally shout and get hysterical about their fear of returning to Haiti for the U.S. Coast Guard to warrant a Credible Fear Interview. None of the rafters I spoke with had any idea they were supposed to scream and shout about their fears of returning.

Furthermore, according to a more senior HCG officer, Richard Bouzl, the USCG has never delivered, in the seven years he has worked for the HCG, even a single interdicted rafter to the U.S.[298] Even if rafters *are* questioned by USCG officers, the task of proving credible fear is nearly impossible. USCG personnel are not trained in determining asylum cases, and most do not speak Creole. Club told me that the Americans are most interested in determining who in the group is the guide—what border crossers call the coyote. The 132 who had been recently interdicted all said they had equally conceived of the idea and financed it. After four days, USCG had still not cracked the coyote mystery and returned the rafters to their Haitian counterparts.[299]

Haiti is a case study in well-founded fear. The norm is gun-ruled chaos, political instability, and extreme poverty. Haiti is the poorest country in the Western Hemisphere, with over two-thirds of its 7.8 million people living in desperate poverty. Some 70 percent of Haitians are unemployed. Two-thirds live on less than one dollar a day.[300] The judicial system is virtually nonexistent, and the International Red Cross says that over 95 percent of those in Haiti's jails do not have a sentence or have not been tried in court.[301] The economy is controlled by foreign powers through the International Monetary Fund (IMF), World Bank, and the U.S. government, allowing it to be flagrantly abused by those in power and leaving the masses to fight over the scraps. Public services like water and electricity do not reach most Haitians. Throughout its history, varying degrees of people have fled Haiti—from the decades-long Duvalier dictatorship to the democratically-elected Aristide and Preval governments, to the post-Aristide U.S.-installed leadership. Throughout, there has been an entirely separate asylum policy for Haitians than there has for other foreign nationals coming to the United States.

Haitians first began fleeing their country en masse during the violent and repressive Duvalier dictatorship that lasted twenty-nine years, ending in 1986. As New York–based Haitian community advocate Jocelyn MaCalla says, "the United States has always had a special set of policies for dealing with Haitians arriving by boat."[302] In December 1972, when one of the first big boatloads of Haitians arrived in the U.S., they were all detained. At the time, refugees were not jailed; they were released into the community and given a court date for an asylum hearing. These 1972 Haitian refugees were the first to be subjected to indefinite detention, which ended only when one of them committed suicide in jail. MaCalla remembers the "furor" this death provoked; the then INS soon showed the Haitians some mercy and freed them on bond.[303]

As the Duvalier reign brought more fear to the everyday lives of people (each village had a "tonton macoute," a section chief, who would pillage, plunder, and even rape villagers), large numbers took to the seas between 1980 and 1982 in makeshift rafts. At this time Ronald Reagan was in power in the U.S. and he saw the political situations of two neighboring countries, Cuba and Haiti, as particularly worrisome for the U.S. While Reagan rolled out a red carpet for Cubans who were fleeing free education and free healthcare, he slammed the door on Haitians who were fleeing political violence. Reagan passed two Executive Orders (EO) that reiterated his support of previous policies that allowed for separate asylum laws for Haitians. In these two swift EO blows, Reagan backed the policy of indefinite detention, while formalizing the policy of interdiction on the high seas. As MaCalla points out, "There were two lines for those arriving in rafts. Cubans were encouraged by the U.S. to come to freedom and were welcomed by family and friends, and the Haitians, if they made it, were taken to jail where they were detained indefinitely."[304] Reagan's second EO mandated that the USCG return any Haitians interdicted on the open seas. In the early 1990s after a minor outcry over this policy, the first president Bush—George Herbert Walker Bush—came up with an ingenious solution: Guantánamo Bay, Cuba.

While his son has made this slice of U.S.-controlled Cuba a place that most everyone in the world now knows as a controversial prison, Bush Senior very quietly brought it into use as a refugee camp exclusively for Haitians. MaCalla was a translator for clients who were stuck in Guantánamo and remembers vividly the sheer injustice of it. "A slot machine has far more legal rights than a Haitian going to Guantánamo," she said. "In the U.S. they would have had access to an attorney, and the attorney would be present during a hearing. They would have [had] a right to counsel with the attorney, and so they would have [had] adequate time to prepare their asylum case, which sometimes requires the assistance of experts. None of that was available in Cuba."[305]

Eerily, critics then, like now, charged the Bush administration with detaining Haitians outside of U.S. soil in order to deny them basic protections. If an individual was lucky enough to convince an asylum officer in Guantánamo that he met the conditions for credible fear, the person was then transferred to a jail on U.S. soil to await the chance to plead his or her case before an immigration judge. Most, however, languished in Guantánamo before being returned to Haiti.

Democrats have also treated Haitian refugees harshly. During President Clinton's first year in office he was faced with the biggest outflow of refugees from Haiti ever. The military coup leaders who had control of Haiti after deposing the elected president Aristide were increasingly cracking down on the population. In 1994 some twenty thousand individuals fled Haiti by boat, and President Clinton continued his Republican predecessor's use of Guantánamo Bay. Of the twenty thousand, half were sent back to Haiti, and the other half were paroled into the U.S. to plead their cases.[306] In May 1994 President Clinton was preparing to interdict more Haitians. "I hope we will not have a new flood of refugees, but we are increasing our naval reserves in case that happens."[307]

The policy of summarily returning Haitians to Haiti when interdicted on the open sea, while not new, has human rights advocates extremely worried. On February 25, 2004, while armed gangs were marauding through Haitian cities, reports of indiscriminate killings were widespread, and the U.S. State Department urged all its citizens in Haiti to evacuate. President Bush then reiterated that all Haitian refugees interdicted by the U.S. Coast Guard would be summarily returned: "I have made it abundantly clear to the Coast Guard that we will turn back *any refugee* that attempts to reach our shore. And the message needs to be very clear as well to the Haitian people."[308]

Human Rights and immigrant advocates had hoped this would be the time when the interdiction policy would be suspended, given that the President himself acknowledged rafters were indeed people fleeing persecution by terming them "refugees," but Bush dealt a swift blow to those hopes. In fact, the U.S. government was anticipating that so many Haitians would flee the violence that it began making preparations for a temporary refugee camp at Guantánamo Bay exclusively for Haitians.[309]

In this light, the contract that the Department of Homeland Security awarded to Halliburton subsidiary Kellogg Brown and Root in early 2006 for $385 million, to plan for multiple "emergency" sites (locations undisclosed) containing up to forty thousand new beds for foreign-born refugees,[310] leaves little doubt that the government plans to continue its incarceration policy for future refugees who may have the misfortune of arriving with a flood of others.

But before such elaborate and expensive contingency plans were in place, back in early 2004, the U.S. appeared to be doing everything it could to stop a massive outflow of people. Alarming reports emerged of U.S.-led security forces in Haiti blocking land borders to prevent Haitians from fleeing during the lawlessness and revenge killings that followed the removal of President Aristide. The Florida Immigrant Advocacy Center compiled these reports, including one sworn affidavit from the Church World Service Refugee representative in Haiti. The representative implicated U.S. forces in stopping refugees fleeing by boat as well. "There are places near the sea where Haitians trying to flee by boat usually go—there are military forces in those areas occupying the places on the ground where they usually go to leave the country . . . [they are] basically U.S. forces."[311]

Such actions, including the policy of interdiction and return, directly violate international law as enshrined in the 1951 United Nations Convention on the Status of Refugees. A person who claims to be fleeing persecution must not, under international law, be stopped from fleeing by a foreign government or forcibly returned to the country where his or her life or freedom would be endangered. International law also forbids the return of refugees to a country where they would not be protected on return. The 1951 Convention instructs that "no Contracting State shall expel or return ('refouler') a refugee in any manner whatsoever to the frontiers of territories where his life or freedom would be threatened on account of his race, religion, nationality, membership of a particular social group or political opinion."[312] The problem with international law is that there is no way of mandating that states open their doors and accept refugees. And while many decades and much human expertise has gone into crafting these international standards for the rights of refugees, there is no enforcement arm, so it is easy for a superpower like the U.S. to ignore them.

Immigrant advocates are flabbergasted at the level of disrespect the current Bush administration has shown for international law. In early March 2004, when armed gangs were plundering Haiti, President Bush warned Haitians not to flee because they would simply be returned. Soon after the U.S. removed President Aristide from Haiti,[313] an announcement was made that the Bush administration would pay the salaries of the Haitian Coast Guard to help prevent a massive outflow of refugees. Administration officials admitted that an influx of Haitian refugees could pose political problems for President Bush in an election year. The salaries of five hundred Haitians for up to three months were set aside, with some extra funds going to refurbish Haitian Coast Guard facilities damaged in the political turmoil.[314] That the U.S. would pay another country to prevent its people from fleeing persecution was unprecedented, and yet this announcement barely made a splash.

As if to further restrict Haitians from access to asylum, the Bush administration even refused to reinstate an in-country refugee processing program.[315] The Department of State was blunt in its rejection of the proposal in 2002: "We do not believe that the extraordinary remedy of an in-country refugee processing program for Haitians is appropriate at this time. Given the level of economic desperation in Haiti, an in-country program is likely to attract many more ineligible than eligible applicants. We believe that existing protection options for Haitians who may be at risk of persecution or torture are sufficient."[316] This drew an angry response from the Women's Commission for Refugee Women and Children, who responded that "it is now clear that this current Administration has no intention of extending refugee protection to Haitians unless they are fortunate enough to make it past the extraordinary hurdles of interdiction, summary return, offshore processing, expedited removal, prolonged detention and fast tracked asylum adjudications."[317]

The treatment of Haitian refugees has long stood in stark contrast to the treatment of refugees from most every other nation. Consideration of how asylum seekers from neighboring Cuba and far-off China are treated is illuminating. Since the early 1960s, Cuban refugees, regardless of which party is in power in the U.S., have always received preferential treatment. Every Cuban who is interdicted at sea by the U.S. Coast Guard receives instructions by a Spanish-speaking officer on how to alert officials if they have a fear of returning to Cuba, and they are all offered an asylum-screening interview. Chinese migrants interdicted at sea are provided with a questionnaire in their native language that guides them through a process that allows them many opportunities to state any fear of returning to China. Advocates have been demanding for years that Haitians get the same treatment.

For his part, President Bush sees no contradiction in America's asylum policies with regard to refugees arriving in boats. "The immigration laws ought to be the same for Haitians and everybody else, except for Cubans. And the difference, of course, is that we don't send people back to Cuba because they're going to be persecuted, and that's why we got a special law on the books as regards to Cubans."[318]

But since 9/11, a select group of other nationalities have joined Haitians in receiving particular attention from the Bush administration. Asylum seekers from countries the Bush administration deems to be sympathetic to al-Qaeda are currently targeted through a DHS program called "Operation Liberty Shield." This patriotically named program, implemented on the eve of the war on Iraq in March 2003, essentially detains asylum seekers from a number of unnamed countries for the entire length of their asylum proceedings, denying them any opportunity to be released on bond or to an alternative program.[319] For "law enforcement sensitive" reasons, the Department of Homeland Security has refused to disclose the list of countries. However, Human Rights First has ascertained that Liberty Shield applies to well over thirty countries including Turkey, Jordan, Egypt, Bahrain, and even the supposedly "liberated" countries of Iraq and Afghanistan.[320] Yet again, the threat of potential terrorists infiltrating the U.S. was the reason given for this program by then Homeland Security Secretary Tom Ridge. "We just want to make sure that those seeking asylum, number one, are who they say they are, and, two, are legitimately seeking refuge in our country because of political repression at home, not because they choose to cause us harm or bring destruction to our shores."[321]

Manhattan

As I waited in the offices of Human Rights First (HRF) to meet with the asylum director, Eleanor Acer, the receptionist fielded a constant stream of calls, at times having two and three on hold. It was surprising to me, though Acer later told me this is usual, that every one of the calls was a person asking for representation in an asylum case. The receptionist went through the same series of questions in rapid succession with each caller. It was obvious to her that some people would be candidates for HRF pro-bono representation, and it was just as obvious that others would not. Acer says their biggest challenge is applying their limited resources to the mountain of cases that accumulate.

Along with a few other human rights organizations, HRF participates in a rotating representation schedule for asylum seekers who are detained in various jails across New York and New Jersey. If this roster of pro bono lawyers does not represent an asylum seeker, the individual will likely go without a lawyer, as the government is not mandated to provide one. In all of Michael Knowles's years of interviewing and adjudicating asylum cases, he has seen time and again that asylum seekers who have legal representation are more likely to win their case. Yet he is quick to note that many lawyers, some that he sees on a weekly basis, are nothing more than sharks, out to make a quick buck on unsuspecting refugees.

In the post-9/11 climate it has become harder to win an asylum case, perhaps because so many asylum seekers go without representation or perhaps because the system itself has slowed down. In 2003, forty-six thousand political asylum cases were filed or reopened in the United States, of which, according to Homeland Security, less than 25 percent were approved. That's down from more than 30 percent in 2000.[322]

The number of people applying for asylum has also dropped dramatically since 9/11. Michael Knowles described this fact as "curious" as we sat in a different Union Station restaurant, the snow of our last meeting now replaced with an eighty-degree day. Knowles's good friend, who had worked with him in the refugee resettlement movement in Southeast Asia some twenty years ago, abruptly disagreed with him. "What's curious about it? If you stifle people's attempts to come here, of course the numbers are going to be down."[323] This man, Kyle Horst, is currently working with the United States Conference of Catholic Bishops. He met us at lunch because Knowles thought he would be a good person for me to talk with.

Kyle Horst worked in refugee resettlement for many years in Southeast Asia. Refugee resettlement is a program that works in collaboration with the

UN High Commission for Refugees. Essentially created and spearheaded for many years by the U.S, it was born out of the massive numbers of refugees who were fleeing persecution and torture and crossing land borders into neighboring countries. These refugees would end up in large camps where they would either languish for years or become victims of further harm, so a program of resettling them in a safe third country was initiated. At its height, the U.S. brought some 200,000 refugees to the U.S. in one year and resettled them. According to government statistics, the average resettlement number between 1975 and 2001 was 95,000 refugees per year. In contrast, the next highest taker was Canada with around 5,000 per year.[324]

Refugee resettlement has been seen as a vital, if imperfect, solution to the world's escalating refugee crisis. When people's lives are threatened they often flee to the nearest safe place, which is almost always another poor country that is ill equipped to handle the massive influx of refugees. Over the years there have been tens of thousands of Afghans who fled to Pakistan, Congolese and Angolans who fled to Zambia, Sierra Leoneans who fled to Guinea, Colombians who fled to Venezuela, Jews who fled various Eastern European countries, and, sadly, the list goes on. One of the major purposes of the Refugee Resettlement program is to encourage all countries to keep their borders open to those fleeing by guaranteeing that other countries will help with the resettlement. If a desperately poor country feels that it cannot possibly cope with such an influx and shuts down its borders, the humanitarian crisis could be devastating. And furthermore, the large camps that refugees are herded into are often not safe for certain populations, especially women, unaccompanied children, and the elderly. Resettlement aimed to use the 1951 UN Refugee Convention to bring those who qualified to a safe third country.

Erin Corcoran was a young New York attorney when she was posted in Zambia for three months to screen potential refugees. The intermediary between the UNHCR and the INS, her position was created after UNHCR and INS officials realized that both bodies had a different set of guidelines for determining who was eligible for resettlement.

Corcoran was greeted every day at her office in Lusaka by lines of people waiting to tell her their story. Her job was to take the tragic and horrific stories she heard and, using her knowledge of U.S. asylum criteria, make a strong case of asylum. An INS officer would decide whether or not to grant asylum based on the paperwork she prepared. Corcoran felt that she was "playing God" by "determining people's futures according to who [she] got to speak to and how they fit the U.S. criteria of a refugee." The process was laborious and wildly random in who it helped. At times Corcoran wondered how plucking a few thousand out of a sea of tens of thousands—many whom she could never meet because they were in regions that were extremely unsafe—was helping the refugee crisis. But, she concluded, it was better than nothing.[325]

After 9/11, the Refugee Resettlement program all but halted. Compared to the pre-9/11 average intake of close to 100,000 refugees per year, the intake in the years since the attacks—around 20,000 per year—is a trickle. And while it is clear that previous U.S. efforts in this area barely scratched the surface in dealing with the magnitude of the problem, it was at least something. In their 2004 annual report, the U.S. Committee for Refugees (USCFR) came down on the world's rich countries for allowing what it called the "warehousing" of refugees. Lavinia Limón, executive director of USCFR, described this as "coercing people who have fled persecution and terror to live in crowded, destitute, and dangerous encampments" for years on end with no hope of returning to a normal life.[326] Limon is adamant that it is "illegal" and "immoral" for millions to be left in refugee camps for ten or more years.

To justify the reduction of the number of refugees admitted, the government claims that it needs to be extremely careful about who it is resettling in a post-9/11 world. Erin Corcoran wonders which potential terrorist would go and live in the middle of a squalid refugee warehouse on the tiny odds that he or she will be selected for resettlement in the U.S. In addition, the already resource-heavy process of determining who to resettle has been made more cumbersome in the security-industry age. Now digital biometrics are recorded, and asylum officers are taking much the same technology that has been implemented inside the U.S. for screening and tracking potential immigrants on the tours-of-duty they are routinely sent on to identify bona fide refugees to resettle.[327]

Refugee advocates like Kyle Horst and Erin Corcoran agree that they saw a clenched fist squeeze even tighter with the passage of the nation's most sweeping immigration bill since the 1996 law. The 2005 REAL ID Act,[328] which was passed as part of the Iraq War and Tsunami Aid Supplemental Bill, made gaining asylum in the U.S. even harder. Included in the law is a provision, section 101, that forces the asylum seeker to prove that one of the five grounds for persecution—race, religion, social group, political opinion, or nationality—is the central reason for the fear of return, not one among other reasons. It also allows for judges to demand corroborating evidence of the torture or persecution experienced, something that in many cases is almost impossible to provide because someone who is fleeing danger rarely stops to think of bringing evidence of their persecution. Furthermore, the law gives judges the power to deny asylum if an applicant does not make eye contact, is flat in their body language, or because of other aspects of their demeanor. Advocates argue that oftentimes there are cultural reasons for a person not making eye contact, which have nothing to do with guilt, while flat body language is common in people who have suffered extreme trauma and become emotionally numb.

The REAL ID law also denies asylum to individuals who do not disclose a claim of rape on arrival at the airport but that do so later, when they come before an immigration judge. This provision of the law completely ignores the discomfort women from different cultures (and in general) feel in talking about violent sexual abuse. Refugee women have complained that airport officers who are always uniformed and armed evoke memories of their attackers, making it almost impossible to talk about the sexual violence they experienced. REAL ID also denies asylum to those who, while personally bearing no responsibility, have relatives that were extorted by so-called terrorist or militant groups. These individuals fall into what Human Rights First calls the "overly broad definitions of 'terrorism' and of what constitutes 'supporting' terrorism."[329]

A coalition of faith-based groups, including the liberal Lutherans and the extremely conservative Southern Baptists, agreed that passage of the REAL ID Act into law would "lead to the deportation of an untold number of bona fide asylum seekers to their persecutors."[330] This act became law without ever being debated on the floor of the United States Senate. In a swift move to avoid any debate or compromise on the bill, it was attached to an Iraq War supplemental by Republican House leadership and quickly became law.

Under the REAL ID Act, all of the people profiled for this chapter—all granted asylum, all bona fide refugees—would most likely have been denied and then deported. The near future seems even bleaker for refugees coming to American shores. A bill, HR 4437, that passed the House in late 2005 contained provisions that would make it a felony for an asylum seeker to be out of status after overstaying a visa, deprive many asylum seekers of the right to appeal a decision to the federal courts, and expand both the detention of asylum seekers and expedited removal. The message is clear: *Refugees be warned: if you're fleeing persecution, don't come to the United States.*

Chapter IV

FOREIGN STUDENTS, FOREIGN WORKERS, AND MILITARY NATURALIZATION

Oladokun Sulaiman came from Nigeria to study at the State University of New York Maritime College when he was twenty-four years old. Vasant Mehta arrived from India when he was twenty-four as well and works for Pixel Systems, Inc., as a computer analyst. Philippe Louis Jean came to the U.S. from Haiti when he was five years old with his parents and younger brother. Three different men, from three different countries, with three completely different immigration experiences. Sulaiman was inspired by his studies in America to write a proposal geared toward poverty alleviation in Africa; Mehta found his calling outside of work, playing tablas for local Indian festivals; Louis Jean joined the Marines and served in Iraq. Yet all three have faced traumatic experiences in the years since 9/11, simply because of their immigration status.

Foreign nationals who come to the U.S. must become citizens to attain the full and equal rights of American citizens. While there is no easy way to enter and stay in the U.S. permanently and legally, for those who are legal permanent residents, naturalization can be a complicated and difficult process. The rungs on the immigration ladder leading to citizenship are most often occupied by foreign students and foreign workers who eventually marry a U.S. citizen or have a family member or employer sponsor their permanent residency application. In the years since 9/11, there have been many changes that have directly and indirectly affected both foreign students and foreign workers. For those willing to put their life on the line and serve the U.S. in war, an expedited path to citizenship has become a promised reward.

Foreign Student Status

Oladokun Sulaiman was born in Burkina Faso and moved to Nigeria, his parents' country of birth, to study. He had an impressive track record in his country of citizenship, Nigeria, when he decided the way ahead for him was to study in America. Sulaiman had graduated in 1996 from the Nigerian Federal College of Fisheries and Marine Technology in Lagos and had a keen interest in the merchant marines. He was not from a wealthy family and had had to work extremely hard to be able to afford college. After graduating, he worked and saved money for a ticket to Singapore where he was able to secure a better-paying job. From Singapore, Sulaiman applied for a tourist visa to the U.S. and, when he was finally granted one, Sulaiman came to visit America with the express purpose of finding a school where he could further his studies. In 2000 Sulaiman was accepted to the State University of New York (SUNY) Maritime College in the Bronx, NY, and legally changed his status from tourist to student by securing an F1 visa from the INS.[331] Sulaiman was overjoyed. He was in New York, a student at SUNY Maritime College, and he was on his way to achieving his dreams.

In most parts of the world, a college degree from a U.S. institution carries prestige. U.S. institutions of higher education, for their part, depend on the influx of foreign students for a variety of reasons, none more crucial than the income they generate. Seventy-five percent of foreign students are self-funded, and in 2001 foreign students and their dependents contributed $11 billion to the U.S. economy.[332]

In 2001 582,996 foreign students studied in the U.S.[333] Three years later the levels had dropped by 2.4 percent.[334] In 2004, applications from foreign students dropped by a staggering 28 percent while graduate school enrollment dropped by 6 percent.[335] The decrease in foreign students has hit certain areas harder than others. According to seventy-nine universities, between autumn 2001 and autumn 2002 there was a 21 percent drop in foreign students admitted to physics programs. University administrators say this has been due to a much tougher climate in the post-9/11 environment in which foreign students are subjected to greater scrutiny from the government. Yale University, for example, has reported that in 2004 complicated visa procedures led to a 9.5 percent fall in foreign post-graduate applications.[336] American universities fear that foreign students are turning to European, British, and Australian universities to complete advanced degrees. On average, international students make up 5 percent of total enrollment in U.S. colleges and universities. In the post-9/11 environment, educational institutions fear this will continue to fall.

Foreign students are also vital to U.S. colleges for reasons beyond the dollars they earn. Over the years, successive U.S. governments have succeeded in maintaining a spider-like reach into many foreign governments via U.S.-trained political scientists and economists who have gone back to their countries to take on leadership roles and implement U.S. neoliberal ideology. Consider the architects of radical free market economic policies in Chile under General Augusto Pinochet. The men, known as the "Chicago Boys," were trained in economics at the University of Chicago.[337]

Professor David Harvey has documented this phenomenon:

> By 1990 or so most economics departments in the major research universities as well as the business schools were dominated by neoliberal schools of thought. . . . The U.S. research universities were and are the training grounds for many foreigners who take what they learn back to their countries of origin—the key figures in Chile's and Mexico's adaptation to neoliberalism were US-trained economists for example—as well as into international institutions such as the IMF, the World Bank, and the UN.[338]

Other schools find it important to maintain a minimum number of foreign students for the diversity they bring to the overall life of the college and to the quality of the education. Sulaiman truly felt that he was giving back to the life of SUNY Maritime as he worked his way through his three-year degree. That is, until he was two months away from graduating. Unlike the other immigrants profiled in this book, Sulaiman is the only one I have never personally met. I came to learn about him only after he was deported, so the Sulaiman I know is through e-mail, telephone, and the rich stories of his friend, whom I met with in New York.

SUNY Maritime College, Bronx, New York

The day was blazing hot when I was taken around the campus of SUNY Maritime. My guide was a graduate of the college, one of Sulaiman's friends from Nigeria. Along with Sulaiman, he was one of only two African students in their class. Yomi Ademuwagun graduated in 2003, and he now has a good job with an American company that makes air conditioners. He is a minister at a local Baptist church, has married an American citizen, and is now a green-card holder. Ademuwagun was visibly distraught over what has happened to his fellow Nigerian, and as we toured the campus of SUNY Maritime, his distress grew as more memories came back to him. "How much my life has changed in the years since I graduated, how much I have achieved. And Sulaiman should have been doing the same. Instead he is dealing with blow after blow because of his deportation and inability to graduate."[339]

The campus is set on the scenic point where New York's East River meets the Long Island Sound. It is steeped in history, as the campus utilizes the original garrisons of Fort Schuyler, a pentagonal granite edifice built in the early 1800s and used extensively during the civil war. Sulaiman was sitting and studying in one of the Fort buildings, which the college has turned into an extensive Maritime library, when the Joint Terrorism Task Force arrived to arrest him.

As mentioned earlier, just weeks after the 9/11 attacks the U.S. Congress passed the USA PATRIOT Act. Among the many controversial powers that this sweeping legislation accorded the government was the ability to scrutinize foreign students by mandating that U.S. institutions disclose students' personal information without their knowledge or consent. This information, which was catalogued in large databases, was pursued aggressively by the FBI and Justice Department on the pretext of determining if foreign students or teachers had ties to terrorism.[340] The government also argued that it needed to be able to track foreign students once they were in the U.S., because one of the 9/11 hijackers was in the country on a student visa and was not, in fact, studying. Most colleges and universities complied with the government's demands, but some were outraged and refused. Prior to the PATRIOT Act, a court order had to be produced for a university to hand over personal records. In the weeks following the World Trade Center attacks and before the passage of the PATRIOT Act, two hundred colleges admitted to handing over private information on its foreign student population without a court order.[341] In most cases, students were not informed that their personal information was being given to the government.

Schools were also being asked for information on foreign students by another government agency—the INS. The INS created the Student and Exchange Visitor Information System (SEVIS) to keep track of all students. Under the PATRIOT Act, schools were mandated to report if a foreign student did not enroll within thirty days of the registration deadline.[342] In this climate, federal government intervention on university campuses became a regular affair. So when the Joint Terrorism Task Force showed up at SUNY Maritime—an event that would have garnered much outside scrutiny prior to the 9/11 attacks—no one questioned it.

Ademuwagun said the suggestion that Sulaiman was connected to terrorism spread quickly throughout the small student body. Rumors swirled that Sulaiman, like the 9/11 hijackers, was studying among them with the ultimate plan of hijacking a ship and one day committing acts of terrorism.

Ademuwagun told me that he could not believe his ears, nor could he believe how quick his fellow classmates were to condemn Sulaiman when no one had any knowledge about why Sulaiman had been arrested. It is not hard to believe that the only African-Muslim student in the overwhelmingly white faculty and student body of Maritime college could so easily be condemned.

In one e-mail, Sulaiman told me that what upset him most was learning how rapidly his classmates forgot his stellar track record. Sulaiman had headed several teams of students on special projects for the State of New York, with each project resulting in a new contract for Maritime College. Sulaiman had even drawn up an extensive plan for the school to start a model UN and a maritime human rights organization. Sulaiman wonders how his history at the school could permit his fellow students to suspect he was a terrorist.

Most of Sulaiman's problems stemmed from his battle with the school's administration over tuition fees. In his second year at this New York State school, the chairman of his department advised Sulaiman that if he could produce proof of NY residency (like a gas bill or other correspondence to his New York City address), he would qualify for in-state tuition. Sulaiman confirmed the information with the bursar and college administration, and was accepted as an in-state student. He never produced any false documentation to make this claim of residency, and it was well known to everyone at SUNY Maritime that he was a foreign student from Nigeria. One year later, the system picked up that he was a noncitizen and charged him accordingly. When Sulaiman questioned the decision, after already paying the in-state rate, the administration would not let him register or attend classes until he paid the difference. He was also asked to retroactively pay the difference from previous semesters, a bill of around $12,000. Ademuwagun says there was no way Sulaiman, who was from a modest family, who worked while he studied to keep up with his school and rent payments, would be able to come up with $12,000 in a matter of weeks or even months.

Sulaiman attempted to fight the charges and attend classes. On the advice of his department chair, Sulaiman threatened to hire a lawyer. Ultimately, he thought he had reached a compromise with the school by agreeing to pay the higher out-of-state rate for the final semester if the school agreed not to charge him extra and accept what he had already paid for previous semesters. Sulaiman knew that he was "too close to graduating to let this matter stop [him] from attending classes."

On March 7, 2003, as he sat studying in the historic Maritime College library, three men in dark suits approached and arrested him. They were from the Joint Terrorism Task Force (JTTF). He was taken from the library to jail.

The exact number of arrests of foreign student since 9/11 is unknown. Some cases received public attention, like the six Middle Eastern students in Colorado who were jailed for ten days after complying with a "special registration" mandate. When the students showed up to register, immigration officials deemed them to be out of status and arrested them because they had enrolled in less than twelve hours of college credit. Each student had to post a $5,000 bond to leave jail.[343]

It is considered an immigration violation for a foreign student to drop a class from their full-time load. While many students may be unaware that this is considered a violation, the new student-tracking system flags authorities. In HR 4437—the immigration bill that passed the House in December 2005—there was a provision that mandated that all immigration violators be added to the National Crime Information Center (NCIC) database. This would effectively place students, like these six men who were arrested in Colorado, into the country's largest criminal database, accessed by all levels of law enforcement around the nation—simply for dropping a class.

While the case of the six Middle Eastern students garnered media coverage, most cases, like Sulaiman's, were kept out of the eye of public scrutiny. Sulaiman is still not quite sure why the JTTF arrested him, though he does know that the JTTF later cleared him of any involvement in terrorist activity. He was never charged with a crime. The JTTF memo stating Sulaiman has no ties to terrorism also acknowledges that "the school contacted the JTTF because of what they believed to be suspicious behavior of the subject."[344] Sulaiman believes the real reason was his race and Muslim faith, and also because he had threatened legal action against the school. The school administration would not return repeated calls seeking clarification.

In 2002 further legislation was passed tightening the grasp of the government on foreign students. The Border Security Act imposed additional reporting requirements on universities while vastly increasing scrutiny on students during the visa application process. In fact, in the years after 9/11, the process of applying for a student or scholar visa in the sciences and technology slowed to a crawl—so much so that in February 2004 the House Science Committee of the U.S. House of Representatives held hearings to examine the extensive visa delays and denials that it believed was weakening the U.S.'s dominant position in scientific research. A specific study into the Visas Mantis program was launched.

The State Department had implemented the Visas Mantis program in 1998, imposing thorough background screening of all incoming foreign students in sensitive scientific areas in an attempt to protect against illegal technology transfer. Sulaiman was one of the science students who had made it through the rigorous screening process. During the House hearings, doubt was cast on the effectiveness of the Visas Mantis's lengthy screening process to keep out potential terrorists. As Committee Chairman Sherwood Boehlert said at the hearings,

> A visa regime that casts too wide a net—that holds up just about everybody for excessive security checks—that regime is not good for security or for science. It's not good for security because it distracts and overwhelms the system, taking resources away from investigations of individuals more likely to present a real threat to our nation. And it's obviously not good for science, given that U.S. success in science has always depended on attracting the best minds from around the world.[345]

After 9/11, the number of applications to be screened increased dramatically, creating a large backlog of pending visas.[346] Moreover, the Government Accountability Office, which had been studying the Visa Mantis program, issued a report that found that, after 9/11, the way in which Visas Mantis information was disseminated at the "headquarters level" made it difficult to resolve cases in an expeditious manner.[347] The national hysteria that led to such heightened background checks and that pegged so many immigrants as terrorists made victims of many, including Sulaiman.

After Sulaiman was arrested by the JTTF, bond for his release was set at an extraordinary $25,000, an amount he obviously could not pay. A week after he was arrested, Sulaiman was scheduled to appear before a SUNY committee to resolve the matter of his tuition fees. He could not attend the meeting because he was in jail, and when he did not appear the school disenrolled him. This immediately revoked his student visa. He was then deportable.

SUNY accused Sulaiman of using forged papers from his Nigerian college in his initial application, according to the JTTF. The JTTF then conducted an investigation into his case. The U.S. embassy in Lagos was asked to verify Sulaiman's credentials with his college in Nigeria.[348] Documents from the U.S. embassy state that the embassy investigator was not able to speak to the office that issues the diplomas, but that the investigator had spoken instead with the student affairs officer. The college's vice provost "pleaded" with the investigator to come back a few days later to meet with the people who would know whether Sulaiman's documents were indeed valid. When the U.S. official returned, students at the university were protesting poor living conditions and would not let the car pass,[349] so the U.S. embassy never completed a full investigation. Based on a later conversation with the student affairs officer, the embassy decided that Sulaiman's documents were false. (The student affairs officer was later severely reprimanded for speaking with U.S. officials when he was not qualified to do so.[350]) The JTTF decisively concluded that Sulaiman had presented "fraudulent documentation."[351]

Ademuwagun finds the charges of false papers particularly troubling because his paperwork was exactly the same as Sulaiman's; if the school genuinely believed that Sulaiman had forged his credentials, they could have compared them to his own. He also adds that in the weeks and months after Sulaiman was arrested, he was very fearful that he, too, would follow Sulaiman to jail, "simply for being a Nigerian student."[352]

While Sulaiman was languishing in an American jail, his father had a heart attack and died. Sulaiman says his father was so distraught on hearing his son was arrested just months shy of graduating that he "caught a heart attack."[353]

Sulaiman is just one of many students who became targets in the days, months, and years after the 9/11 attacks. Because some of the hijackers had used student visas and had enrolled in schools, the government immediately heightened its vigilance of foreign students. The post-9/11 period fostered an environment in which foreign students of Arab, South Asian, Muslim, and African descent fell under immediate suspicion. Students like Sulaiman suffered the consequences.

While anecdotal evidence indicates that applications for F1 student visas picked up again during 2005–2006, foreign students continue to be attacked. In a barely noticed move in March 2005, the Department of Commerce quietly announced changes to regulations that will undoubtedly affect the composition of foreign students in the sciences in the coming years. It will also have a dramatic impact on U.S. prominence at the head of scientific discoveries and advancements.

At issue are certain pieces of equipment, known as "dual use" equipment, that are in use on university campuses around the country and that are deemed to have both military and commercial purposes. Under new Commerce Department regulations, foreign students from twelve so-called countries of concern—China, Cuba, India, Iran, Iraq, Israel, Libya, North Korea, Pakistan, Russia, Sudan, and Syria—must apply for a "deemed export license" to use any such equipment.[354] The government considers the passage of knowledge to foreign students and their participation in research projects to be an "export" because they are a national of another country and will be taking that knowledge with them when they complete their studies.

The 2005 regulations involve extensive background checking if a student is required to use any dual-use equipment. In some cases it could be as simple as a microscope or a textbook. In early 2005, when a ninety-day comment period was quietly announced by the Department of Commerce, Stanford University warned its faculty in a circular memo that the licenses could "take months to process" and that "multiple licenses could be needed for the same person to work with multiple pieces of equipment/technology."[355] Stanford further warned its faculty that penalties are "severe and could involve criminal charges against individuals as well as institutional liability" for failure to license students from the twelve "countries of concern."

The only substantive media coverage of these potentially huge changes appeared when it was almost too late. *San Francisco Weekly* found, with only weeks left to the ninety-day comment period, that many universities and foreign student bodies did not even know that these changes were slated to take place.[356] The changes not only singled out nationals of twelve countries, they also changed a fundamental tenant of U.S. immigration policy. This new regulation, one that did not have to clear the House and Senate, mandates that foreign nationals be treated according to their country of birth, *not* their country of citizenship. Accordingly, a person born in India but raised all her life in Australia and holding Australian citizenship and an Australian passport would be deemed to be from India and hence required to apply for a license for any dual-purpose equipment usage.

Because many universities across the country were not aware of the regulation changes when they were first announced, few schools took full stock of what the changes would mean for them in terms of costs. One school that did do the math, the University of Maryland, estimated that it would cost them upward of $1.5 million to comply because it would be necessary to determine whether each piece of equipment is subject to licensing.[357]

Criticism of these new restrictions has come from many quarters, including a research commission comprised of scientists with strong government connections. The Commission on Scientific Communication and National Security, chaired by Harold Brown, a former defense secretary, and Nobel Laureate David Baltimore, president of the California Institute of Technology, concluded that "by imposing unnecessary barriers on the research activities on U.S. institutions, an overly zealous or inflexible export control system will make it impossible for U.S. researchers to keep abreast of technical activity conducted outside the United States, and the United States will necessarily fall behind."[358]

The commission found the new regulations completely out of sync with reality, arguing that "most universities do not conduct classified research on campus because the associated constraints are incompatible with their educational mission."[359] It went on to blast the government for its outright "discrimination on the basis of nationality," saying that "many leading research universities have made it clear that they have neither the human resources nor the will to selectively segregate their research facilities in this fashion."[360] Perhaps most significant in this bipartisan commission's findings is that the changes are virtually useless in protecting against terrorism, as "they provide little or no security benefit, and only serve to damage the U.S. research enterprise."[361]

H-1B—Skilled Worker Visa

Not just foreign students complain about new tougher rules and regulations. Corporate executives also lament the dramatic fall in foreign student numbers. For General Electric Chairman and CEO Jeff Immelt, the heightened vigilance around student visas is "a case where our policy to close down on access boomerangs."[362] Microsoft Chairman Bill Gates has said that the fall in foreign computing students is a "disaster" for the U.S. and that America's position as "IQ magnet of the world" has been threatened.[363] Many of these young, U.S.-trained foreign students go on to be employed under the H-1B visa that companies like Microsoft and GE use extensively.[364]

Dayton, Ohio

Vasant Mehta's routine rarely changed, as exhausting and demeaning as it was. He worked all night at a local motel or gas station where he earned five dollars an hour. After a ten- to twelve-hour shift, Mehta would sleep for a few hours and then get up and study a little before driving his roommates to their various jobs around town. He was the only one with a car. After he concluded his taxi duties, Mehta would go to class and then back to his graveyard shift at the motel or gas station.

Since arriving as a foreign student at Wright State University in 2000, the same year that Sulaiman entered SUNY Maritime College, Mehta was determined to study hard and get a good job upon graduating. He planned to complete a masters degree in electrical engineering in a maximum of two years, find work, and then soon after return to his home in Andra Pradesh, India, to look after his parents and get married. Five years later, Mehta is part of the high-tech sweatshops that have come to characterize the exploitive skilled-worker visa category of immigration.

Mehta is currently in the U.S. on an H-1B visa, known to many as the Microsoft Visa because the computer giant has largely been behind the creation and growth of this visa category to fulfill its purported need for foreign information technology specialists. The H-1B visa has played the dual role of creating opportunity for foreign workers while also allowing U.S. corporations to shuffle in a largely subservient and cheaper workforce. H-1B visas have met the wrath of the far Right and organized U.S. labor who protest that this incoming foreign workforce has led to a loss of jobs for U.S. workers while simultaneously lowering the wages and working conditions of those still employed.

Foreign workers have historically been brought to the United States when industry has had shortages of U.S. workers or has sought a less costly labor force, most notably during the industrialization of the 1800s and then again during the first and second World Wars.

The professional work-visa category was born in the context of the Cold War, when there was a great paranoia in the U.S. that the USSR was outpacing it in terms of technology. In the early 1960s President Kennedy delivered a bill that opened up employment for foreign nationals who fell into specific technology fields. For the first time, this work-visa system was structured through the U.S. higher education system. The system allowed for individuals with basic degrees from foreign universities to come to the U.S. on a student visa and to complete a more advanced degree. On completion of that degree, the individual could transfer to an H-1 visa, filling such elite positions in the workforce as advanced research engineers or highly specialized information systems analysts.[365]

U.S. corporations have always aggressively sought the lowest-costing workforce. In the years before the rise of globalization and neoliberal economic policies, before U.S. companies began relocating production and service centers to other countries, cheap, skilled workers were sought in America. By the 1990s the H-1 had become the H-1B visa. It was no longer as elite as it once was, with 65,000 non-immigrant midlevel skilled occupation visas issued per year. In the decade since, corporations and organized labor have clashed over the necessity for and the numbers of skilled foreigners needed. Unions have argued that there are enough skilled workers in the U.S. to do the jobs, and that Congress together with the high-tech lobby have sought to replace them with a workforce that can be paid less and denied crucial worker rights.

Over the years the numbers of H-1B visas issued have risen and fallen as per congressional mandates resulting from direct high-tech lobby pressure. In fact, the high-tech lobby has consistently pushed for more medium-skilled foreign workers while cloaking it as a demand for highly skilled workers. This has created a glut in the market and decreased wages. The IT bust in early 2000 simply facilitated a quick decline in the jobs available and in the prevailing wage for those jobs.

At his suggestion, I first met Mehta in a coffee shop right next door to his office in midtown Manhattan. He is a very sweet man with a personality that exudes warmth mixed with an intense shyness. Mehta seems willing to do anything for anyone. And as he told me his story, it was clear that he puts most people in his life before himself, except when it comes to the individuals who seem to exploit him routinely for monetary gain.

Vasant Mehta always planned on beginning his master's degree as a fully paying foreign student and then later applying for financial assistance, which the school boasted would be available after one year of study. Mehta, however, like most of the foreign students in his year, never received financial assistance and so had to apply for multiple credit cards to pay tuition. His debts accrued quickly, but Mehta was confident that he would get a high-paying job that would take care of the growing amount he owed. But around the time that he began attending job fairs at Wright State University, the place where medium-level IT companies shopped for talent, 9/11 happened. And as young South Asian men, Mehta and all his friends found that there was suddenly no one interested in them when they graduated. The IT bust also no doubt narrowed the field even further for Mehta and his friends.

Along with many foreign students, Mehta found himself in a fix. If he graduated and could not find a job, he would be out of status. Yet he had such large student debts to pay off that he needed to find a job in the U.S. so that he could at least take care of his debts. Mehta says he could never find a job in India that would pay enough to cover his U.S.-dollar student loans. He decided to drag out his studies and not graduate in order to maintain his legal status in the U.S. as a student. So began a lengthy period of being a nearly graduated masters student in computer science and electrical engineering and working as the night clerk at a Dayton motel and gas station for five dollars an hour.

It cannot be conclusively argued that post-9/11 xenophobia was the sole reason that Mehta and his fellow Indian classmates were locked out of the job market. But the fact that so many South Asian midlevel engineers and computer scientists were desperately looking for work allowed unregulated work-visa sharks to swarm in. These highly profitable middlemen, who have come to control the H-1B visa domain and are completely unregulated by the government, are yet another critical cog in the profitable U.S. immigration machine.

Supplying H-1B workers to American businesses is immensely profitable. There are currently over one hundred H-1B "vendor" firms of Indian origin that are registered U.S. businesses. According to Javed, who runs an H-1B agency in New York, there are so many people in India with the required qualifications and two to five years of experience that "recruiting IT workers in India is like putting a bucket in a gushing stream to collect water."[366] These "vendors" hire a potential candidate, run through the H-1B paperwork, and then bring the worker to the U.S. They then shop them around the various clients they service. These Indian-origin firms usually end up contracting their H-1B worker out to another, bigger American vendor who, in turn, contracts the worker out to companies like JP Morgan Chase, Merrill Lynch, and Microsoft.

To avoid this second-level vendor, also known as a recruiter or recruitment firm, a worker would have to accept working for a smaller, lesser known, lesser paying company. In return, the original Indian vendor—not the company that has actually hired the H-1B worker—provides all benefits to the worker and pays all taxes to the U.S. government. Thus American companies avoid having to do any visa paperwork and paying the costs usually associated with hiring a worker. The client firm (Microsoft or JP Morgan Chase, for example) pays the vendor directly per hour for the H-1B worker. Of the money received for the worker's services, the vendor keeps a certain percentage, deducts for costs like healthcare, and gives the remainder to the employee.

Vending H-1B companies usually use a two-prong strategy for finding new workers. Abroad, vendors often have offices based in India or China and recruit heavily in these two countries. And in the U.S., they most often find prospective H-1B workers, like Vasant Mehta, on Web sites where job seekers post their résumés.

On graduating from an American university, a foreign student is allowed to work for one year under what is known as an Optional Practical Training (OPT). If during this yearlong OPT a student can find an employer and apply for an H-1B visa, then the student can continue to live and work in the United States. Prior to 9/11, for most midlevel IT graduates like Mehta, this was fairly easy to do. But when Mehta could not find a job and his OPT was nearing its end, he posted his résumé on Monster.com and other employment-related Web sites, including Dice.com. Mehta says that Dice.com is "the lowest on the totem pole of Web sites for IT job recruitment." But he was desperate. Within days of posting on Dice.com, Mehta received a call from an H-1B recruiter. The man had seen Mehta's résumé and was calling to offer him a job with one of his clients. Mehta considered going directly to the firm, but he knew all too well that American IT companies work hand in glove with recruiter firms. They feel they can trust the prospective employee more if she comes through a recruiter. They also save themselves the cost and trouble of providing all the extras like health insurance or payroll taxes. Mehta says this simply allows recruiters to "get rich quick" and for corporations to "save huge amounts by hiring foreigners rather than locals."[367]

The man who called Mehta was from a firm called Pixel Systems. His company's purpose is to find contract employees for American firms. Its Web site states, "Pixel Systems encourages dynamic, aggressive and motivated candidates to apply for IT contract job opportunities here at Pixel Systems. When you join us, we will provide you [with] an opportunity to grow. Unlike . . . other companies, we have a long-term growth plan for you. We will provide you [with] a path and we will encourage you to partner with Pixel Systems."[368] Mehta was about to become an employee of Pixel Systems, even though his job was with One to One Communications.

One more company stood between Mehta as a worker and One to One as an employer. Information Technology Providers (ITP) was the extra "middleman," according to Mehta, something that occurs frequently. One to One paid ITP, who paid Pixel Systems, who paid Mehta. One to One paid ITP $55 per hour for Mehta's services. From that, ITP paid Pixel $37 per hour for Mehta's services, and from that, Pixel paid Mehta $29.60. Mehta calculates a forty-hour week totaling 160 hours per month. At this hourly rate, ITP pockets $2,880 per month and Pixel gets $1,184. Per year, ITP is making $34,560 and Pixel is making $14,208.

Like many other foreign workers, Mehta feels robbed. He could understand a one-time fee for job placement, but $48,768 each year for the length of the job is "highway robbery," according to him. He says he deserves to be paid what the American company is paying for his services. Mehta also pays, through Pixel, for government unemployment insurance, which he decries as "ridiculous," because "H-1B people can't claim the unemployment benefits if they are laid off." Mehta also pays for his own health insurance and even contributes to Pixel's office expenses. Thus, in contrast to the claim on Pixel's Web site that they pay their employees "up to a whopping Ninety Percent of their client-billing rate," Mehta receives only 55 percent.[369]

Mehta is essentially trapped. To leave his job and find another, he must apply for a new H-1B visa. On his current visa, he can only work for Pixel

Systems (and Pixel Systems will decide which company to contract Mehta to). On an H-1B, a foreign worker cannot earn money from any other source. No independent contract work, no freelancing, no babysitting for friends. Any of these would violate the terms of the H-1B and render a foreign worker out of legal status. Mehta's visa is held by Pixel Systems and he can only be paid by Pixel. The chances of another U.S. firm applying to change the H-1B visa to its name are very low. So Mehta's only chance is to have Pixel, who holds his visa, find him another job and contract him out again. No wonder Pixel's Web site boasts that "believe it or not, very few of our associates, and management who joined us left us in the last four years."[370]

If the government's rhetoric about clamping down on immigration in the interests of national security is sincere, then why not sharply scrutinize the H-1B workers that are employed by middleman companies? One imagines that all a would-be terrorist would have to do is have minimal computer engineering skills, post a resume on Dice.com, and wait for the sharks to bite. It couldn't be easier to get into the country legally. And most H-1B workers, even after the exploitation of their wages, still make between $30,000 and $80,000 per year.

H-1B contracts and subcontracts by no means relegate the foreign worker, in this case largely of South Asian and Asian origin, into poverty. However, it has allowed for this arm of the U.S. immigration system to become a cash cow with plenty of money for the making. H-1B workers are the pawns of high-tech sweatshops, and DHS is doing very little to regulate the middlemen or the corporations that ultimately use this cheaper foreign labor.

Despite the fact that an exploited H-1B worker will probably earn substantially more in the U.S. than she would earn in her home country, many H-1B workers, like Mehta, have high levels of college and accrued debts to pay off. Moreover, once their six-year visa term is up, an H-1B worker must leave the U.S. Scholar Vijay Prasad surmises that this makes immigrant workers "high-tech coolies,"[371] a derogatory term bandied at nineteenth-century Asian workers brought to the U.S. to work during the gold rush.

An H-1B worker does not qualify for any path to legal permanent residency that could then lead to citizenship. Requests by workers to have their H-1B status lead to a green card after the six-year cap is reached have not been supported by the U.S. corporations that use H-1B labor or the vendors that supply them. H-1B is just too profitable to change the equation. And besides, there is an ever-ready and ever-growing pool of qualified foreigners who will more easily accept the exploitation that more seasoned workers like Mehta have grown increasingly upset with.

U.S. citizenship is the final rung on the immigration ladder. Eligibility requirements are many. While none of the steps leading up to it are simple, citizenship has traditionally been tied to meeting the more patriotic criteria of displaying adequate dedication to the nation. Testing applicants on the history and workings of the U.S. government has been one way of proving loyalty to the United States. And in times of war, taking up arms for the country has often expedited the process.

Baghdad, Iraq

"I couldn't call my mom to tell her I was alive, I was fighting a war," Philippe Louis Jean said. "She lived in fear every single day that I was dead. But I wasn't. I was just doing my job."[372] Louis Jean was one of the first U.S. Marines to cross into Iraq after President Bush declared war in March 2003. Louis Jean had just spent twenty weeks as part of the 1st battalion 5th Marines Weapons Company making the dangerous trip from the Kuwaiti border into Baghdad. His battalion's task was to secure Saddam Hussein's palace. On the outskirts of Baghdad, where things were incalculably dangerous, his unit took the most fire. But Louis Jean made it safely to Baghdad, and not long after President Bush declared the mission "accomplished" and major hostilities had ended. In Brooklyn, Louis Jean's family did not know whether he was alive or dead.

After securing Saddam's palace, Louis Jean's function changed to a less dangerous patrol duty, and his family first learned that he was alive when they saw him on a television news program talking to some Iraqi men as the camera panned the scene. With no direct communication, Louis Jean's mother became glued to the television news hoping for even a fleeting glimpse of her eldest son.

Louis Jean is a soft-spoken, bright-eyed young man whose parents brought him and his younger brother to the U.S. from Haiti, his country of birth, at age five. Speaking Creole and French when he arrived, he quickly learned English, and by high school Louis Jean knew only America as his home. He attended James Madison High School in Brooklyn while his parents (both American citizens) had three more children in the U.S. Somehow in the struggle to raise five children in Brooklyn and deal with political instability back in Haiti, Louis Jean's parents never had him naturalized. He and his younger brother were noncitizens in a family of U.S. citizens.

After graduating from high school, Louis Jean enlisted. He didn't really think he would see battle so soon after joining the Marines, but he liked the idea of fighting for his country. To Louis Jean, enlisting in the Marines was a career "which toward the end of, I might see battle,"[373] he told me. But as he watched the twin towers collapse on 9/11, Louis Jean says he knew he would soon be headed to war.

Baghdad and the realities of war were nothing like he imagined, but he rose to the challenge. Louis Jean realized that he was a good marine. He was promoted quickly on the battlefield, and his superiors saw him as the kind of soldier who should be an example for new recruits. Louis Jean wanted to study and advance. He was not in Iraq for an adventure or to kill innocent people, and he did not drink or partake in the mindless revelry of his fellow marines. "I was proud to serve what I never doubted was *my* country,"[374] he told me.

Putting his life on the line in Baghdad and wearing the fatigues of the U.S. Marines, Louis Jean could not have guessed that dying in the war may have been the best solution to the nightmare that began when he left Iraq. Ironically, death in combat would have granted him U.S. citizenship—a consolation benefit for the family members who survive him that may fast track their own status as a result. Instead, in 2008 when his green card expires, this combat veteran will probably be denied a new green card, rendering him out of legal status. He is one of the tens of thousands of noncitizen members of the U.S. armed forces.

U.S. Citizenship and Immigration Services (USCIS) says that 40,000 noncitizens have served in the U.S. military since 9/11, roughly 15,000 of them for less than three years.[375] Under immigration law, noncitizens must serve in the U.S. military for three years before they are eligible to apply for U.S. citizenship. However, an Executive Order issued by President Bush on July 3, 2002, allowed noncitizens on active duty to become eligible for citizenship before completing the three-year service requirement. A senior administration official told CNN this expedited citizenship was a "reward" for serving the country.[376]

Camp Pendleton, San Diego

July 4, 2005, was a particularly hard day for Philippe Louis Jean. In the past, he had always immensely enjoyed the Independence Day holiday. He would go to the beach with his family and friends to celebrate and would round out the day by watching fireworks. But in 2005, Louis Jean was in no mood for celebrating. Instead he stayed home, which beat the jail cell he had been locked in the previous July 4. As he sat down to watch the Padres-Giants game, Louis

Jean was riveted to his seat as the match was preceded by a naturalization ceremony for marines from his home base of Camp Pendleton. It felt like a cruel slap in the face to watch something that should have been his, too. The marines were sworn in, the crowd applauded, and then the Padres beat the Giants.

Sunny, carefree Southern California could not be more starkly different from dusty, bombed-out Baghdad. Thousands of U.S. troops have been in the spinning wheel of rotating realities, one moment cruising the coast with heroic salutations from fellow Americans, the next on alert with weapons drawn to protect against the threat of attack. While he longed to be with his family and back in the safety of America, Louis Jean knew his mission relied on not thinking too much about the comparatively easy life he led back "home."

In May 2003, Louis Jean's unit was rotated out of Iraq and back to Camp Pendleton. There Louis Jean underwent surgery for an aggravated shoulder injury, and he was not able to redeploy with his unit. It was around this time that Louis Jean's troubles began. Now with a new unit, his superiors refused to honor his battlefield promotions, saying that it was impossible that such a young marine had received so many promotions in such a short space of time. When Louis Jean provided proof from his battlefield commander, his new superiors brought up an old military conviction for which Louis Jean had served thirty-seven days in a military brig in 2002. This thirty-seven-day conviction, his superiors told Louis Jean, made him deportable because he was not a U.S. citizen. "I laughed," Louis Jean told me. "I'm a combat veteran, I've been to war and put my life on the line for this country. That automatically makes me a citizen. Plus, my parents are U.S. citizens, my wife is a U.S. citizen, so I thought that made me a U.S. citizen."[377]

It didn't. The president's Executive Order didn't apply to Louis Jean because of the military criminal record for which he was sentenced to thirty-seven days in prison the year before the Iraq war. Louis Jean could not believe that after doing his time in the military brig and then proceeding to do much more time in Iraq in defense of the U.S., the country would deny him citizenship.

But in this young Haitian-American's case, it was much worse than just being locked out of naturalization. Louis Jean was reported to immigration officials by his new superiors for his old thirty-seven-day conviction. Immigration officials arrested Louis Jean and threw him into a San Diego correctional facility. After five months in jail, Louis Jean was ordered deported to Haiti because of his previous conviction for oral sex, which the military falsely charged as adultery and sodomy.[378] Even though his crime was so minor that he was sentenced to only thirty-seven days in a military brig, an immigration judge deemed it to be an aggravated felony. This made Louis Jean deportable. "What kind of a country sees no problem in allowing a noncitizen with a criminal conviction to go fight a war, but on his return the laws say he is not allowed to be in the country any longer and puts him in jail and then deports him?" Louis Jean demanded to know.

There are no government statistics on how many noncitizen military personnel have been deported.

As the occupation of Iraq dragged on and the level of new recruits dwindled, the "reward" of a quick path to citizenship was a way to fill the ranks. Since President Bush made his declaration of an expedited naturalization process for soldiers who go to battle, eight thousand green-card holders have signed up to join the military.[379] Recruiters in Los Angeles say that 50 percent of new recruits are green-card holders, which they attribute to a blitz of military advertisements in English and Spanish highlighting this shortcut to citizenship.[380] And when legal permanent residents didn't come forth to enlist, the Army went to them. Approaching individuals at all manner of immigrant and ethnic events, from the United Latin American Citizens National Convention in Little Rock, Arkansas, to an immigrant heavy high school in New York City, recruiters have been able to lure many young noncitizens into their ranks.[381]

Furthermore, not only does military service grant expedited citizenship under the president's EO, it also waives all fees associated with the process of naturalization, and the military offers free legal services to complete the complicated application process, which can save the applicant up to six thousand dollars.

Since the EO was issued, USCIS says that as of February 2005 close to sixteen thousand active-duty personnel have taken advantage of the executive order to receive citizenship.[382] However, the reality of citizenship for combat duty is sobering if one considers that between 9/11 and early March 2006, seventy-five military personnel killed in the line of duty have received posthumous citizenship.[383] The *New York Times* reported in March 2005 that immigrants from Mexico were the largest group of casualties. In fact, when President Bush announced this expedited citizenship for military service, the U.S. embassy in Mexico City was flooded with people wanting to sign up. The embassy quickly put the word out that the EO applied only to legal permanent residents of the U.S., not to any foreign national willing to join the U.S. military.

The temporary EO was made somewhat permanent when the National Defense Authorization Act for fiscal year 2004 was passed in November 2003. The new law reduced the qualifying service time from three years to one year and also permanently waived all fees. Further augmentation to the EO made military service even more tempting for those struggling to legalize the status of some members of their family. The 2004 law says that if a noncitizen soldier dies in battle and is awarded citizenship posthumously, then other members of that dead soldier's family are eligible for citizenship even if they are not legal permanent residents. Moreover, their citizenship petitions are moved to the front of the line to ensure expedited service.[384]

Despite the honorable completion of service in Iraq that he thought made him a citizen, Philippe Louis Jean found himself in a San Diego jail awaiting deportation to Haiti, a country known for its extreme human rights abuses toward U.S. deportees.[385]

Louis Jean's thirty-seven day conviction put him in the gray area between civilian law and military law, and between criminal law and immigration law. He was in a legal no-man's-land.

While he was in prison Louis Jean met another marine from his unit who was also an inmate. This marine, who was born in Venezuela, was also a noncitizen Iraq War combat veteran. He told Louis Jean that after the success their unit's sergeant had in calling immigration on Louis Jean, the same sergeant targeted all the people of color and those with accents in the unit. Another marine, originally from Africa and with a thick accent, had to find his naturalization papers to prove that he was a citizen to the sergeant and to immigration officials.

Ten months after being thrown into the San Diego Correctional Facility—on a conviction whose sentence he had already fully served, a sentence that was one-tenth as long as his immigration incarceration—the Board of Immigration Appeals dismissed Louis Jean's case. The appeals judge accepted the defense lawyer's argument that the zealous prosecutors forgot to certify the records of Louis Jean's military conviction. This technicality rendered the case invalid. On January 28, 2005, Louis Jean became a free man again. Almost.

In our current post-9/11 climate where local police can cross-check immigration status with criminal background, Louis Jean will always be potentially deportable given that his record still shows that he has a criminal conviction and that he is a noncitizen. It doesn't matter that he has been through one trial and had it dismissed. That was in California. If he gets stopped by police anywhere else, and they check his records, it is probable that they will arrest him and hand him over to immigration authorities.

A criminal record is not a bar to serving in the military, but it is a potential bar to citizenship, no matter how minor the crime. In fact, in legislation that passed the House in December 2005, there were two clauses embedded in the massive bill that would make it much harder for a legal permanent resident with *no* criminal conviction to get citizenship. Sections 609 and 612 expand broadly the offenses that are considered violations of "good moral character," which is required of those applying for citizenship. These sections would also cut off all appeals access in the federal courts if USCIS denies a citizenship application. Traci Hong of the Asian American Justice Center gave me an example of just how "egregious" these clauses are:

> Take the case of a man in Seattle who once got a $350 fine for clam fishing at a beach. Well, USCIS determined that because of that civil violation, that is equivalent to a traffic violation, the man did not have good moral character. They denied him. Luckily, back then he had access to the federal courts, and he sued and won.[386]

But worse still, Hong warned, "laws like this would serve to create a class of people who are permanently disenfranchised. They can't become citizens and they are not deportable because whatever they have done to merit a decision of bad moral character obviously is not enough to deport them. It's ludicrous."[387]

In fact, the rosy path-to-citizenship picture that has become such a selling point for new recruits to the armed forces also has its built-in limitations. Perhaps the most obvious one is that a noncitizen service member must apply for citizenship within six months of being discharged or lose the privileges gained from serving. As the veteran's organization Operation Truth points out, "service members coming home will have to bear the burden of what the frontlines have left them: financial problems, depression, post-traumatic stress disorder, injuries, and/or even the loss of limbs. They should not be faced with the additional burden of needing to take care of their naturalization issues upon the first six months of their return."[388]

Louis Jean just wants this ordeal to be over. Because of his criminal record he stands virtually no chance of getting citizenship, and his lawyers have advised him that when he reapplies for his green card after it expires in 2008, he will probably be denied because of his record.

Perhaps the worst insult for Louis Jean came five days after his release from prison. "So my mother gets a call from a military recruiter seeing if I would volunteer to go back to Iraq because they needed more soldiers." Louis Jean still has three years on his contract as an inactive reservist. The cruel irony is that after trying to deport him, the military can force him back to Iraq. Right now, they are just calling him regularly to see if he will return voluntarily, but should things get tight and troop levels drop, Louis Jean can be ordered to serve. "The Marine Corps still has control over my life," Louis Jean says, "and at any time they could call me and send me back to Iraq to die for America. And there is nothing I can do about it."

After all he has been through, you would imagine that Louis Jean would be bitter and angry. But he says he just wants to get on with his life. "I succeeded in the military, and I know I will be a success at whatever I dedicate myself to." If only this country would let him.

On hearing my accent, Louis Jean asked me if I thought he had a chance of getting citizenship in Australia. "Because," he told me with hope in his eyes, "at least to be deported there would be better than Haiti."

The two visas discussed in this chapter, the F-1 and H-1B, are crucial immigration tracks for those who come to the United States. Both have been vigorously supported by American corporations, which have profited from immigrants with these visas. For a foreign student or a foreign worker in the post-9/11 years, changes to laws and regulations have made life increasingly difficult. These immigrants were made easy targets as the government pursued an aggressive war to supposedly root out terrorists. On many occasions the corporate pressure that had previously kept these immigration tracks somewhat insulated from anti-immigration attacks failed to protect immigrants. However, as the regulation and law changes began to hurt the bottom line, corporate and academic America stepped in—not to protect immigrant rights, but to guarantee a cheap labor pool.

The stories of the three young men told in this chapter serve to illustrate that immigrants are welcome in America only *if* they are benefiting the nation. These relatively privileged immigrants, who serve in wars and fulfill industries' need for cheap skilled labor, are subjected to a standard of productivity higher than that of other citizens. This shatters the much-promulgated myth that immigrants are simply a drain on the resources of the local community and the country. These three men's stories are extraordinary, but unfortunately not uncommon. They are men who have given an immense amount to the country, and yet are being pushed out. The country has been enriched by each one's contributions, and at a time when they need the country to stand up for them, the country has abandoned them.

PART II

Chapter V

THE IMMIGRATION-INDUSTRIAL COMPLEX: BOOMING BUSINESS AT THE EXPENSE OF IMMIGRANT RIGHTS?

> I like to think of us not as a company that is out to make money, but we're out to help the federal government, you know, be more accurate in taking prints. I mean if that's what they are going to do and we have the technology to build whatever they want, why not give it to them?
>
> —Adam M. Forman, Program Manager, Federal Programs, Cross Match Technologies Inc.

America is a proudly capitalist country where individuals and corporations are celebrated for making money. The American Dream, which has brought many an immigrant to the United States, promises happiness attained through the accumulation of wealth. Examples of successful immigrants—those who arrived with nothing and achieved economic and political power—are plentiful. Yet for every successful immigrant, there are thousands who struggle to rise out of poverty and thousands more who will never have a political voice. For them, the American Dream will never be realized.

However, an unrealized American Dream is perhaps the least of an immigrant's worries these days. What is more alarming is the way in which immigrants and noncitizens have become the latest targets in the country's capitalistic appetite. As with the cotton, tobacco, and steel industries of the past, money is always made on someone else's back. Historically, the peoples targeted have been Native Americans and African Americans. And during certain periods of history, immigrants, too, have been used to accumulate wealth for others.

Today, enforcing immigration policy has become the latest way to make a quick buck. Enacting and implementing harsh immigration policies has been equated with protecting the nation, allowing those selling immigration-enforcement goods and services to the government to do so with the high moral imperative of ensuring homeland security.

In the days after the 9/11 attacks, as the nation mourned and the Bush administration began retaliatory strikes on Afghanistan, the country was in a state of high alert. Everyone knew that the U.S. would take dramatic measures to ensure that another attack did not occur. The progressive Left, with little representation in Congress, argued that U.S. foreign and economic policies needed to radically change to prevent another attack. The Right, led by the Bush administration, decided on a "war on terror." Democrats and Republicans sided with the Bush administration and gave almost unanimous consent for the use of force. Right, Left, Democrat, Republican, or somewhere in between, the country was mobilized. While some held vigils and protests, others enlisted in the armed services. Still others, including the nation's corporate leaders, met to plan how they could be of service to the nation.

Being of service to the nation, however, did not imply community service. What corporate executives anticipated and lobbied for in the months following the attacks was the beginning of what Ohio State University law professor Peter Swire calls the security-industrial complex.[389] I call it the immigration-industrial complex. There is big money to be made as the government dramatically increases its reliance on the private sector to help carry out its war on terror. On the home front, the prime targets of this war are immigrants.

As discussed earlier, one of the first major steps in linking immigration with terrorism occurred with the creation of the Department of Homeland Security in 2003. DHS immediately subsumed twenty-two existing government agencies and was given a staff of 179,241 and a first-year budget of almost $30 billion.[390] DHS's creation was in direct response to the 9/11 attacks and the subsequent public pressure to ensure that another such attack did not occur. For the federal government, bringing DHS into existence was the single largest reorganization since the creation of the Department of Defense in 1947.

The stated mission for creating the Department of Homeland Security is to "unite much of the federal government's effort to secure the homeland, with the primary goal being an America that is stronger, safer, and more secure."[391] Although the Department incorporated all immigration-related agencies, the six-point mission of DHS as listed under Section 101(b) of the Homeland Security Act of 2002 does not include a single mention of immigrants or immigration.[392]

In the years since the creation of DHS, there has been little assessment of the Department's progress in fulfilling its mission. In fact, there was virtually no public scrutiny of what the DHS's mission would be when it was first created. In assessing the Department's functioning today, it is instructive to revisit the thinking that led to its creation. As we'll see, the roots of DHS—the U.S. government department that deals with all the nation's immigration matters—are not buried in the concerns of homeland security, but in the concerns of big business.

Indian Treaty Room, Eisenhower Executive Office

In October 2002 a very important and secret meeting took place a stone's throw from the White House. It was the fourth such meeting of President Bush's Homeland Security Advisory Council (HSAC), created by the White House to help President Bush develop homeland security strategy. The council was so secretive that many lawmakers did not even know of its existence as this hand-picked group sat down for its fourth meeting.[393] One can only guess at the agenda of this meeting because it was never released to the public.

The chosen attendees, thirteen in total, were representatives of big business, law enforcement, and the intelligence community. Eli Lilly CEO Sidney Taurel was on the Council, as was a woman that *Fortune Magazine* named one of the fifty most powerful women in business, Kathleen Bader, president of Dow Chemical's Business Council. Another CEO, Joseph J. Grano of UBS Paine Webber, was in attendance, as was L. Paul Bremer, who was then the CEO of a risk insurance company called Marsh and who subsequently became the chief administrator of Iraq. The HSAC also counted among its chosen few several paid consultants to government contractors, as well as two ex-CIA directors and Utah governor Michael Leavitt.[394]

What would later, and much more publicly, be expanded to a council of eighteen by then-Secretary of Homeland Security Tom Ridge, began in secret. The many potential conflicts of interest did not seem to bother the White House as it used the HSAC to plot the course of Homeland Security. While the later enlarged council would be even more blatantly steeped in administration-favored businesses (two additions were current and former CEOs of Lockheed Martin), it is the initial thirteen that bear examination, as their critical input laid the foundation for the Department of Homeland Security.

At the very same time that Eli Lilly's CEO was advising the highest office on matters of homeland security, his company managed to slip into the 2002 Homeland Security Act a startling provision to protect itself from lawsuits. *New York Times* columnist Bob Herbert exposed this piece of covert legislation in a November 25, 2002, column: "Buried in this massive bill, snuck into it in the dark of night by persons unknown . . . was a provision that—incredibly—will protect Eli Lilly and a few other big pharmaceutical outfits from lawsuits by parents who believe their children were harmed by thimerosal."[395] Believed to cause injury to children, thimerosal is a mercury-based preservative used until 1999 in childhood vaccines. This spotlight embarrassed lawmakers and brought about a repeal of what came to be known as the Lillygate section of the Homeland Security Act in early 2003. But the drug company nearly succeeded in using its extensive political connections to indemnify itself from over forty-five existing class-action lawsuits—lawsuits that protected its bottom line but had no connection to homeland security.

The Project on Government Oversight warned, "Eli Lilly's inappropriate manipulation of the Homeland Security Act, in order to protect themselves from unrelated litigation, may indicate where their interests lie on HSAC."[396]

But Eli Lilly was not the only HSAC member actively using its position to put its company's bottom line ahead of homeland security interests. Consider the role of Dow Chemicals. Chemical security is critical to protecting the homeland, yet during the time that Kathleen Bader was on the HSAC, Dow joined lobbyists in the oil and fertilizer industries to successfully quash the 2002 Chemical Security Act. This act would have mandated security measures by companies like Dow to protect millions of residents who live near the 110 chemical plants across the country.[397]

In June 2003 Democratic Senator Jon Corzine reintroduced the bill as an amendment to the 9/11 legislation and made sure to cite the statements of Secretary Ridge about the inadequacy of the country's chemical security.[398] Senator Corzine argued that the amendment should be part of the Homeland Security Act. After much lobbying by the chemical industry, which included Dow, the Senate declined to consider Corzine's amendment.[399] That Dow would protect its profit margins is to be expected, as its success depends on it, but one has to question why such a company should then be permitted to advise the government on matters of homeland security when its priority is obviously not the safety of millions of residents living in the path of a chemical plant.

Consider as well one of the greatest scandals that occurred while the hand-picked HSAC was helping the president determine the future of Homeland Security. Revealed through a random investigation by New York's Attorney General Eliot Spitzer, in 2004 the inquiry accused Paul Bremer's company, Marsh Inc., of being a "corrupt contractor" in the insurance industry. Spitzer alleged that unsuspecting insurance clients were deliberately steered to specific firms in return for lucrative kickbacks, a move that pushed up prices. Spitzer also charged Marsh with bid rigging: offering quotes that appeared to be competitive but that were, in fact, fixed. The charges were indeed grave given that Marsh's parent company, Marsh & McLennan Companies Inc., was the world's biggest insurance broker at the time of the Spitzer lawsuit.[400] Spitzer's inquiry was touted as having the potential to "change the face of the industry forever."[401]

In 2005 Marsh & McLennan Companies Inc. settled out of court with Spitzer for $850 million. Marsh announced the agreement in a press release, saying that the company had agreed to "enact reforms to lead the industry in transparency and service to clients and establish an $850 million fund to compensate clients."[402]

In conducting his investigation, Spitzer refused to negotiate with the Marsh & McLennan management team because he said that his office's investigations had been "misled at the very highest levels of that company."[403] While not part of the management team that foiled Spitzer's investigation, Paul Bremer was the head of Marsh when it was carrying out these widespread fraudulent activities. He was also on the HSAC advising President Bush on how best to protect the homeland from fraudulent activities.

DHS was conceived and created in a way that made it possible for private industry to become the driving force behind much of its operations. DHS was born with a massive budget, and those who were present at its creation undoubtedly saw the huge revenue potential for big business. This may well cloud the judgment of many in instances when protecting the homeland and making a profit clash. The billion-dollar question that faces the Bush administration is, which interest will win out?

In December 2003 the administration also created another group to advise on DHS's spending and policy. The Academe and Policy Research Senior Advisory Committee (APRSAC), as the body is known, became the brain of homeland security strategy. The Bush administration clearly understood the need to have its policy and regulatory changes backed up by research. Yet there was little balance in the ideology of those research institutions chosen. The APRSAC was made up wholly of conservative academics and researchers. Many were from federally contracted research facilities that were funded by the government to pump out the research that supported government policy. Investigative journalist Wayne Madsen calls the actions of these think tanks and research institutes, particularly one called Advancing National Strategies and Enabling Results (ANSER), "policy laundering."[404] ANSER Analytical Services Inc. describes itself as an independent, not-for-profit, public service research institution. A substantial part of ANSER's income comes from the federal government in the form of research contracts.

Dr. Ruth David, the CEO of ANSER, was one of the appointed panel members to the Academe and Policy Research Senior Advisory Committee on homeland security. ANSER has been a prime contractor with the Pentagon for years, ranking fifty-eight on the list of the top hundred Department of Defense contractors in 1993. In 2000, ANSER's federal contracts totaled over $74 million.[405] In 1999 ANSER developed a homeland security branch, but it was a minor side of operations until April 2004. Five months after Dr. David began advising the president on homeland security, ANSER was awarded a lucrative $130 million contract for over four and a half years to operate the newly created Homeland Security Institute.[406] As per section 312 of the 2002 Homeland Security Act, ANSER's institute takes its orders from the Secretary of Homeland Security and receives all its funds from the government, yet it is touted as an independent institution.[407]

The corporate side of the academic panel includes former NYPD Commissioner Bernard Kerik. When nominated by Bush to be the secretary of DHS, Kerik resigned from the boards of two companies, including CamelBak, which produces hands-free water bottles for athletes. Before his nomination, while Kerik was advising the president on homeland security, Kerik did not see fit to resign from his leadership role at either company, nor relinquish his financial interests. Moreover, during his tenure on the advisory panel his companies received lucrative contracts.

Post-9/11, CamelBak immediately developed an interest in homeland security and pitched itself to the government as a company that could keep drinking water safe in the event of a chemical or biological attack. By the time Kerik resigned from CamelBak's board in 2004, the company had received $16 million in contracts from the federal government to provide water-carrying pouches to troops in Iraq and to border patrol agents.[408] CamelBak simply took its consumer product that retailed for $25 and "developed sturdier materials and a silver-based, antigerm lining to keep water clean for troops."[409] These upgrades increased the cost of the backpack water flask to around $200 when the government bought it. CamelBak also changed its motto from "Hydration on the Move" to "Hydrate or Die."[410]

Before the concept of homeland security became so critical to the federal government after 9/11, Washington spent just over $13 billion on it in fiscal year 2000. In 2006 DHS will spend nearly $50 billion, an increase of nearly 300 percent.[411]

In 2004 DHS awarded $9 billion in contracts to nongovernment organizations and corporations, close to one quarter of the total DHS budget for the year. That increased to $11 billion for fiscal year 2005.[412] All these contracts have created a bonanza for businesses of all shapes and sizes. DHS has become the latest federal cash cow, and companies are lining up to milk.

While there are many companies providing valuable and important services to DHS, there are also plenty of examples of contracts being awarded to protect the homeland against terrorism that, in fact, end up targeting immigrants and noncitizens while doing little to secure the nation. With minimal regulation or oversight from DHS, companies are overcharging, providing faulty products, and convincing the government to purchase products that do not protect against terrorism.

Ronald Reagan International Trade Center, Washington, DC

The conference slogan seemed daring: "The New Culture—No More Excuses!" It was simultaneously accusing the federal government of not taking responsibility for the 9/11 attacks while encouraging it to embrace new action. It was the fourth annual AFCEA[413] Homeland Security Conference. The conference attracted a plethora of companies that were trying to crack the DHS market by promising information on how to get a lucrative contract, combined with the opportunity to mingle with invited government representatives. It cost $525 to attend the two-day affair, a pittance for companies intent on doing business with DHS.

The AFCEA trade conference, one of many that occur on a regular basis at fancy hotels and conventions centers around Capitol Hill, provided a fascinating insight into a world where corporations meet the federal government. The trade fairs are full of patriotic slogans; soaring eagles; red, white, and blue pens; key chains; and other company giveaways. From "SAIC: Helping Keep the Beacon of Freedom Shining" to Intrusion Network Security Solutions' products, which are "Defending Our Nation . . . with Five Star Results," from small family-based companies to big multinational corporations, business representatives at the Washington trade fairs all told me that their companies had the solution for homeland security. It was simply a matter of making the case to the government.

The display booth of ManTech International Corporation on the main floor of the AFCEA conference showroom was not much different from the others. It had an oversized television screen, company posters and a bunch of logo pens for the taking. ManTech's screen caught my attention because it had a larger-than-life map on it, which could zoom in tight enough to display the houses on a street. John Foley, ManTech's technical trainer, enthusiastically explained that the mapping system was part of a contract his company had just gotten with DHS to implement the "Homeland Security Information Network" (HSIN). The contract was awarded in January 2004 and was worth $33.1 million.[414]

According to DHS, the HSIN is a Web-based portal that ManTech was paid to build and operate, which will "significantly strengthen the flow of real-time threat information to state, local, and private sector partners at the Sensitive-but-Unclassified level, and provides a platform for communications through the classified SECRET level to state offices."[415] John Foley told me much the same, as he zoomed in and out and jumped between threat-warning screens to demonstrate his point. Foley explained that any police officer could enter information about a suspected threat, which would then be available in real time for any other police officer anywhere in the country. "So law enforcement in Iowa can search through and find documents from New York [and] Florida quickly and easily."[416] It seemed like a fabulous program to help protect against terrorism.

Integral to Foley's demonstration is the premise that this technology could only be used for the good of the nation, that this expensive equipment was only going to help the government protect its citizens. Foley gave me an example from the 2005 presidential inauguration. When someone from law enforcement spotted what looked like a suspicious package, it was entered into the system, and instantly, backup officers arrived and other law enforcement were warned. The big television screen was dotted with indications of a "suspicious package" or "smell of natural gas" or "right-to-life demo" or "suspicious person."

When I asked Foley about the suspicious person category, he told me that once information about a person was entered into the computer's database, it would remain there for five years. I was curious about the criteria law enforcement were encouraged to use to judge who was suspicious, and Foley told me that any "weird occurrence" would be entered, even if there may not be anything immediately illegal about it. So if it just seems "weird" to law enforcement, "it gets reported back and it gets stored."[417]

Remembering the incident of the Pakistani man who was arrested, jailed for six months, and then deported because he seemed suspicious to a police officer for videotaping tourist attractions in North Carolina,[418] I pushed Foley as to who might be deemed suspicious. He responded enthusiastically with a "success story":

> Someone was pulled over in California.... They put their name up there and it came back "yeah, you know what, this guy crossed into the country illegally" and that's just an example. And they knew that in under five minutes. [And] someone was able to tell them that, "you should hold this person," and this was just a regular small city law enforcement. Pulled 'em over, routine traffic stop that turned into a bigger thing.[419]

The HSIN is an example of new technology that is making it easier to profile immigrants. The system is storing unvetted information about individuals, based, at times, on the whim or suspicion of any law enforcement officer anywhere in the country.

HSIN, as exemplified by Foley's "success story," is catching immigrants in the name of protecting against potential terrorist threats. The fact of the matter is that HSIN has not been successful in stopping terrorism nor in warning against any pending threats. HSIN counts the roundup of criminal-aliens—easy targets—as its successes, but in no way is this protecting the homeland from a terrorist threat. To round up undocumented working migrants, legal permanent residents with criminal records for which they have already served their time, and those who just generally look suspicious, $33.1 million is being spent.

ManTech is one of the bigger companies with a long record of working under contract with the federal government. Its business exists almost solely on contracts with various government agencies, and in 2005 achieved annual revenues in excess of $900 million.[420] ManTech knows how to play the contracting game, and in June 2005 scored a great coup by appointing to its board of directors Richard L. Armitage, former Deputy Secretary of State, former Ambassador, and former Assistant Secretary of Defense. As various company representatives at the Washington trade fairs told me repeatedly—though curiously always off the record—contracts with DHS depend on your board's connections to the Bush administration and DHS officials, not on what the company is selling.

This practice of hiring ex-government officials to executive or board positions has seen many government officials, particularly high-level officials from DHS, leave the government to join private industry, including former DHS Secretary Tom Ridge.[421] In April 2005 Ridge joined the board of directors of Savi Technologies, a multinational corporation that supplies radio frequency identification technology to the Department of Defense to track supplies and equipment to U.S. forces in Iraq.[422] DHS is currently considering implanting radio frequency chips into passports and border-crossing cards. Not surprisingly, the companies that are lucky enough, or wealthy enough, to lure these ex-government officials are soon after rewarded with lucrative federal contracts.

Among top DHS officials to make the move to private industry is Asa Hutchinson, former Undersecretary for Border and Transportation Security. Hutchinson held this position from January 2003 to March 2005 and is now the chair of a homeland security law firm, Venable LLP, and a board member of a biometrics company, Saflink Corp. Another to leave DHS is Lt. General Frank Libutti, who was the former Undersecretary of Information and Analysis and Infrastructure Protection. He is now the vice chairman of Digital Fusion Inc., a big contractor with the Defense Department that has agreed to provide DHS with unmanned aerial vehicles and ground sensors. Consider also Stewart Verdery, who was the former assistant secretary for border and transportation security policy and planning, and is now with a lobbying firm that works for IBM and Hewlett-Packard on pushing for IT-related investments at DHS. The 2006 budget calls for almost $6 billion for IT services through the border entry-exit screening program called US VISIT. Carol Dibattiste was the former deputy administrator of the Transportation Security Administration (TSA). She is now with Choice Point, the company that is running a pilot program, under contract with DHS, to register frequent and safe travelers.[423]

Lobbying, in the form of petitions or letter-writing campaigns, was once the tool of concerned citizens who were working to make their elected representative aware of issues that needed their attention. Over the past decade, lobbying has become the domain of big-budget corporations. Multimillion-dollar firms operate on K Street in Washington, DC, and one of the most lucrative jobs for a high-level administration official is to become a lobbyist for private industry. The Center for Public Integrity, a nonprofit organization that monitors the world of congressional lobbying, says that "it is common for former lawmakers, staffers and regulators to lobby on the very issues they worked on during their public service. In fact, 82 percent of lobbyists who were former government officials as identified by the Center have reported lobbying their former agency or government office since registering as a lobbyist."[424]

Another Washington-based nonprofit organization, the Project on Government Oversight, has documented that the Department of Homeland Security has seen an unprecedented migration of its highest-level staff to K Street.[425]

So how has this high-powered lobbying machine impacted DHS legislation and spending? In 2003 there were 490 companies and organizations employing 2,260 individuals actively lobbying the government for homeland security-related legislation, policy, and contracts. This is about four times the number of companies that lobbied for defense-related legislation or contracts in the same year.[426] Not surprisingly, the biggest DHS contractors, like Accenture Ltd., Northrop Grumman, and Lockheed Martin, were among the biggest lobbyists.[427]

In 2004, Accenture Ltd. was awarded the bulk of the contract for US VISIT, an entry-exit screening program for all foreign nationals arriving and leaving the United States. It could end up being worth $10 billion.[428] While there were three bidders for the contract, according to Peter Swire's contacts inside the government, "the contract was awarded even before the bidder had any clear plan in line for the system."[429] What's more, the contract is an Indefinite-Delivery, Indefinite-Quantity contract (IDIQ). This is not a contract for specific work, but practically a blank check for an unspecified amount of future work. The Project on Government Oversight has called these contracts "the federal acquisition equivalent of a hunting license."[430] The government justifies the IDIQ contract by saying that it can cancel the project at any point and that the contractor is paid for specific tasks along the way. Yet even if the overall system ultimately does not work, under an IDIQ, the contractor is still paid.[431] In short, this type of contract is a very sweet deal for a company. Accenture will make it up as it goes along, and the taxpayer will foot the bill.

There are many aspects of Accenture's contract that are highly questionable. It is interesting to note that until 2001, Accenture was known as Andersen Consulting, part of Arthur Andersen LLP, which became defunct as a result of the Enron scandal. While it would have been extremely suspicious to award a contract to a company so steeped in wrongdoing, a simple name change made all the difference. Accenture was also one of the many companies that quickly developed a homeland security focus after 9/11. According to a *Washington Post* investigation, Accenture has lobbied hard to get a firm foot in the DHS door, and its reward was the $10 billion IDIQ.[432]

Back amid the patriotically decorated booths of the Ronald Reagan International Trade Center, I found one of the subcontractors under US VISIT, Cross Match Technologies Inc. The friendly company representative, Adam M. Forman, was more than willing to grab my index finger and demonstrate how his digital-fingerprinting machine works. Forman's booth had the standard big-screen television with company promos running, and it also had the little boxes to which I have submitted my fingers many times as I have been through my own green-card application process over the last few years. Most people, however, have probably never seen, much less used, a digital-fingerprinting machine. Forman walks me through the sales pitch, telling me that his company is one of only three that makes these digital biometric readers. He enthusiastically describes the advantages for the government and law enforcement in finding criminals and terrorists—a very convincing sales pitch.

Cross Match is a small company that has been in business since 1996. Its digital-fingerprinting machines, which Forman describes as producing "forensic-quality fingerprints,"[433] were used on a small scale prior to 9/11 by local and state law enforcement, and by schools and childcare facilities to keep track of students. After 9/11, Cross Match won a contract program to have its machines placed in airports around the nation as part of the US VISIT. At a cost of $10 billion, this program, which tracks all incoming visitors by collecting their digital biometrics,[434] began on January 5, 2004, when Cross Match digital biometric scanners were deployed at 115 airports and 14 seaports of entry. The contract deal is worth $2 million,[435] significantly less than ManTech's risk-advisor information networks, but significant nonetheless.

Former DHS Secretary Tom Ridge touted US VISIT as a primary enforcement tool in catching terrorists. At the launch of the program he said that US VISIT "will be easy for travelers to use but hard for terrorists to avoid."[436]

Forman is quite open when I ask him about the level of competition to get a contract like US VISIT. "We're pretty aggressive. We're a well-trusted name in the industry, we're well known in the FBI, we have a lot of retired FBI people in our company as well as the chief of staff of the FBI. So we have a lot of political pull." Did that mean his company had "ins"? Forman responded, "Ins? Yes." When I ask him if "ins" were "pretty critical" to the process of securing a contract, Forman replied, "Yup. When you're talking something like this, it gets extremely political and having those 'ins' is almost a necessity. It helps, it really does. There's a level of trust that's incorporated around that and it is used."[437]

Cross Match's "ins" begin with the chief executive, Ted Johnson, who came to the company after being a senior executive at Paine Webber. CEO of Paine Webber, Joseph J. Grano was one of President Bush's chosen few on the Homeland Security Advisory Council. A former FBI chief of staff, Robert Bucknam heads Cross Match's office in Washington, DC, while the former FBI head William Sessions is the company director. Add to the list two former congressmen, Charles Wilson and Bob Davis, who are lobbyists for the company, and you have a pretty good "in" crowd.[438]

Cross Match has provided over six hundred biometric detection units for vocal recognition, iris scans, and fingerprinting that have been used in Afghanistan and Iraq by the Department of Defense to log detainees. When

I asked Forman how successful the fingerprinting machines used at U.S. airports have been, he responded, "Over 1,500 people have been detained from entering the U.S. on many different levels . . . terrorists have been stopped, known terrorists that have entered the country. Captured at one point and they were in Guantánamo Bay and then released and they came back . . . That's pretty good."[439]

Unless these arrests of "known terrorists" thanks to the US VISIT airport screening program were kept from the public, which is highly unlikely because the government has trumpeted all of its arrests of alleged terrorists, there is no record that Forman's success stories actually happened.[440]

In a follow-up interview with Forman six months later, he triumphantly told me that of the 45 million fingerprinted so far, 1,800 border crossers have been detained for having a criminal record.[441] For Forman, these 1,800 arrests illustrate that this is "obviously a very successful program."[442] Interestingly, in January 2005, DHS's number of arrests was drastically smaller, claiming just 370.[443] A Freedom of Information Act request, which proved to be the only way to access the real numbers of those denied entry through US VISIT, disclosed that between January 5, 2004, and September 26, 2005, US VISIT had denied entry to 1,091 international travelers. The FOIA breakdown counted 385 denials for a "criminal record," 518 for an "immigration record," and 188 for "both criminal and immigration records."[444] The FOIA information also had no record of a former Guantánamo Bay detainee being stopped on entry to the United States, nor were any of those stopped among those on the international terrorist watch lists. Every single one of the foreign nationals stopped were either in the National Crime Information Center (NCIC) database or had violated a clause of the Immigration and Nationality Act.

Since neither Foreman nor DHS can clarify the discrepancy in their numbers, it bears examining just who is getting arrested.

Because only immigrants are fingerprinted on entry to the United States, the arrestees are largely foreign nationals and noncitizens. The fingerprint divulges whether a noncitizen has ever been convicted of a crime, which would make the person deportable from the country if the crime is considered an aggravated felony. A noncitizen can be deported even if they have already served the sentence for their crime, and even if the crime had happened years earlier.[445] While there obviously have been captures of "criminal aliens" with outstanding records or foreign nationals who are wanted for more serious crimes,[446] most of the arrests are for time already served, past visa violations, or minor offenses like driving infractions.[447]

US VISIT was originally proposed to protect the U.S. by preventing terrorists from entering the country, but the government seems to have shifted goals. In March 2004, Asa Hutchinson, Undersecretary for Border and Transportation Security in the Department of Homeland Security, spoke before the House Committee on Government Reform about US VISIT. He began by touting the success of the program, which notably did not include any mention of terrorists. "Since the US-VISIT entry procedures were implemented, we have caught a fugitive who escaped from prison 20 years ago. We have caught and extradited a felon wanted for manslaughter. We stopped a drug dealer who had entered our country more than 60 times in the past four years using different names and dates of birth."[448]

Hutchinson did not say that the security measures are catching would-be terrorists; he said, "It is important to note that these important security measures currently are not just capturing those that are attempting to enter our country under false identity and with previous convictions, many times under orders to be expelled from the country. But it also serves as a deterrent as the word goes out that we have this capability."[449]

There are grave concerns over the ability of the technology to correctly identify people. The Electronic Privacy Information Center (EPIC) says, "The program's fingerprint identification system has resulted in many cases of mistaken identity."[450] EPIC requested information from DHS under the Freedom of Information Act, and the material provided was stunning.[451] DHS's own records show how susceptible the technology is to error, and the letters that DHS has sent out in apology document the cases of those who put their complaint in writing to DHS.[452]

Every fingerprint taken is run against the country's largest national crime database, the NCIC. Over 650,000 local, state, and federal law enforcement officials have access to this collection of information on an individual's criminal violations. The database is full of inaccuracies. Shockingly, the Justice Department, in a quiet ruling in March 2003, decided that data in the NCIC does not have to be accurate. This stunning ruling was justified on the grounds that requiring the data to be accurate would interfere with efficient law enforcement.[453] To make matters worse, buried in legislation that passed the House in late 2005, there was a section that mandated that the name of any immigration violator be added to the NCIC regardless of whether "sufficient identifying information is available on the alien."[454] As worrying as it is that the names of hundreds of thousands of noncitizens believed to have an immigration infraction could be added to the NCIC, the fact that insufficient information on any of these will not prevent it from being added to the national crime registry means that local law enforcement and airport immigration inspectors in any part of the country will be able to detain a person who fits a description in an inaccurate record.

Then there are the concerns raised in September 2003 by the Government Accountability Office and again in a December 2004 Office of the Inspector General report,[455] which called US VISIT a "risky" program. [456] The GAO report found officials in charge of the program had not demonstrated how their computers, networks, and databases would work effectively together, nor had it sorted out how to coordinate the activities of a huge border-screening program with the agencies in charge of customs operations. The OIG report warned that DHS was inadequately prepared to manage and oversee a contract with a $10 billion price tag. Both reports questioned the management of the program and cited a multitude of problems likely to occur when integrating several immigration databases, surmising that the complexity of the system could lead to cost overruns and serious errors.[457] Given that the material being collected, processed, and stored includes personal biometrics, there are also deep concerns about issues of privacy.

In its attempt to alert citizens to the pending breach of their privacy, EPIC has published extensively on the civil liberties problems with the vast collection and storage of biometric information. EPIC's concerns range from a lack of details about how the data is stored, to how vulnerable the data is to theft and abuse. EPIC also questions how wide a margin of error is in the technology's authentication process.[458] The fact that the bulk of biometrics now being collected are those of noncitizens, who have few of the rights of citizens, is of great concern.

While some in Congress have taken DHS to task over its failure to comply with certain parts of the Privacy Act in implementing US VISIT,[459] the Privacy Act, as Ohio State law professor Peter Swire points out, applies only to U.S. citizens and to legal permanent residents, but not to nonresident individuals. At a time when the government is collecting unprecedented amounts of personal information from immigrants and noncitizens, "it is extremely worrying that Privacy Act protections simply do not exist for immigrants."[460]

Despite the questions surrounding the success of the current digital biometric technology, Cross Match has bigger and better plans for the future. On the horizon is technology that may be able to detect a change in blood flow when an individual has a print taken. Cross Match asserts this change would indicate that an individual is anxious.[461] The machine would register this change in much the same way a lie detector test works, and law enforcement would be notified. That way, even those who are not listed in criminal databases may be captured.

The experience of crossing into the U.S. for any noncitizen can be extremely disconcerting. I myself can attest to the fact that even though I have never committed any crime or broken any immigration law, I am always anxious. I have no doubt that my fear of immigration authorities, based on many years of maltreatment by immigration officials, both in the U.S. and in Australia, would register.

The accuracy of polygraph testing, which is based on the same principle of heart rate and blood flow, has always been questioned. In a 1998 decision upholding the absolute ban on the use of polygraph tests in court-martial proceedings, the U.S. Supreme Court said that

> there is simply no consensus that polygraph evidence is reliable. To this day, the scientific community remains extremely polarized about the reliability of polygraph techniques . . . The degree of reliability of polygraph evidence may depend upon a variety of identifiable factors. There is simply no way to know in a particular case whether a polygraph examiner's conclusion is accurate because certain doubts and uncertainties plague even the best polygraph exams.[462]

Furthermore, the World Wide Web is full of handy techniques to beat a polygraph test.

With no clear indication of what US VISIT will ultimately compromise in its broad mandate to screen all incoming and outgoing foreign nationals, this program raises significant questions about the targeting of immigrants. Peter Swire points out how successful government and industry have been in switching the focus from capturing terrorists to capturing immigrants, making it seem like an unanticipated success of the program. "Imagine that you are working in one of the companies, and you are selling a system that is going to improve homeland security and will supposedly make your family and your neighbors safer—you can feel good when you go home at night. If I told you that your job was to find a technology for finding the terrorists, for protecting us from these attacks, many people would feel that it is a high version of patriotism."[463] But would these same employees, average American citizens, feel the same sense of patriotic duty if they were told their job was solely to use technology to keep immigrants out of America? Swire asks.

He goes on to warn U.S. citizens that if they are not alarmed that civil-liberty breaches are happening to immigrants, then they should consider that they might be next. "The Bush administration has made a big distinction between the treatment of immigrants and the treatment of citizens. . . . The technologies that get tested against immigrants are then used later against citizens. It would be harder to try out these new systems on ordinary Americans; if you try them out on people who can't complain so loudly, then the surveillance systems get tested out in greater settings."[464] The NSA domestic spying scandal is a prime example. There was a national outcry when the government was exposed for secretly listening in on communications of Americans without permission of the Foreign Intelligence Surveillance Act (FISA) court. Yet when the government was open about spying on noncitizens, there was no outcry, no congressional investigation. Surveillance of noncitizens, many who have been in the U.S. for decades as legal permanent residents, should be as alarming as the surveillance of citizens.

Cross Match and ManTech are just two of many companies that are servicing the government's immigration needs. However, after attending a slew of DHS trade fairs, one of my primary concerns is that it is not the government that is determining its immigration outsourcing needs, but rather corporate America. Corporations, like the two profiled here, are eager to prove that they can take a basic idea and enhance it in different ways, which of course enhances the price tag as well, and DHS has been all too willing to consume. The danger with this kind of operation is that the people who end up getting targeted are a population with few rights and nowhere near the economic and political power of the businesses that are profiting from them.

Sierra Vista, Arizona

Glenn Spencer is losing his voice because he has spent too much time growling at the German shepherd pups he is raising just miles from the U.S.-Mexico border. Spencer wants his pups to be disciplined, as he plans on using some of them in his border-patrolling operations, and he says growling at them will ensure this.[465] Spencer moved to Arizona from California in 2002 because he felt his actions to halt undocumented migrants crossing the border stood no chance of succeeding in the heavily Democratic state. Spencer casts himself as a regular American citizen who is concerned about the Mexican "invasion" and what it means for the future of the country. As I document in the next chapter, Spencer has deep ties to white supremacist and hate groups.

In Arizona, Spencer started a new company, Border Technologies Inc. It is one of the many small new companies trying to crack the federal government contract market. Unlike the slick, high-budget public relations machines of the bigger and much more established companies doing business with DHS, which all seem to be highly suspicious of press coverage, Glenn Spencer has his personal telephone number on his Web site.

Spencer believes that successive U.S. governments are "allowing Mexico to colonize the American Southwest."[466] He believes that "Mexican culture is based on deceit," saying "Chicanos and Mexicanos lie as a means of survival."[467]

To solve these problems, Spencer advocates the use of technology to seal up the border. In 2003, Spencer said, "We knew we needed something like the unmanned drones. We couldn't buy one, we had to build our own."[468] So that is exactly what this newly transplanted Southwestern border resident did. Through his anti-immigration group, American Border Patrol, Spencer teamed up with technical experts who built "from scratch"[469] a robotic flying machine that used cameras to capture where and when unlawful crossings of the border took place. The twenty-pound wooden plane was tested on the border by Spencer and his crew without the permission of U.S. Border Patrol.

Spencer boasts that these early robotic flying machines have "the capability of staying airborne for more than two hours and can scan the border with its onboard camera equipment."[470] Spencer also boasts that it was his three-man operation that first put the idea of using Unmanned Aerial Vehicles (UAVs) to patrol the border on the government's agenda. Spencer takes "full credit for forcing the government into using that technology, and I don't think you'll find a journalist in southern Arizona who would disagree with that statement."[471]

Calling his UAV patrols "Border Hawk missions," Spencer attracted the attention of the Department of Defense, which sent two officials to meet with him and examine his UAVs. When the army representatives told him what improvements would make the machines more attractive to the DOD for use in Iraq, Spencer spent six months working on it. He never got the contract and decided to make the product he originally intended and sell it to DHS.

Spencer's product is cheap. He does not have the big profit margins that large companies have, but he also doesn't have an expensive managerial staff to maintain. Spencer's costs include himself, his few partners who built the UAVs, and the cost of the technology, which adds up to between twelve and twenty-one thousand dollars per drone.[472]

In June 2004 Border Patrol units began using Israeli-made unmanned aerial vehicles leased from the Defense Department for the Arizona Border Control Initiative. The primary goal of the initiative was "anti-terrorism"[473] activities under which large expenditures are justified. During the four-month trial, which cost $4 million,[474] not a single terrorist was identified or caught.

Moreover, in the eight months that the unmanned drones patrolled the skies over Arizona, they accounted for less than half a percent of the sector's total apprehensions of undocumented entrants for the 2004 fiscal year.[475]

Despite the poor results from this first test, the Department of Homeland Security was won over by UAV technology.[476] In his November 2005 immigration speech, President Bush reiterated his administration's commitment to UAV technology and boasted that the $139 million price tag had been budgeted for 2006. "Listen, technology can help an individual agent have broader reach and more effectiveness," President Bush said. He went on to tout the success of the technology, saying that "in Tucson, agents on the ground are directing unmanned aerial technology in the sky, and they're acting rapidly on illegal immigration or illegal activities they may see from the drones."[477] By late 2005, with no terrorists captured on the southern border, the rhetoric of rooting out terrorists, which was originally used to sell the expensive program, was completely absent from officials' references to the Arizona Border Control Initiative.

Glenn Spencer still hopes to get the UAV contract, but if he does not, he will continue his own extralegal patrols of the border.[478] Spencer says explicitly that he wants to use the technology to apprehend "illegals." The government's initiative is hardly as honest; instead, it makes immigrants the targets of a large so-called antiterrorism expenditure.

Perhaps the Electronic Privacy Information Center best summarizes the situation: "The federal government's redirection of military technology toward the civilian population is troubling. The use of UAVs gives the federal government a new capability to monitor citizens clandestinely, while the effectiveness of the expensive, crash-prone surveillance planes in border patrol operations has not been proven. The costs of these unmanned aerial vehicles outweigh the benefits."[479] When the technology does work, immigrants are targeted.

Another small Arizona-based company that saw a business opportunity in the rapidly increasing DHS budget is Sensor Technologies. Executives at Sensor started planning seven years ago, when patrolling the border became a viable business venture. Yet the big-name corporations were getting the contracts, and so Sensor had to be creative. They came up with a winning product: a ground-based radar system that could detect human movement. It is still in the testing phase with DHS, but the company has sold fifteen long-range radars to the Department of Defense. Radar systems representative at Sensor, Steven Ware told me that it has not been easy to convince DHS to buy their product. "Border Patrol are used to driving around in jeeps and finding illegals as they cross. They want more jeeps and more men. They think of a product like ours as a loss of man power. But we talk to them and convince them that there is something in this for them, too."[480] His boss, Walker Butler, is more diplomatic. "We are a small company competing with large companies. We have to find niches and create markets. That's what we did in this case."[481]

And while the likes of Glenn Spencer and Sensor jockey for the lower-end contracts to patrol the southern border, there are much larger contracts on offer from DHS. A new proposal, currently one of the largest DHS has to offer at $2.5 billion, is focused on catching terrorists and aims to expand widely the militarized border. Preceeded by a smaller pre-9/11 contract called ISIS, which was designed to catch and curb undocumented *migrants*, this contract is being sold as the surefire solution to protecting against *terrorists* trying to cross the border. According to Border Patrol, the American Shield Initiative (ASI) will "significantly strengthen our ability to detect, intercept, and secure the borders against illegal aliens, potential terrorists, weapons of mass destruction, illegal drugs and other contraband."[482]

Major corporations such as Isilon and Northrop Grumman are gunning hard for the ASI contract. And as with other billion-dollar contracts that the Bush administration has dangled, the main contenders for ASI are well connected to the White House and have donated heavily to the Republican Party. Between 1990 and 2002, Northrop Grumman gave over $8.5 million in federal campaign contributions. [483] Northrop Grumman has received a very profitable contract with the Pentagon for a missile defense system estimated at $10 billion, making it the third largest defense company in the U.S., following Lockheed Martin and Boeing.[484]

As most every company represented at the DHS trade fairs held regularly in Washington told me, the key to standing out in the tight competition for contracts is to get as close to the decision makers as possible. This translates into luring present and former government employees onto staff or management. Northrop Grumman is particularly good at this. Former systems chief James Roche served as President Bush's Secretary of the Air Force for two years, while seven former officials, consultants, or shareholders of Grumman currently hold or held posts in the Bush administration—Paul Wolfowitz, Lewis Libby, Pentagon comptroller Dov Zakheim, and director of NASA Sean O'Keefe. In fact, in August 2005 President Bush nominated Grumman's vice president and president of the company's missile system division, Donald Winter, to be the Navy Secretary.

The company that wins the ASI contract will be called on to provide a sweeping number of products and services, from unmanned drone planes and databases to storage for the millions of fingerprints currently being amassed. ASI will be one of the biggest DHS contracts to further lock down the borders and lock up immigrants.

Unnamed Location on the U.S.-Mexico Border, Via the Crystal Hyatt Regency, Virginia

At another Washington, DC, trade fair in 2005, I was surprised to see my favorite New York City–based electronics store: B&H. I was instantly curious to know what they were pitching to DHS at the Crystal Hyatt Regency trade fair. B&H is like a bigger version of Circuit City and certainly not a company its local customers know has such deep ties to the federal government.

The B&H sales representative at the trade fair practically pounced on me, and when I asked what he was selling the government, he began a dramatic thirty-second role-play. The energetic theatrical display was a pleasant change from the overstimulating high-tech machines and screens of other companies. I watched in amusement as the sales representative leaped around the B&H booth as he described the following scenario.

Border Patrol is on the hunt for terrorists and illegal immigrants, he said. Sitting squarely on the officer's helmet is a tiny but high-quality digital camera. The sales representative made a little circle with his index finger and thumb, indicating the size of the camera. He then wrapped all his fingers into a small circle and thumped his hand onto the top of his head where his imaginary helmet-cam would have been. He hunched over and began scouting around as if he were in the jungle on the prowl for dangerous or exotic animals. He then sprang up and, with a look of conquest on his face, told me that this tiny camera would capture digital images of the terrorists who had illegally crossed the border and then instantly transmit them to a central database, wiping the image from the camera and never putting Border Patrol officers' lives in danger.

It was not quite clear to me why the image in the camera would need to be deleted instantly, or why the officer's life was in danger, but the sales representative was so triumphant, it seemed irrelevant to ask.

The sales representative completed his role-play by telling me that with a growing central database of photo images, the government would have concrete proof that a person crossed the border illegally—enough to stop a person and demand proof of immigration status (it is not legal for law enforcement to stop an individual and question their immigration status without reasonable cause). The B&H helmet-cam would create a database of photos of those who supposedly crossed into the U.S. illegally, and I surmised that this could be used to justify more stops of suspected undocumented immigrants. Then, according to the B&H representative, while the individual was under arrest, the government could look for the individual's terrorist connections, and if none were found, deport the person based on illegal entry.

After this energetic performance, I asked the B&H rep if he could repeat it for my tape recorder, and he suddenly clammed up. He thought I was with DHS. He didn't know journalists were invited to the conference. He wouldn't even give me his name.

The potential new use of this technology is alarming. While it is legal for local or state law enforcement to ask for immigration status in the course of another investigation, it is illegal in all states except Florida and Alabama for a person to be stopped simply because local law enforcement believes the person is undocumented. A legal opinion published on February 5, 1996, by the Justice Department's Office of Legal Counsel (OLC) states that "subject to the provisions of state law, state and local police may constitutionally detain or arrest aliens for violating the criminal provisions of the Immigration and Naturalization Act [*sic*]."[485] However, the opinion also clearly stated that "state and local police *lack* recognized legal authority to stop and detain an alien solely on suspicion of *civil deportability*, as opposed to a criminal violation of the immigration laws or other laws [emphasis added]."[486]

In April 2002 reports leaked from the Ashcroft Justice Department indicated that the OLC had reversed its 1996 opinion allowing local police to stop a person solely on immigration-related grounds. Yet the Justice Department has refused to release this analysis to the public, fueling much speculation that the highest levels of government have approved the profiling of immigrants who appear undocumented.[487]

Back in New York City, I followed up with B&H directly. According to Mutty Strulovic, director of government and corporate sales, two-thirds of all of this consumer store's inventory is sold to the federal government. This amounts to 110,000–177,000 products.[488] As I was passed among many B&H employees, I finally got some concrete answers from Dan Waxell. He told me that "every product in [their] store is in use with DHS."[489] It appears that B&H has a variety of contracts with DHS, though Waxell used consumer terms, describing all the government contracts as "purchase orders." The contracts are officially called Blanket Purchase Agreements (BPAs). A BPA allows the government agency to simply order what supplies it needs without having to repeat the whole contracting process. BPAs are necessary, according to the government, to avoid lengthy bureaucratic delays for simple and repetitive governmental needs.[490] For example, should a department run out of staples, it should not have to waste time waiting for approval of a resupply order. Critics say that these large and vaguely worded contracts are subject to little government oversight. Indeed, there is a big difference for taxpayers between government employees stocking up on staples and stocking up on digital cameras.

According to Waxell, DHS is "as much a user of photographic and video equipment as anyone."[491] Though he claimed not to know what DHS uses the products for ("we never ask a client what they will use a camera for when they come in to buy one, so why would we ask DHS?"), he did give a few examples, which ranged from a police officer taking photos of a suspicious car after stopping it to the computer monitors that airport officials use. Waxell acknowledged that the nameless Washington representative's example of a helmet-cam for border patrol is "most likely" in the works, though he wouldn't confirm it. No B&H official would tell me the value of its contracts with the government. It was stunning how secretive my favorite electronics store was being. And when I asked how B&H's products were being used to prevent terrorism, the openness and energy of the trade fair was replaced with quick rebuttals. No consumer store, after all, wants to be associated with terrorism, even if they're helping to combat it.

Florence, Arizona

If you're driving to Florence from Tucson, it's impossible to get lost. The one-lane highway runs right through the middle of Arizona's colorful desert, with cacti, red rock, and occasional mountains forming a picturesque backdrop. It's the perfect drive for a city girl, and as I got closer to Florence, I felt miles away from civilization. In fact, as the harsh midday heat baked the desert around me, I began to wonder whether life could even exist out there. And then, almost out of nowhere, a roadside sign broke the spell: "State Prison: Do Not Pick Up Hitchhikers." That was my welcome to Florence, a desert prison town.

The next roadside sign announced that Florence has a population of around seventeen thousand. But that is a figure that is always up for debate in Florence as locals are divided over whether to include the prisoners in the count or not. Home to Arizona's state prison, two privately run prison complexes, and one DHS immigration jail, Florence is the quintessential prison town. "It has a prison economy and a prison consciousness," says Victoria López, an attorney who runs the town's only pro bono legal center that helps immigrant detainees fight their cases. "And I don't mean a prison consciousness in the abolish-prisons sense," she goes on to tell me. "Florence is another world. Here most locals are people whose families have for generations worked in the prison system. Life revolves around the prisons."[492]

López's husband is one such local. He was born and raised in a family of prison workers. Many locals have family roots in the mining industry that once was the lifeblood of Florence. As this industry went into decline, locals turned to the only other industry in town: incarceration. The private prison boom has regenerated this historic and fiercely proud town. After Corrections Corporation of America built two prisons in Florence, and the INS began renting bed space and then built its own prison, the town really came back to life.

> In September 2000, a *Business Week* article documented what many in the corrections industry and on Capitol Hill had come to fear—that "the [correction] industry's heyday may already be history." Corrections Corporation of America, one of the biggest prison companies, saw its stock plummet 93 percent in 2000.[493] On September 10, 2001 another article was published in the *American Prospect* magazine. On that day, it wasn't particularly significant to mainstream America. It opens like this: The private-prison industry is in trouble. For close to a decade, its business boomed and its stock prices soared because state legislators across the country thought they could look both tough on crime and fiscally conservative if they contracted with private companies to handle the growing multitudes being sent to prison under the new, more severe sentencing laws. But then reality set in: accumulating press reports about gross deficiencies and abuses at private prisons; lawsuits; million-dollar fines. By last year, not a single state was soliciting new private-prison contracts. Many existing contracts were rolled back or even rescinded. The companies' stock prices went through the floor.[494]

It went on to explain how the federal government, rather than let bad businesses accept their market-dictated demise, actively bailed them out. That is, until the day after the article was published, September 11, 2001. In the aftermath of 9/11, the private-prison industry has once again experienced a boom as national security has been invoked to sweep up and jail an unprecedented number of immigrants. Immigrants are currently the fastest growing segment of the prison population in the U.S. today.[495]

In the 1980s the INS turned Florence's old World War II prisoner-of-war camp into a Special Processing Center (SPC). SPCs are massive, self-contained, immigrant jail complexes. These complexes are one-stop-shops where an immigrant can be jailed, tried in an immigration court, appealed before an immigration judge, and then finally ordered deported—all without leaving the compound. While DHS does not refer to its facilities as jails, the SPC in Florence has all the hallmarks of a jail. Ringed by concertina wire, surrounded by chain-link fences with inmates locked into cells, no one who has ever been to this immigration detention facility would deny that it is a jail.

The changes to immigration laws in 1996 began a gradual increase in the immigrant prison population. [496] In the aftermath of 9/11, that legislation has been harshly enforced,[497] and towns across the U.S. have seen their once dwindling prison populations swell each year. In most cases, the INS, and now DHS, pay local, county, and private prisons to house noncitizen detainees. In Florence, the two private prisons that are run by CCA are paid between sixty and seventy dollars per day, per detainee by DHS.[498] In addition, DHS has its own facilities around the country that have been built to house immigrant detainees.

There are currently over nine hundred jails across the U.S. that rent bed space to DHS. The average cost to DHS per day to detain a noncitizen is between eighty-five and ninety dollars.[499] In the months after the 9/11 attacks, especially around New York and New Jersey, the government relied on county jails and private prisons for additional space, as there was a lack of immigration jails. At the time, the state of New Jersey paid sixty-two dollars per prisoner per day to private and county jailers, making an INS detainee worth at least twenty more dollars per day. [500]

It's always hot in Florence, and for those just passing through, the desert dust might make the small town seem unbearable, especially when a large portion of the population are criminals. But for those who live and work in Florence, prisons are their lifeline. As the desert town of Florence attests, prisons can in fact sustain a community while making private companies a lot of money. Since the number of immigrant prisoners has boomed in recent years, Florence has seen a plethora of new housing complexes spring up on the outskirts of town, followed by big retailers like Wal-Mart.

For those noncitizens who are inside the prison walls, there is a strong case to be made that they are being zealously prosecuted, sentenced, and in many cases left to languish for weeks and months without trial or sentencing.[501] Each day a noncitizen sits in jail, U.S. taxpayers are filling the coffers of those who incarcerate them.

The need for immigrant detention space dramatically increased after 9/11.

The government began to target noncitizens with mass arrests during sweeps through immigrant communities, increased prosecutions of undocumented border crossers, and the deliberate use of immigration law to hold people while looking for criminal or terrorist charges against them. For those without legal status who are picked up, the government continues to claim that locking them up is the only way to ensure that they do not disappear into the country. A December 2004 DHS report from the Office of the Inspector General concluded that all the evidence proved the "importance of detention in relation to the eventual removal of an alien. Hence effective management of detention bed space can substantially contribute to immigration enforcement efforts."[502]

The average time an immigrant is detained is 42.5 days from arrest to deportation.[503] To detain an immigrant at $85 per day equals $3,612.50 per detainee. In 2003 DHS was holding 231,500 detainees,[504] and the budget to cover this was $1.3 billion.[505] Since 9/11, the DHS budget for detention bed space has increased each fiscal year. In 2003 there was more than $50 million slated for the construction of immigrant jails.[506]

The speed with which the Bush administration rounded up and jailed noncitizens after 9/11 saved the corrections industry. For example, in 2000 Corrections Corporation of America carried more than $1 billion in debt and was violating its existing credit agreements. Then the federal government awarded the failing company two large prison contracts. At the time, the company's CEO, John D. Ferguson, admitted that CCA would have been forced into bankruptcy without the government's help.[507]

CCA has been plagued by scandals in its decades-long existence. Stemming from poor management, the charge sheet includes understaffing prisons, denying pensions to workers, abuse of inmates by prison guards, violence, and escapes. Worse still, CCA prisons have not provided adequate medical treatment to inmates and have maintained substandard prison conditions that have led to prison protests and uprisings. Yet CCA continues to be awarded government contracts.

CCA's favorable status with elected officials has deep roots. In addition to the $100,000 that CCA has contributed to the Republican Party since 1997, there are also significant connections between executives and government officials. J. Michael Quinlan, former head of the Federal Bureau of Prisons, has been an executive at CCA for the past decade. CCA's chief lobbyist in the state of Tennessee is married to the Speaker of the House. And CCA is a member of the American Legislative Exchange Council, a conservative group that writes and pushes bills on policy such as sentencing guidelines.[508]

In the post-9/11 years, CCA has increased its profits and won more government contracts. For the second quarter of 2005, CCA announced that its revenue had increased 3 percent over last year, for a total of $295.8 million.[509] CCA calculates that it spends $28.89 per inmate, per day and profits $50.26 on each inmate per day.[510] Meanwhile, on July 1, 2005, the Bureau of Immigration and Customs Enforcement awarded CCA contracts to continue running the 300-bed Elizabeth Detention Center in New Jersey and the 1,216-bed San Diego Correctional Facility. Both of these contracts are for three years with five three-year renewal options. In 2005 CCA also secured new prison contracts with the Kentucky Department of Corrections, the state of Kansas, and the Florida Department of Management Services.[511] Business is good for CCA.

Wackenhut has also received a great boost in the years since 9/11. For a company that is getting multimillion dollar contracts from the government, Wackenhut's record is astonishing. Prior to 9/11, Wackenhut, like CCA, had been at the center of all manner of inmate-abuse scandals: guards were caught having sex with underage inmates, there were routine reports of extreme mistreatment of inmates, and there was even a disproportionately high level of deaths in their facilities.[512] CEO George Zoley has been flippant about the cases of abuse. After a CBS report exposed the repeated rape of a fourteen-year-old girl at a Wackenhut juvenile jail and two guards were found guilty, Zoley said, commenting on the abuse, "It's a tough business. The people in prison are not Sunday-school children."[513] Still more worrying was Wackenhut's record with inmate-on-inmate killings, which, contrary to public opinion, are not very common in America's prisons. In 1998–99 alone, Wackenhut's New Mexico facilities had a death rate of one murder for every four hundred prisoners. For the same period in all U.S. prisons, the rate was about one in twenty-two thousand.[514]

With so many scandals and documented cases of abuse at its prisons around the country and the world, Wackenhut changed its name to the GEO Group Inc.[515] GEO has not only continued to run the Wackenhut facilities and kept George Zoley as CEO, it has also continued to get new contracts. In 2005 the State of California Department of Corrections gave GEO the contract for the housing of minimum security adult male inmates at the 224-bed McFarland Community Correctional Facility estimated to be worth $4.1 million in revenue each year.[516] The Broward Transitional Center[517] in Miami is owned and run by the GEO Group Inc., which won its contract from Immigration and Customs Enforcement (ICE) on August 8, 2002. The contract was later extended to October 1, 2003, and again recently for another five years to September 30, 2008.

In another contract granted in 2005 by the Bureau of Immigration and Customs Enforcement, GEO will manage and operate the Queens Private Correctional Facility; it expects to earn $10.5 million in annual revenues.[518] The Mississippi Department of Corrections also renewed its contract for the continued management and operation of the one thousand-bed Marshall County Correctional Facility.[519] Meanwhile, also in 2005, GEO announced a merger with another major corrections company, Correctional Services Corporation (CSC). GEO says CSC's operations will add approximately $100 million in revenue to GEO's coffers. GEO is especially excited about the earning potential from CSC's one-thousand-bed expansion of its State Prison in Florence, Arizona.[520]

The major problem with privately run jails is that the government doesn't consistently regulate what goes on inside. The corrections industry has routinely argued that private corporations will run a prison at a dramatically lower cost than the government. A 1996 U.S. General Accounting Office report concluded, however, that there was no clear evidence supporting this.[521] In the cases in which a privately run prison is cheaper per inmate than a government-run facility, prison companies have cut costs primarily to boost their profits. And as has been well documented, this comes at the expense of those they are locking up.

San Diego, California

Philippe Louis Jean, the noncitizen Iraq combat veteran introduced earlier, had ended up in the San Diego Correctional Facility (SDCF). His Marine commander had reported him to the Department of Homeland Security for an old conviction, whose sentence he had already served.[522] Louis Jean had advanced quickly though Marine ranks and had just come back from serving in Iraq when he was detained at SDCF. His experiences inside were shocking to him—he found the treatment inside SDCF appalling.

> The guards would scream and shout at us as if we were little kids. If we would ask them to stop, they would threaten to lock us down for a few days, which would happen constantly. Three people being locked in a two-man cell, in a 12 x 7 room. This happened a lot; sometimes as punishment for the actions of one or two inmates, the other 105–115 detainees would suffer. Other times, it seemed 'just because.' A lot of the detainees would be missing money on

> their accounts, which I was recently told by a detainee who keeps in contact with me was being stolen by the staff, according to [an] OIG investigation. We would get underserved during meal times. When we complained to the unit manager she would say that we were given the right amounts, which in my opinion is the appropriate portion for a ten or eleven year old. Some of the guards and staff would curse at us. They would purposely lower the televisions so we couldn't hear them, just to mess with us. During our free time they would take their time turning on the phones so we wouldn't be able to call our families. Just to be cruel.[523]

One of the guards at SDCF while Louis Jean was locked up was an ex-marine. This guard often talked with him and tried to explain why the treatment was so bad. "What he told me was that in his training to be a prison guard he was taught that we were all second-class citizens . . . that all we do is complain about everything and most of us are getting deported anyway, so he was taught to not really pay attention to our complaining and to treat us like second-class citizens."[524]

As this book goes to press, the U.S. government's Office of the Inspector General (OIG) is preparing to release its findings from its own investigation of the conditions at SDCF in 2005.

The OIG report that most forcefully condemned the treatment of immigrants inside various jails was released in 2003: "The September 11 Detainees: A Review of the Treatment of Aliens Held on Immigration Charges in Connection with the Investigation of the September 11 Attacks."[525] The findings were shocking. Infractions included routine abuse of basic prisoner rights, mental and physical abuse, denial of health care and medical treatment, prison overcrowding, and a lack of working showers and toilets.

Prison companies are able to save large amounts of money on labor costs that no other corporation would legally get away with. Prisons are notorious for paying a pittance to inmates for jobs that would earn them at least minimum wage on the outside. Immigrant prisons are even worse. The Department of Homeland Security has written guidelines that mandate that while noncitizen prisoners are allowed to work in their detention centers, they are not allowed to earn more than one dollar per day.[526] In this way, jails that detain and use immigrant labor have been able to save enormous amounts of money, as they employ prisoners to do much of the janitorial and prison maintenance work. From cleaning the prison to running the laundry, from cooking or sewing to tending the grounds, labor costs for private prisons are very low.

There are also subcontracts that go out to corporations to provide services, like telephone usage, to detained immigrants. To make a telephone call from inside a detention center costs a great deal more than a regular call made outside the center. MCI has all the telephone contracts for New York–area jails. In return, New York State has a very profitable deal with MCI where the telecommunications corporation pays 57.5 percent of all calls made from jails to the state.[527] The Center for Constitutional Rights (CCR) in New York is pursuing legal action to end MCI's stranglehold. CCR charges that since 2000, New York State "has received approximately $125 million from inmate telephone calls, in what has essentially been an unlegislated tax on inmates' families and friends."[528] CCR also documents a 630 percent markup over consumer rates to receive a collect call from a prisoner. In most New York state prisons inmates can only call collect, and they are charged sixteen cents per minute plus a three-dollar surcharge. CCR research shows that the average prison phone call costs around six dollars and is billed at nineteen minutes, which adds up to a monthly phone bill of about four hundred dollars per prisoner.[529]

MCI, like other companies that hold contracts to provide telephone service to prisoners, claims that it needs to charge higher rates because it has to record all conversations and sometimes block lines. While MCI, AT&T, and Sprint have many of the contracts with states and prisons around the country to provide telephone service,[530] smaller, unknown telephone companies, like Evercom, also have significant contracts. I learned about Evercom when detainees at the Broward Transitional Center in Miami angrily thrust their yellow Evercom calling cards at me, complaining of the exorbitant rates.[531] This company's record is very disturbing. In a 2004 FCC hearing regarding anticompetitive actions, Evercom was consistently highlighted for its poor service and for overcharging prisoners.[532] In a 2000 lawsuit in New Mexico, Evercom was charged with conspiring with the four largest private prison companies in the United States, including CCA and Wackenhut, to establish a monopoly over prison telephone services. The deal would have included "commission kickbacks" of up to 60 percent of gross revenue generated by Evercom in return for the contract.[533] In its home state of Texas, Evercom has a near monopoly, holding the telephone service contract for two thousand state, county, local, and immigration jails.[534]

Detainee advocates have decried the treatment of immigrant inmates. They accuse prison companies of cutting corners in training guards and in providing basic services. The government has done little to regulate prison administration, but, as with labor practices and telephone costs, has, in fact, sanctioned it. Moreover, the budget for detention beds continues to rise each year, and more and more contracts are awarded.

With the increase in prison beds to house immigrants comes the pressure to fill them, a scenario that has immigrant advocates extremely worried. Isabel García, attorney and human rights activist in Tucson, sees this as maintaining the prison-industrial complex that first flourished with the war on drugs. "The war on drugs has conveniently become a war on immigrants," says García, "and there is a lot of money to be made in detaining immigrants."[535] She worries that the profit motive behind detaining immigrants will only lead to an expansion of the system that criminalizes immigrants. Given the tight connections between the private-prison industry and the federal government, this is very likely.

The Department of Homeland Security has been built by private industry working very closely with the government to implement systems and procedures that purport to protect America from future terrorist attacks. The Department of Homeland Security has let industry lead the way in designing technology to aid in this task. However, in many cases, the systems and procedures end up getting immigrants and noncitizens who have no connections to terrorism tangled in their nets.

This book only scratches the surface of how immigration and immigration enforcement are extremely profitable for American business at the expense of immigrant rights. There are *many* more areas that need to be investigated. We should ask how much the government is paying American Airlines to transport deportees. It's been proposed that jail bondsmen be paid exorbitant sums to round up removable immigrants. We should demand to know why a water flask or a cell phone or a digital camera costs the government so much more for use by a Border Patrol agent than it costs a regular consumer. Questions should be raised about why "nonlethal" chili-powder guns, which have caused so many serious injuries, are still being used by Border Patrol agents. Each of these small contracts, and many more not mentioned here, are trampling the rights of noncitizens. Yet these profitable and questionable contracts continue to proliferate because they have a powerful lobby behind them that is closely connected to government officials. Only a mass citizen's movement that demands justice for immigrants and noncitizens could possibly trump the power of corporate America.

Isabel García's concern about industry profits driving punitive immigration policy must be addressed in a national dialogue. Progressive grassroots organizers worked for years to bring the issue of the prison-industrial complex to the national agenda. The movement forced the nation to look at who was being incarcerated, the nature of the crimes, and who profits from the prison industry. With a prison population of over 2 million, that struggle is very much alive. The movement must continue its efforts to expose the growing immigration-industrial complex and to demand that human rights not be ignored for the sake of private profit.

But as the next chapter illustrates, business interests are only half the battle in restoring rights to noncitizens in the United States. The other lobby, which forms a small yet powerful part of the Republican base, is the nativist movement.

Chapter VI

U.S. IMMIGRATION POLICY AND RACISM

HOW WHITE SUPREMACISTS ARE WRITING IMMIGRATION POLICY AND DEMOCRATS ARE ASLEEP AT THE WHEEL

> It should be legal to kill illegals. Just shoot 'em on sight. That's my immigration policy recommendation. You break into my country, you die.
>
> —Carl, a sixty-nine-year-old veteran of the U.S. Army's Special Forces and the Vietnam War

> Something needs to be done about the way in which aliens are sneaking into the United States of America along the Canadian and Mexican Borders. Many of these individuals have criminal records and are known as communists.
>
> —From "Canadian Border Scandal," an article that appeared in the June 1948 issue of *The Cross and the Flag*, a Christian Nationalist Crusade publication

When I first met the man who infiltrates white nationalist and hate groups, I anticipated a tattooed, head-shaven, mean-looking man. I did not expect the shaggy-haired, warm-eyed man with a brightly colored ethnic-print shirt who greeted me with a huge smile and a bear hug. Peter Smith was the furthest thing from a stereotypical skinhead, and my initial trepidations quickly dissipated. Smith says that in all the years he has been attending white supremacist and neo-Nazi events, he has yet to be outed as an infiltrator. And from his first hate event, a cross burning in Pennsylvania in 1993 billed as a "white unity rally," Smith realized he had entered another world, a dangerous world his progressive ideals had sheltered him from.

I undertook a crash course on these so-called hate groups, an umbrella term used to describe groups who believe that as a group they are inherently superior to another and who actively work to suppress the other. As I began to research white nationalist and neo-Nazi individuals and groups, I kept coming back to a couple of sources: the Southern Poverty Law Center (SPLC) and the Center for New Community. Both nonprofit groups have dedicated much of the last decade to tracking, monitoring, and documenting the activities of hate groups. Mark Potok, director of the Intelligence Project at the SPLC, told me that his definition of a hate group "has nothing to do with violence, criminality, or any kind of judgment on our part about potential future violence. We list groups as 'hate groups' based strictly on ideology. If a group says—via its plank, Web site, speeches, or writings of its leaders—that any other whole group of people, defined by their group characteristics, is somehow less, then that's a hate group."[536] I used this as my benchmark in judging the actions of individuals and groups toward other individuals and groups.

Peter Smith spent years stealthily entering and exiting the world of these groups. In his Washington, DC, home and tiny office in a local community church, Smith shared with me the archive of materials collected at hate-group events over the years. He has photos that he has taken at various events as well as pamphlets, fliers, and various types of hateful propaganda. Smith also has an incredible stockpile of stories that emerged as we drank tea and took care of his day's errands.

In 1996 Smith was at a KKK rally in Washington, DC, where he posed as a window washer who was pissed off because "illegals" had taken his job and had made it impossible for him to find another job. His story won him many racist friends who sympathized. Smith showed them his bruised knuckles and said he had taken matters directly into his own hands because the government had done nothing. This won him legitimacy in the eyes of those attending the KKK rally. They plied him with potential solutions, and Smith says he was stunned at their ideas. His KKK friends wanted a complete halt to all immigration, legal and illegal, and demanded that all the basic rights of noncitizens in the country be stripped.

Smith believes that what is happening to immigrants in America today is due to the adoption of the far-Right agenda, an agenda driven by individuals who are members of and directly connected to white nationalist groups. My research in the months after meeting Smith confirms his claim. And one man, John Tanton, surfaced at almost every turn. As I discovered, this ophthalmologist from Michigan, who founded one of the country's most influential anti-immigration organizations, the Federation for American Immigration

Reform (FAIR), can be credited as the major influence in current immigration policy. Yet, as my research also uncovered, John Tanton and the movement that surrounds him is not just anti-immigrant—it is racist.

However, considering that the history of the United States is steeped in racist policies, this story does not begin with Tanton. From the early and current efforts to remove indigenous peoples by stripping these communities of their homelands and several attempts at literal and cultural genocide, to the enslavement of Africans and the segregation of African Americans, the United States has routinely legislated against certain groups. Immigrants, too, have a history of being targeted and scapegoated for such societal problems as a poor economy or a terrorist attack. What John Tanton and others have been able to do so successfully is take advantage of moments of vulnerability to affect mainstream America's views toward immigrants and then follow up with concrete policy ideas that restrict immigration and immigrant rights.

Tanton's very clever planning laid the groundwork for a decades-long effort to bring his visions for immigration to fruition. Along the way he managed to win over prominent elected officials, the media, and all manner of hate groups to make the victory much more than just his. Tanton's biggest success has been capturing the public discourse around immigration and bringing it firmly into his court. It's a chilling story indeed.

The Ballot Initiative Strategy

In 1994, in a ballot initiative that stunned the nation, California voters passed Proposition 187, a highly loaded measure that denied undocumented immigrants access to nonemergency medical services and public education. Prop 187 was extremely provocative, and had controversial provisions requiring that public employees "turn in" undocumented immigrants, an immigration enforcement strategy that had never before gained any mainstream currency.

Prop 187 was not engineered by anti-immigrant groups, but by those with overt white supremacist ties and ideology. One of the two main groups behind Prop 187 was the California Coalition for Immigration Reform (CCIR) headed by Barbara Coe, who is not shy about referring to Mexicans as "savages."[537] Coe has described undocumented migrants as "illegal barbarians who are cutting off heads and appendages of blind, white, disabled gringos."[538] Coe recently told the *Denver Post* that she is a member of the Council of Conservative Citizens (CCC),[539] a white supremacist group that states on its Web site that it rejects "all efforts to mix the races of mankind [and] to promote non-white races over the European-American people."[540] CCC has sold t-shirts that declare: "White Pride. Save our Culture."[541]

Coe is one of the later pioneers who fight overtly racist anti-immigrant battles couched in decidedly "I'm not racist" rhetoric. Yet Coe, as with many of the anti-immigrant groups and leaders, is exposed for her white nationalist ideology when one examines who she works with and who she is connected to, as well as what she actually says herself.

In the Prop 187 battle, CCIR worked closely with the very hard-line anti-immigrant organization Voices of Citizens Together (VCT). According to the Southern Poverty Law Center, both CCIR and VCT are bona fide hate groups.[542]

> Coe and VCT chief Glenn Spencer stage annual Fourth of July rallies that have drawn prominent neo-Nazis. Barbara Coe's political activities convinced the *Orange County Weekly* to name her in 1999 one of the "scariest" people in Orange County. CCIR has sponsored billboards along the Arizona-California border that read, "Welcome to California, the Illegal Immigration State. Don't Let This Happen to Your State."[543]

Spencer told the *Los Angeles Times* that "the Mexican culture is based on deceit. Chicanos and Mexicanos lie as a means of survival."[544]

Toward the end of the Prop 187 debate in the late 1990s and early into 2000, Coe and fellow anti-immigrationist Spencer were participants and featured speakers at major gatherings of anti-immigration extremists. In May 2000 in Sierra Vista, Arizona, Coe stood before an eager audience and denounced immigrants as "alien savages."[545] She incited her audience to embrace border control because every immigrant caught at the border would be "one less illegal alien bringing in communicable diseases, one less illegal alien smuggling deadly drugs, one less illegal alien gang member to rob, rape and murder innocent U.S. citizens."[546]

Making it a multimedia event, Spencer treated the crowd to a homemade racist video. *The Intelligence Report*, a publication of the Southern Poverty Law Center, describes the video like this:

> A Mexican invasion, Spencer warns in his own videotape, is racing across America "like wildfire." There are drugs in Iowa, gang takeovers in Nevada, and "traitors" in the Democratic Party, the Catholic Church and among the "corporate globalists."

> Bringing crime, drugs, squalor and "immigration via the birth canal," Mexicans are a "cultural cancer" from which Western civilization "must be rescued." They are threatening the birthright left by the white colonists who "earned the right to stewardship of the land." And this invasion is no accident.
>
> Working in league with communist Chicano activists and their allies in America, Spencer warns, Mexico is using a little-known but highly effective plan—a scheme already successful in "seizing power" in California—"to defeat America."
>
> The name of the conspiracy is the "Plan de Aztlán."[547]

Glenn Spencer also took out full-page ads for this video in the newspaper of the overtly racist Council of Conservative Citizens, which recently had the following comment posted on the Web site of its Florida chapter, next to a photo of an asylum seeker: "THIS WORTHLESS, DIRT POOR, HAITIAN LEACH [*sic*] and her 3 BRATS have ABSOLUTELY NO RIGHT to be in this COUNTRY!"[548]

While Barbara Coe and Glenn Spencer riled up the crowd in Sierra Vista, which consisted of members of former Ku Klux Klan leader David Duke's organization, as well as unrobed members of the Knights of the Klan, all the surrounding cars were adorned with Klan fliers.[549] The anti-immigration movement has been very successful in making the legislative work (like the Prop 187 campaign) appear completely unrelated to these peripheral activities of hate.

Beginning in the late 1980s, a new strategy incorporating a more palatable kind of hate replaced regular cross-burning and other hate events.[550] Long-time analyst of American white-nationalist movements, Leonard Zeskind has called it the "bullet-to-ballot strategy." Consider Glenn Spencer. He did not make his video just to rile up angry white crowds—he wanted lawmakers to see it, too. In 1999, Spencer's people hand-delivered copies of the racist anti-immigration video to every member of Congress. The messenger was Bettina McCann, the fiancée of Steven Barry, the military coordinator of the neo-Nazi group the National Alliance.[551]

The National Alliance recently displayed a recruitment billboard in Las Vegas that stated: "Stop Immigration. Join the National Alliance." Zeskind has described the National Alliance as a "national socialist sect known best for producing *The Turner Diaries*, the race-war terror novel carried by Oklahoma City bomber Timothy McVeigh."[552] The members of this group are Glenn Spencer's friends and confidants.

Spencer also coordinates citizen patrols in the southern border region under his organization American Patrol. In talking about why he thinks it is necessary to patrol the border, Spencer says, "This gang is here to subvert our immigration laws," referring to Mexican nationals. He went on to tell *Salon.com* journalist Max Blumenthal, "If we lose the United States to that cesspool of a culture, how would you like to give 15,000 nuclear weapons to Mexico? It will be the death of this country when hot-blooded, Latin-American macho people bomb the crap out of China or whomever gets in their way."[553] American Patrol boasts an advisory board with members such as FAIR founder John Tanton. Tanton's organizations U.S. Inc. and FAIR have donated $50,050 to Spencer's American Patrol and Voices of Citizens Together over a three-year period beginning in 1998.[554]

What Coe and Spencer were able to do with Prop 187 was extremely significant. Although it was immediately challenged in court and eventually ruled largely unconstitutional, Prop 187 signaled a major shift in the public debate on immigration. For the first time, a significantly anti-immigrant agenda, which for years had been accepted only on the margins of the far Right, had successfully been sold to an electorate. Hate-group infiltrator Peter Smith sees the Prop 187 battle as the bellwether for elements of the white supremacist movement that had chosen electoral politics over violent acts as their way forward.[555]

Lawsuits against Prop 187 were filed soon after the 1994 election. The proposition's death knell sounded when U.S. District Court judge Marina Pfaelzer issued a permanent injunction, employing as precedent a 1980 Texas case (Plyler v. Doe) where Texas's attempt to deny public education to undocumented immigrants was ruled unconstitutional since the state's denial of education violated the Fourteenth Amendment's equal protection clause. In a thirty-two-page opinion, Judge Pfaelzer found that Proposition 187 was a "scheme" designed to regulate immigration in California. And, according to the Constitution, immigration law is the exclusive domain of the federal government, not the state.

For the extremist groups who had dreamed up and advanced Prop 187, the ability to sell these harsh anti-immigrant laws to a majority of Californians marked a victory. To Coe and her crew, the later decisions of the high court to strike down much of the proposition as unconstitutional merely proved that the judiciary was out of touch with what the people wanted.

Prop 187's success at the ballot box, while specific to California, allowed groups around the country, such as Voices of Citizens Together and other white supremacists, to translate messages of hate into less overtly offensive messages of "anti-immigration."

The Federation for American Immigration Reform (FAIR), John Tanton's Washington, DC-based policy organization, was one of the groups that eagerly—if quietly—supported Prop 187 and gained a lot of ground from the victory at the ballot box. In fact, Tanton had been calling for the measures included in Prop 187 back in the early 1980s.

Along with his early 1980s ideas of barring certain groups of immigrants from receiving social services and public benefits, Tanton and FAIR also began talking about sanctions against employers who hire undocumented workers, beefing up border enforcement, and conducting concentrated sweeps, arrests, and deportations of immigrants as early as 1979. Not surprisingly, FAIR also opposed guest-worker programs and asylum for refugees from Haiti and the Central American wars.[556]

On the other side of the congressional immigration debates is Rick Swartz, a man who has been described as the godfather of the proimmigrant agenda in Congress. Swartz, a twenty-five-year veteran of immigration battles on Capitol Hill, was the organizing and lobbying genius behind the amnesty proposals and the relief visas for Central Americans and Haitians in the 1980s. He was also present for all the big immigration battles dating back to the late 1970s. Swartz was often at loggerheads with Tanton and FAIR and other anti-immigration groups that enjoyed overwhelmingly better funding. "In the late 80s," according to Swartz, "Tanton's groups had $30 million a year between them to focus and concentrate on one single issue: restricting immigration."[557]

Long before Prop 187 surfaced in California, Tanton and his colleagues were actively writing and lobbying for very restrictive immigration measures. In the 1986 immigration legislation, "Tanton and FAIR were pushing for big cutbacks to family and employment visas, restrictions on political asylum, restricting access to counsel for noncitizens, restricting judicial review, among many other restrictions."[558] Swartz explains that his coalition fought all these provisions and was successful in getting them stripped from the 1986 law. But he knew that they would resurface, and sure enough, by 1996, much of the restrictionist agenda that was staved off in 1986 had returned. Swartz says that "these ideas were percolating around and in the pots in the early '86 debates. We stripped them all out. But they were certainly not going to simply go away."[559]

Not long after the "success" of Prop 187, federal legislation followed that strongly echoed the anti-immigrant sentiment of Prop 187, as well as other of Tanton's early-1980s ideas for reducing the number of immigrants in the United States. This restrictionist agenda involved vastly expanding the ability to remove, via deportation, those already legally in the country.

Two 1996 acts tackled immigration: the Illegal Immigration Reform and Immigrant Responsibility Act (IIRAIRA)[560] and the Antiterrorism and Effective Death Penalty Act (AEDPA).[561] Together, they introduced many clauses that left immigrant advocates reeling. One part greatly increased the scope of the grounds for deportation of legal permanent residents who had committed a crime deemed an aggravated felony by the INS. It went further, however, by severely restricting the power of a judge to suspend the deportation, a reprieve that was traditionally available to deportable immigrants who had resided in the U.S. for considerable periods of time and had deep family and work ties.

The 1996 laws increased to ten years the time period that an out-of-status individual had to have resided in the United States to claim relief from deportation. They also required demonstration that being deported, with a permanent bar to reentry (in nonaggravated felony cases a ten-year bar was imposed), would cause "exceptional and extremely unusual hardship" to a lawful permanent resident or U.S.-citizen spouse, parent, or child. Immigrant advocates decried this as a legal way of denying relief from deportation to those who were not legal permanent residents and who had no other way to adjust their status.

As the restrictionist agenda took root in federal legislation, there were grave fears at the time that this was the first step toward a state-sanctioned immigrant cleansing of the United States. When one looks at the numbers deported since the laws were enacted, currently well over 1 million,[562] this charge of immigrant cleansing seems well founded, especially when one considers the types of minor infractions for which many of the deportations are ordered and the fact that the majority of those deported are permanently prohibited from reentering the United States.[563]

IIRAIRA also signaled a major change in the way the country would deal with those fleeing life-threatening and dangerous situations by giving immigration authorities the discretion to jail any arriving person stating a fear of returning to their country, or those without proper documentation or legal visa status on arrival in the United States. Formalizing what had previously been an ad hoc policy applied selectively, and mostly to arriving Haitians, the use of the prison system by immigration authorities to streamline its bureaucratic processes is found in just one other nation—Australia. Only three Senate Democrats voted against IIRAIRA when it came before the 104th Congress: Senator Russ Feingold (D-WI), Senator Paul Simon (D-IL), and Senator Bob Graham (D-FL). Given that much of this bill had its roots in restrictionist ideology, were the other Democratic senators simply asleep?

As the 1996 immigration debates raged, Rick Swartz was then at the National Immigration Forum, the organization he founded and ran for many years. Swartz says it was a compromised bill that "the Left lost." At the time, Bill Clinton was president, but Congress was controlled by Republicans.

Democrats were deeply split on how to stop certain provisions, like big cuts to legal immigration levels and the implementation of a national identification card. One faction refused to compromise on elements such as the harsh enforcement provisions for those illegally in the country or those arriving without proper documentation. Rick Swartz says he was on the other side, feeling that "if the Left did not compromise on this, then legal immigration would be dealt a severe blow."[564] In the end, all categories of immigrants, including legal permanent residents, legal visa holders, and undocumented migrants lost out. Tanton, FAIR and the far-Right sailed to victory.

The 1996 assault on immigrants came from many directions. Another bill to pass that year was tied to so-called welfare reform—the Personal Responsibility and Work Opportunity Reconciliation Act.[565] This act all but halted social services available to undocumented *and* documented immigrants, including health care and food stamps. It shifted immigration policy enforcement from the federal to the state level, giving state officials substantial authority to determine which types of immigrants would receive which kinds of public benefits. Consider, for example, Medicaid. Under the new law, states would determine which *legal* immigrants would be eligible for the medical benefits based on the date they arrived in the United States.[566] Additionally, the complete financial burden for providing medical treatment to legal immigrants was passed on to the states, relieving the federal government of this responsibility. So if a state was to provide basic social benefits, it would also have to cough up to pay for them. Not a great incentive for states to sign up. Furthermore, this legislation completely barred undocumented immigrants from these public benefits by not listing them in the "qualified aliens" section and simultaneously limiting the rights of those legally in the United States.[567] The authors of Prop 187 could not have hoped for more.

Passed in an election year, this legislation became a focal point of the 1996 presidential race between Bill Clinton and Bob Dole. Although he had commented publicly on the harshness of some of the Prop 187-ish provisions of the 1996 legislation, Clinton ultimately signed each one into law.

In fact, as election day neared, Clinton's campaign spokesman on immigration, Democratic congressman Howard Berman, was jubilant as he lauded the Clinton administration's record on immigration. "They have deported nearly 200,000 illegal immigrants, over a hundred thousand of those are criminal aliens, and this is the first administration to put money into its budget and to support funding to reimburse the states and the local governments who have the cost of incarcerating criminal aliens. It is the most proactive administration on this issue that we have ever had."[568]

When some of these ideas were first floated, many of which comprised the substance of Prop 187, they were seen as extreme and limited to far-Right groups like CCIR and VCT. Prominent Democrats fought strongly against Prop 187, yet thanks to strategic work by FAIR and John Tanton, these once-extreme ideas took less than a decade to wind their way into the policy speeches of both Republicans and Democrats, and also into law.

In his 1996 State of the Union address President Clinton promised to increase "border controls by 50 percent" and announced an executive order to "deny federal contracts to businesses that hire illegal immigrants."[569] In his 1996 book, *Between Hope and History*, President Clinton wrote that "since 1992, we have increased our Border Patrol by over thirty five percent; deployed underground sensors, infrared night scopes and encrypted radios; built miles of new fences; and installed massive amounts of new lighting. We have moved forcefully to protect American jobs by calling on Congress to enact increased civil and criminal sanctions against employers who hire illegal workers. Since 1993, we have removed 30,000 illegal workers from jobs across the country."[570]

Led by President Clinton, Democrats were learning that just as they could appeal to a certain section of the electorate by appearing tough on crime, there was also growing mainstream acceptance for policies that were tough on immigration. The public debate on immigration had shifted with Prop 187, and even though the courts ultimately blocked it, the Prop 187 lobby had taken their fight to mainstream America and tapped into the country's deep fears of an immigrant takeover.

Bullet-to-Ballot Strategy: The Origins of the 1996 Legislation

One of the more virulent racists who expresses anti-immigration sentiments is David Duke. In the years before he was elected to the Louisiana House of Representatives in 1989, Duke was openly associated with Nazi, neo-Nazi, and Ku Klux Klan groups.[571] While in the House, he managed to introduce and pass a bill to severely curtail affirmative action programs in Louisiana. His other bills, aimed at restricting the rights of welfare recipients and mandating drug tests as part of the driver's license application, were soundly rejected. Duke attempted to run for the U.S. Senate in 1990 and lost, but received a stunning 44 percent of the vote.[572]

In May 2005 Duke spearheaded a conference, which many European neo-Nazi groups attended. From his experience as an elected local official, Duke had learned the power of a toned-down message when the occasion warranted it. His presentation to the conference, according to longtime watcher of the far Right Leonard Zeskind, "repeated his mantra that 'local politics is the soft underbelly' of the political establishment—and most of his European speakers were out to prove this point."[573] Duke was one of the earliest pioneers of pursuing an electoral strategy to try to get elected to public office to advance goals of hate.

However, before Duke went the electoral route he had been outspoken about immigration issues since the mid-1970s. When he was the head of the Knights of the Ku Klux Klan and participating in KKK patrols of the southern border, Duke talked about what his immigration policy would look like. "I'd make the Mexican-American border almost like a Maginot Line," he said, referring to the fortifications that France built on its eastern border before World War II to keep immigrants out. On October 16, 1977, as his KKK patrol of the border was preparing to launch, Duke told reporters who had flocked to cover this openly white supremacist event that, in addition to walls along the border, he would prohibit businesses from hiring undocumented workers and that he would round up everyone without legal papers and deport them.[574] While these now seem like very common solutions to immigration problems, newspapers from that time report that residents and law enforcement found them extreme and limited to the likes of the KKK.[575]

Duke was certainly not the first to claim that immigrants were swarming the United States. However, Duke connected this "rising tide of color" to welfare benefits.[576] He referred to immigrants as "parasites" who were coming to the U.S. to leach off the system.[577] It was a theme that was revived very successfully in the Prop 187 battle and later enshrined into law in the 1996 welfare reform legislation.

Drawing on Duke's success, more white supremacists, KKK members, and neo-Nazis decided to run for public office, beginning in the early 1990s. It was clear to them that they would not likely win (although David Duke did) but they believed their ideas could gain more currency and that their extremist and racist beliefs could move into the mainstream. Although immigration was not the only area of concern, severely limiting it and curtailing nonwhite immigrants' rights were a prominent part of their agenda. It was the beginning of the movement of these ideas from the margins to the center of political thought, both in the halls of power around the country and in the general American population.

Plotting the Infiltration

It is no coincidence that extremist immigration policy passed in 1996. In fact, it was tactical and thoroughly planned. Again, all roads seem to lead back to John Tanton. While David Duke put himself forward as a candidate to lead the unofficial bullet-to-ballot movement, years of investigations by the Southern Poverty Law Center have uncovered that it was Tanton who was the architect and brains behind engineering the margins-to-mainstream strategy for this anti-immigrant movement that had grown to embrace all stripes of white supremacists and neo-Nazis.

From the early days of FAIR, Tanton was adept at framing his immigration policy suggestions as beneficial for the environment or as simple population control mechanisms. Tanton and FAIR have always emphatically denied any racist intent behind their actions. Yet in 1988, years before Prop 187 and soon after the 1986 amnesty, a number of secret memos were leaked that clearly illustrate not only Tanton's long-term strategy for pushing through his immigration policies, but also their racist underpinnings.[578]

The memos, called WITAN, were written in 1986 by Tanton and then executive director of FAIR, Roger Conner. WITAN is an abbreviation of "witenagemot," an old English word for a council of wise men. WITAN memos detailed a plan to infiltrate Congress, the judiciary, and liberal groups like the Sierra Club to position the anti-immigrant agenda at the forefront of policy. Reading the 1986 WITAN memos almost twenty years after they were written is chilling. Tanton realized back in the mid-1980s that he needed to win the American public's hearts and minds. He needed them to believe that immigrants were criminals and a threat to society. If he could win the public debate on immigration, then it would be possible to get his agenda passed into law.

The memos outline the prime goal of Tanton's early anti-immigrant agenda: swaying public perception to allow for a "moratorium" on immigration. Initial thoughts are offered on how to sell the idea to the public: "here are some phrases that could be used: 'The pause that refreshes.' 'A seventh inning stretch.' 'Take a break, catch-up, eliminate a backlog, take a breather.'"[579]

The memos also suggest multiple ways to foment anti-immigrant sentiment. Ideas range from equating migrants coming across the southern border with drug smugglers to using a tax strategy that would impose an immigrant tax on those who employ non-Americans and that would get the IRS firmly on board. The memos touch on educational strategies, judicial strategies, congressional strategies, and activist strategies. They are a powerful documentation of Tanton's early anti-immigrant dreams.

Tanton was attempting to sway public opinion so firmly that, years later, elected officials would not be able to dismiss the anti-immigrant agenda because it would represent mainstream consensus. As Ray Ybarra of the ACLU in Texas points out, "We lost the battle for public opinion years ago, and since then we have simply been compromising our way out of the very extreme and settling for harsh."[580]

The WITAN memos also display concrete proof of Tanton's racism. Their public exposure allowed critics to charge that Tanton's racism was now firmly sewn on his sleeve for all to see. For example, Tanton wrote, among many other questionable statements, "As Whites see their power and control over their lives declining, will they simply go quietly into the night? . . . Can *homo contraceptivus* compete with *homo progenitiva* if borders aren't controlled? . . . Perhaps this is the first instance in which those with their pants up are going to get caught by those with their pants down!"[581]

The WITAN memos contained racist references to Latinos and provoked major defections from Tanton's various anti-immigration groups. Linda Chávez, executive director of Tanton's group U.S. English, quit her post, as did board member Walter Cronkite. Chávez, after years of being the Hispanic face rebutting charges that U.S. English was motivated by racism, finally seemed unable to deny Tanton's motives. "This nexus of issues—population control, immigration control, and language policy—certainly gives the impression that [U.S. English] is biased against Hispanics."[582] Cronkite called the memos "embarrassing." U.S. English was harshly condemned by Latino activists, including Raul Yzaguirre, president of the National Council of La Raza, who blasted the organization. "U.S. English is to Hispanics as the Ku Klux Klan is to blacks."[583]

While the leak of the WITAN memos caused defections and threw some negative light on John Tanton and his organizations for a short period, there was never a mass exposé. Tanton simply weathered the brief storm and all seemed to be forgotten. What mattered to Tanton was that he remain focused on to his goal making his beliefs about immigrants and immigration the beliefs of mainstream America.

Over the years, Tanton has been closely associated with thirteen anti-immigrant groups, founding many and funding others. The Southern Poverty Law Center lists three of the groups that Tanton funds, one of which he also founded, as "hate groups."[584] Tanton has been described as the "puppeteer" of these various anti-immigrant groups, each of which espouses independence, though tax records reveal how closely linked they are.[585]

Tanton's devotion to the racist novel *The Camp of the Saints* by Frenchman

Jean Raspail is revealing. The *Intelligence Report* describes the novel, first published in 1973, as depicting "an invasion of the white, Western world by a fleet of starving, dark-skinned refugees." The magazine goes on to note that "Tanton helped get the novel published in English and soon was promoting what he considered the book's prophetic argument. 'Their [Third World] "huddled masses" cast longing eyes on the apparent riches of the industrial west,' Tanton wrote in 1975. 'The developed countries lie directly in the path of a great storm.'"[586] At the same time that he was embracing this white racist's call to arms, Tanton wrote an essay that addressed immigration as a global problem of developed countries. Some of his early ideas on restricting immigration and immigrant rights included calls for all immigrants to carry "identity cards to establish one's right to social benefits, a job and to be in the country."[587]

Tanton clearly understands the importance of projecting a more mainstream agenda while at the same time supporting and promoting white supremacist ideology. Toward this end, the Tanton empire also targets those who write immigration policy. In 1996 John Tanton founded—and until 2003 funded—a direct lobbying organization with the benign name of NumbersUSA. Within Tanton's elaborate network, NumbersUSA is perhaps the most significant organization when it comes to direct policy work. Situated in Washington, DC, NumbersUSA operates a short distance from the Capitol in its "government relations office." Over the years, it has gained recognition from elected representatives such as Tom Tancredo (R-CO) and anti-immigrationists such as Barbara Coe, architect of Prop 187. Its claim that it is simply worried about the rising levels of immigration and is not a bigoted organization was exposed as a falsehood at a recent NumbersUSA event. Among the reading materials on offer was the white supremacist tabloid the *Citizens Informer*, published by the hate group the Council of Conservative Citizens.[588]

FAIR, the best known and most mainstream of Tanton's anti-immigration organizations, does not escape racism charges either. FAIR has received a large portion of its funding from the overtly racist Pioneer Fund. The Center for New Community, which tracks and documents white supremacist groups, has described the Pioneer Fund as "a centerpiece in keeping scientific racism alive through allocating grants for pseudo-scientific studies."[589] FAIR's receipt of over $1 million from the Pioneer Fund and its continual defense of this fact show clearly where the true roots of FAIR lie.[590]

But the Tanton-FAIR connections to extremist hate groups go beyond funding. In fact, multiple FAIR staffers have been directly connected with the white hate group the Council of Conservative Citizens (CCC). The Center for New Community says that the CCC is the largest white supremacist group in the

United States today. Its main work revolves around racially charged issues like battles over the Confederate flag and restoring monuments of the Confederacy. The group also tries to stop nonwhite immigration.[591] The CCC has said that blacks are 'a retrograde species of humanity,' compared singer Michael Jackson to an ape, and promoted neo-Nazi and Holocaust-denial materials."[592]

FAIR staffers participate in CCC events—one member even claims to be a member of CCC—yet FAIR leadership does not fire them, nor even reprimand them in any way.[593] One FAIR staff member, Peter Gemma, is also employed by the CCC newsletter with a job title of "Design, Marketing, and Advertising." In 2003 and 2004 Gemma also worked for the FAIR political action committee, the U.S. Immigration Reform Political Action Committee (USIRP). USIRP was established in 1993 to support "immigration reform" candidates. For the November 2004 general election, USIRP contributed $25,500 to twenty candidates. In 2004 they also contributed $31,761 to fourteen primary candidates in twelve states.[594] As a representative of FAIR with ties to the white supremacist group Council of Conservative Citizens, Gemma's direct funding connections to federal congressional candidates raises grave questions.

FAIR was a strong advocate of detaining arriving Haitian refugees, denying it had anything to do with race. In October 1985 when the Supreme Court heard the case of *Jean v. Nelson*, which claimed that the detention of two hundred Haitian asylum seekers was discriminatory, FAIR submitted an Amicus Curiae brief arguing that the policy was justified and had nothing to do with race.[595] At the time there were no other nationalities detained on arrival.

Rick Swartz told the *Intelligence Report* that John Tanton was the "puppeteer" of the movement. He said, "Tanton is a brilliant tactician. He has created a system where he can have his cake and eat it, too. He has a political movement on the extremist, racial fringe that is stirring up popular discontent and hatred with its harsh rhetoric. There is a lot of fertile ground out there, and the fringe is increasingly significant in areas like what is going on in Iowa right now. At the same time, other Tanton groups are getting invited to testify before Congress on a regular basis."[596]

In the summer of 1998, ten years after the WITAN exposure, Tanton seemed to abandon all pretense of not being racist when his publishing house, the Social Contract Press, released a special issue of its journal, *The Social Contract*. Entitled "Europhobia: The Hostility Toward European-Descended Americans," the main article argued that "multiculturalism" was replacing "successful Euro-American culture" with "dysfunctional Third World cultures." It was written by John Vinson, head of the Tanton-supported American Immigration Control Foundation. More disturbing, however, was Tanton's public support of Vinson's article. Tanton elaborated on Vinson's remarks by accusing "multiculturalists" of being behind this takeover of white culture stating that an "unwarranted hatred and fear" of white Americans was developing.[597]

In a 1994 essay Tanton wrote that immigrants "should enjoy a lesser 'bundle of rights' than citizens," while for asylum seekers "the emphasis should be on *temporary* succor with eventual repatriation, rather than permanent settlement."[598] That lesser "bundle of rights" was directly written into the 1996 legislation. In fact, it was the most overt stripping of noncitizen rights in recent history. It is important to remember that prior to 1996 noncitizens were not so easily deportable, had more relief available to them from deportation, and were eligible for access to social services.

Tanton's ultimate mission, according to his own WITAN memos, is to influence anti-immigration legislation. In section A of the 1986 WITAN memos, titled "Congressional Strategy," subsection A2 reads:

> Infiltrate the Judiciary Committees. This is a long-range project. We should make every effort to get legislators sympathetic to our point of view appointed to the House and Senate Judiciary Committees, and their Immigration Sub-Committees. Think how much different our prospects would be if someone espousing our ideas had the chairmanship! If we secure the appointment of our people as freshmen members of the committee, we will eventually secure the chairmanship. Remember: we're in this for the long haul.[599]

This infiltration of Congress began in the early 1990s, while Roger Conner was executive director at FAIR. Conner hired Cordia Strom as FAIR's legal director. There was almost immediate success in achieving Tanton's vision of infiltrating congressional committees when Strom was hired as the minority counsel to the Senate Judiciary Committee's Subcommittee on Immigration and Refugee Affairs. Strom worked there from 1992–1995.[600] She then became part of the staff of Representative Lamar Smith (R-Texas) and from 1995–1998 was chief counsel to Smith, who was the Chair of the House Judiciary Subcommittee in Immigration and Claims. Strom was extraordinarily well placed during the 1996 immigration debate.

The very harsh legislation that eventually passed into law was written and introduced by subcommittee chairman Lamar Smith. Rick Swartz, who was intricately involved in the battles over the 1996 legislation, says it was the ultimate victory for Tanton when a "FAIR plant like Cordia Strom is ghostwriting Lamar Smith's immigration legislation."[601] INS commissioner at the time,

Doris Meissner was more blunt, telling me that Cordia Strom did not ghost-write the legislation, "she directly wrote it."[602] This was the first big victory at the national level for the extremist and white supremacist electoral strategy.

Lamar Smith was an easy target for the likes of FAIR in its plans for infiltrating Congress. Immigration attorney Ira Kurzban, who is the author of a widely used textbook on immigration law and who worked closely with Democrats during the 1996 immigration debates, says that Lamar Smith, in effect, turned the congressional immigration subcommittee over to FAIR.[603] While it is usual practice for lobby groups to pressure lawmakers and even write sample legislation, it was detrimental to immigrant rights that the chair of an important congressional subcommittee would allow an extremist group such access. Lamar Smith is no longer chairman of the immigration subcommittee, but his legacy to immigration is significant and profound. Kurzban says that Lamar Smith "did more to undermine the basic principles of due process and equal protection in our society than probably any Congressman in the century."[604] Smith's right-hand woman was Cordia Strom.

Cordia Strom remained a member of FAIR while she worked on Capitol Hill. According to Tom Olson, former public relations director for U.S. English, Strom was one of Tanton's chosen few: an elite hand-picked associate of FAIR who attended WITAN retreats. Strom, according to Olsen, was present at the 1989 meetings where the primary goals were to "to sit around talking about action plans to solve the world's problems."[605] After the exposure of the WITAN memos, even the most conservative Republicans tied to Tanton anti-immigration groups could not deny the organizations' racist intent. Thus those like Strom, who chose to continue participating in WITAN retreats, appear unequivocal in their support of these groups' racist ideals.

Cordia Strom went from success to success in her immigration infiltration work on Capitol Hill. On the heels of the 1996 legislation, Strom left her position as a staffer for Representative Smith for the Executive Office for Immigration Review, where she was appointed senior advisor to the director. One of the functions of this body was to hear the administrative appeals from INS decisions and make final decisions on such matters as deportations. Strom was paid a salary of $110,028 a year, about $14,000 less than she was making previously.[606]

Strom, curiously, was not appointed by her ever-supportive Republican allies, but by the Clinton White House.[607] Her immigration ideology is clear from her record, and she had worked for Republicans who were bent on halting immigration, not merely reducing it. According to Rick Swartz, "everyone knew she was a FAIR plant."[608] So how could the Clinton White House have found her an appealing candidate? Perhaps because she had been a prominent player in the 1996 immigration debates, the Democrats saw no problem in appointing her to such a high position. Perhaps it was an easy compromise, a backroom deal that was not thoroughly considered. Whatever went on behind the scenes, however, the end result was that a white supremacist agenda was firmly planted inside a critical committee that makes immigration policy. It was a great victory for Tanton and his plans for infiltrating Congress.[609] In August 2005 Strom was named Assistant Director for Legislative Affairs at the administrative office of the United States Courts.[610]

The Clinton White House must take responsibility for promoting and supporting Strom, because a little bit of homework would have revealed her personal ties and background. Ray Ybarra of the Texas ACLU believes that the dehumanizing of migrants, to the degree that the white supremacist lobby has achieved, has gained acceptance among a vast number of the Democrats as well. "Democrats and Republicans are equally on the anti-immigrant band wagon. It's all about pandering to this notion of security and being tough on those who are undocumented. It didn't start with 9/11, it began much before that."[611]

In a May 2003 hearing before the Subcommittee on Immigration, Border Security, and Claims,[612] the architect of the 1996 immigration legislation and then chair of the Immigration Subcommittee, Representative Lamar Smith, ended his presentation by praising how valuable Cordia Strom had been to the lawmakers bent on reforming immigration. Smith said, "I would like to recognize a former staff member of the Immigration Subcommittee, Cordia Strom, who happens to be in the front row and who served us so well for the six years she was here. But, Cordia, in an effort to embarrass you, I am glad you are here and glad to see you."[613]

Strom has become a fixture on Capitol Hill as an immigration staffer. She has played many roles, including completing simple administrative tasks, accompanying congressional delegations, and visiting immigration facilities and jails.[614] Undoubtedly, though, her biggest achievement, as corroborated by the then INS commissioner Doris Meissner, has been her significant contribution to immigration legislation.

Another insider, though not as influential as Cordia Strom, is Rosemary Jenks. Jenks has never worked for Congress, but has been on staff at two significant right-wing immigration-lobbying organizations: the Center for Immigration Studies and NumbersUSA. Both these organizations, while purporting to be nonpartisan and even apolitical, are open about their philosophies of dramatically slowing, if not ending altogether, the legal and illegal flow of immigrants into the country. While Jenks has not been on staff or worked directly in Congress, she is no stranger to Capitol Hill. She has been called on frequently to testify before the House on matters of immigration, and she is well known to all the staff of the House Judiciary Committee and its Immigration Subcommittee.

Rosemary Jenks graduated from Harvard Law School and then worked as one of NumbersUSA's top lobbyists. Before that she had been a senior fellow for the Tanton group, the Center for Immigration Studies. Jenks has been published in Tanton's *The Social Contract*, which the Southern Poverty Law Center lists as a hate publication. She was also chosen for publication by Tanton in a booklet meant as a primer on immigration for the 2004 election campaign. The booklet, called "Common Sense on Mass Immigration,"[615] is far from a benign informational source and contains the writings of well-known white supremacists like Peter Brimelow.[616]

Both Cordia Strom and Rosemary Jenks have more intricate knowledge of immigration laws and the immigration system than most elected lawmakers. In the majority of Jenks's testimonies before Congress, she commands attention because of the extent of her knowledge and because she presents information in an authoritative and persuasive manner. She is particularly skilled at making presentations that are so technical, one has to struggle through the jargon to understand the political implications of what she is proposing.[617]

Within the interconnected web of white supremacist and anti-immigration groups, both Cordia Strom and Rosemary Jenks are inextricably tied to John Tanton and FAIR. Jenks is not shy about her ties to Representative Tom Tancredo (R-CO), who receives support from white supremacist and neo-Nazi groups. At a recent lobbying event in Washington, which Representative Tancredo attended, Jenks announced that if anyone was looking for her, they could find her in the offices of Representative Tancredo, where she and Linda Purdue (who has long worked with Tanton) were "virtual staffers."[618]

Given Rosemary Jenks's close ties to various hate groups and racist individuals, it is instructive to look at her early ideas for immigration reform. Jenks's writing on refugee and asylum policy is perhaps most illustrative of the white supremacist agenda she represents. In a 1992 article, Jenks laid out what she sees as the endemic problems of a too-liberal asylum system: "The right of aliens to apply for asylum, which was strengthened in the 1980 Act, has become a powerful magnet for illegal immigration and a major obstacle to quick and consistent removal of illegal entrants. Aliens applying for asylum can pursue a chain of tedious and time-consuming hearings and appeals through the INS adjudication machinery, the Department of

Justice's immigration courts, and the Federal court system—a process that can easily take several years."[619] What Jenks deems tedious and time-consuming, refugee advocates call the basis for a fair and humane system.

Jenks not only thinks that asylum seekers do not deserve a fair chance to make their claim of persecution, she also believes that many countries wouldn't qualify as nations where people are being persecuted. Jenks writes that, based simply on individual countries' human rights standards, the U.S. government should be able to determine "in advance the countries from which it will accept refugees."[620] Jenks goes on to suggest that the U.S.

> should maintain a specific limited list, subject to periodic revisions, of countries whose residents would not be eligible to claim asylum. Included on this list would be a sizable number of the world's countries where human rights standards are adequate, where evidence of persecution is weak, or where sufficient alternative remedies for those problems are available to the aggrieved citizen at home. Asylum seekers from countries not listed as ineligible for asylum consideration would receive prompt and rigorous screening to determine their suitability for full asylum adjudication. Those found in screening to have no arguable basis for pursuing asylum would be promptly repatriated to their home countries. The prospect of a rapid decision and quick repatriation would deter others seeking to immigrate through the asylum channel.[621]

While lawmakers have yet to adopt the list of asylum-ineligible countries that Jenks advocates—a measure that would be in direct violation of the UN Charter on Refugees—the 1996 legislation did enact a version of Jenks's other plan: the quick screen-and-return process known as expedited removal. Under this new regulation, anyone who enters without a valid visa or travel document is subject to immediate removal, and it is the sole purview of low-level immigration officers to determine who stays and who gets immediately sent back. The Bush administration recently expanded the application of expedited removal to all land-border ports, authorizing Border Patrol to employ this process with people found within one hundred miles of the border who do not have a valid visa. The more lengthy process that allows incoming immigrants to make a case for asylum or prove that they do actually have valid status in the U.S. was substantially curtailed by the 1996 legislation. While it is impossible to determine how directly Jenks influenced the 1996 legislation, it is safe to say that in the realm of immigration policy advisors, Jenks, who worked very closely with FAIR, was a strong advocate for these harsh asylum provisions. The passage into law of expedited removal represents a victory for Jenks and the white nationalist agenda she represents.

The power of Rosemary Jenks and her colleagues lies in their ability to influence mainstream American thought. Consider the plan to construct an exclusive list of asylum-eligible countries, which many people today might view as extreme and even ridiculous. What Tanton, Jenks, and their network have been able to do in the past is build a public case for a certain immigration enforcement strategy, thereby moving it from a place where it has marginal support to a place where it has enough mainstream backing to pass into law.

It is interesting to note that since 2003 Jenks's so-called nonpartisan organization, NumbersUSA, has been the tenth biggest spender on lobbyists to the Department of Homeland Security. In 2004 alone, NumbersUSA spent $120,000 on lobbyists, $80,000 of which went to the firm Olive, Edwards & Brinkmann (OEB) to aggressively advocate on its behalf.[622] Jenks and OEB partner James Edwards have formed a great team, working their "inside sources on the Hill" to be able to send out emergency alerts to like-minded colleagues and activists at any sign that legislation that does not fit their agenda is brewing in Congress.[623]

Arizona, Ten Years after Proposition 187 in California

Thanks in large part to the work of Tanton and other tenacious racists, the public debate on immigration and immigrants shifted significantly to the Right with the passage of Proposition 187. Its popularity in the Democratic stronghold of California made anything seem possible, and national political actors of all stripes began to take notice.

Ten years after the success of Proposition 187 and further success at the federal level with the 1996 immigration legislation, the racist fringe again sought to use a local ballot initiative to advance its goals. With fertile ground being created in the border state of Arizona, where hate groups have been busy for years laying siege to migrant crossers and even carrying out unknown numbers of vigilante killings,[624] Proposition 200 passed in the 2004 election.

To get Prop 200 on the ballot, FAIR put up half a million dollars to fund the campaign.[625] The proposition included almost exactly the same elements of Prop 187 that FAIR had lobbied for a decade earlier; it should therefore be no surprise that this supposedly Washington-based policy group had its paws all over it, even though it was a ballot initiative in a southwestern border state.

Called the Taxpayer and Citizen Protection Act, Prop 200 mandates that all residents of the state prove they are citizens by presenting a passport or birth certificate in order to receive any public services or to vote. Proposition 200 requires that public employees alert federal immigration authorities if anyone fails to prove their legal status (or their citizenship if they want to vote) or face criminal charges. This means public librarians will be forced to ask anyone applying for a library card for proof of legal immigration status or face prosecution. The same applies to hospital workers before attending to sick patients, police officers answering domestic violence calls, or public school administrators registering new students. On November 2, 2004, the proposition passed 56 percent to 44 percent.

Civil liberties groups immediately challenged Prop 200 in the federal courts, but the outcome was not as fruitful as the court ruling on Prop 187. In fact, in August 2005 the Ninth Circuit Court of Appeals dismissed a lawsuit brought by the Mexican American Legal Defense and Education Fund by ruling that the plaintiffs lacked the "legal standing" necessary to challenge the initiative approved by Arizona voters in November 2004. FAIR, which had played a large supportive role in preparing for the legal battle, was jubilant at the ruling. The president of FAIR, Dan Stein, was quoted as saying, "we are delighted the Ninth Circuit has rejected this naked attempt to place the interests of illegal immigrants ahead of the democratic will of U.S. citizens in Arizona. The question of legal standing has long been a barrier to American citizens seeking redress in the courts when their interests have been harmed by mass illegal immigration."[626]

Stein was clear in what his Washington-based organization had to gain from the successful implementation of Prop 200 in Arizona. "We worked closely with local groups in Arizona because we believe what they have done there can be a model for citizen action all across the country. The Ninth Circuit's decision will undoubtedly be a tremendous boost to that effort as Americans use the political process to force government to control illegal immigration and to protect their interests and resources."[627]

Similar legislation is currently being proposed in North Carolina, Tennessee, Minnesota, Colorado, and Arkansas. In North Carolina, State Senator Hugh Webster introduced legislation modeled after Arizona's Proposition 200 but with a crucial addition: Senate bill 976 requires employers to repay whatever costs the state incurs for the healthcare and education of undocumented workers. In Colorado, Defend Colorado Now, a group modeled after Arizona's Defend Arizona Now, is trying to gather the necessary signatures to introduce a bill similar to Prop 200 on the ballot in 2006. Representative David Schultheis, the Republican who introduced the legislation, justified the bill saying, "This is what the people of Colorado want and the Legislature should be in line with it."[628] The Colorado branch of the ACLU cites the egregious nature of the bill's requirements, highlighting that residents could be required to prove immigration status to board a public bus or enter a public park.

The true roots of this growing Prop 200 national movement are perhaps most clearly illustrated in Arkansas. On January 26, 2005, a bill was introduced into the Arkansas legislature by Senator Jim Holt (R-Springdale) and Senator Denny Altes (R-Fort Smith) called the Arkansas Taxpayer and Citizen Protection Act.[629] Modeled on Prop 200, the bill requires proof of residency for anyone applying for state services. While it is sold as a bill to stop undocumented immigrants from voting and getting public assistance, it also precludes access to such state services as prenatal care and immunizations, and requires that immigration status be reported to federal authorities.

The main lobbying group behind the bill is Protect Arkansas Now (PAN), and when Senator Holt introduced the bill he also introduced a man named Joe McCutchen as the head of PAN. The *Intelligence Report* has extensively researched McCutchen. It found that in June 2003, McCutchen wrote an anti-Semitic letter to his local paper, the *Southwest Times Record*.[630] The *Report* also found that in 2001 McCutchen was a member of the racist Council of Conservative Citizens (CCC), according to the group's own newspaper, the *Citizen's Informer*.[631] He also spoke at the annual CCC conference the same year on a panel titled "Immigration Invasion." McCutchen has written to *American Renaissance* seeking support for an anti-immigration group he had formed in Michigan.[632] Despite the evidence, McCutchen denies his ties to CCC,[633] and the issue has quickly disappeared from public discourse. The legislation is still pending.

Capitol Hill, 1999

While local government elections and state ballot initiatives around the country are two means by which the white supremacist agenda is being infiltrated into electoral politics, the trifecta is completed with the election of federal representatives.

Each day, it seems, the far-right and nativist agenda for immigration is more acceptable in Congress. In large part this is due to the successful use of the 9/11 tragedy to frame national security as paramount to immigration and immigrant issues. Colorado representative Tom Tancredo is at the head of this movement in Congress.

Tom Tancredo was elected to the House of Representatives as a congressman from Colorado's sixth congressional district in 1998. Before coming to Washington, Tancredo was elected twice to the Colorado statehouse and was later appointed by President Reagan to a cabinet-level position in the Education Department.

Tancredo's popularity stemmed from his days as a local junior high school teacher. In his early days as an elected official his mantras were reducing taxes and cutting social services. But very quickly Tancredo discovered the issue of immigration. It didn't take him long to begin courting any element that would support his agenda for ending immigration. According to Leonard Zeskind, who has studied the congressman extensively, "Tancredo epitomizes an ominous overlap between seemingly respectable Republican anti-immigration activists and the white nationalist movement."[634]

In the aftermath of the London bombings in the summer of 2005, Tancredo made comments suggesting that the United States should target Muslim holy sites like Mecca if radical Islamic terrorists detonate nuclear devices in U.S. cities. Some called for his resignation following his statements, but there was only a murmur of disapproval from the Democrats. Tancredo refused to apologize. "It was a deterrent," Tancredo said of his comments when questioned by a caller on a radio talk-show interview in South Carolina. "I'm telling you, nothing should be taken off the table when you're trying to defend your own country."[635]

One of the first things Tancredo did on arriving on Capitol Hill in 1999 was form the Congressional Immigration Reform Caucus. Membership was sparse in the early years as Tancredo's immigration platforms—which boiled down to eliminating immigration altogether—were a hard sell. After 9/11 the Tancredo public relations machine went into action almost overnight and declared that protecting the homeland against terrorism was primarily an immigration issue. He spoke of Islamic prayer rugs and a diary written in Arabic that had been found in the scrublands of the U.S.-Mexico border.[636] No evidence was ever produced, but little was done to counter the powerful and lingering image that immigrant-terrorists were indeed coming into the U.S. via the southern border.

The mainstream very quickly picked up the link made between national security and immigrants. Tancredo himself seems thankful for the terrorist attacks, telling journalist Michael Scherer how the ranks of his sparsely membered Congressional Immigration Reform Caucus instantly swelled:

"9/11 happened and everything changed. We got sixty members overnight."[637] Tancredo also began to attract members of the Democratic Party, and by 2005 three Democrats in his ranks had joined the caucus.

Tancredo attracts audiences that contain white supremacist or neo-Nazi elements. A simple Google search shows that Tancredo has spoken before members of various white nationalist groups. When he addresses his supremacist audiences, Tancredo is more outspoken with his messages of hate. For example, while campaigning with a senatorial candidate in Illinois, Tancredo told the crowd that illegal immigrants "are coming here to kill you and to kill me and our families."[638] As Mark Potok of the *Intelligence Report* points out, "such statements aren't very different from the messages being emitted by *bona fide* hate groups."[639]

Tancredo has worked closely with John Tanton over the years. Tanton has directly contributed to Tancredo's campaign coffers, as evidenced by the Federal Election Commission.[640] According to an extensive Salon.com piece on Tancredo in 2003, the senator had received significant sums of money ("$5,000 to his 2002 campaign . . . and thousands more in personal donations") for his reelection campaign through the FAIR Political Action Committee.[641] It also documents how Tancredo's Immigration Reform Caucus Web site

> contained links to FAIR, NumbersUSA, CIS and virtually every other Tanton creation. It also contained a link to VDare, a white nationalist Web site run by British writer Peter Brimelow that is named after Virginia Dare, the first white child born in the New World. When asked about the link, Tancredo was befuddled and indignant.
>
> "If we are connected to VDare, and I don't think we are," says Tancredo, "then I will take action . . . I do not want the support of these kinds of people and I do not need their support." After the interview, the links had mysteriously moved from the Web site's front page and were buried next to an essay Tancredo wrote called "Showing Immigrants Respect."[642]

Tancredo's mission goes far beyond rallying supporters around the country to back him and his end-immigration agenda. Like Tanton, he wants to see more like-minded lawmakers in Congress so that more extremist legislation can be passed. In 2004 Tancredo formed a Political Action Committee—Team America PAC—to find and support people who subscribed to his very specific immigration agenda. Tancredo and cofounder Bay Buchanan, sister of former

Reform Party presidential candidate Pat Buchanan, are clear in what they want from candidates: (1) will oppose any sort of amnesty; (2) will support a "time out" on immigration until serious reforms can be enacted; (3) will support the use of American military forces on the border until Border Patrol is at full strength; and (4) will join the Congressional Immigration Reform Caucus.[643]

The explicitly stated goal of Tancredo's Team America PAC is to "provide these Patriots with the ability to pool their financial resources so as to build a war chest to battle those who profit from open borders and lax immigration policies."[644] In 2004 Team America managed to elect one of its endorsees to national office, Representative Tom Price of Georgia.[645] Price's campaign Web site states clearly his immigration ideology: "We must return common sense to this matter by . . . securing our borders through whatever means necessary."[646] One of Price's first actions as a new congressman was to loudly support the renewal of the sunset clauses of the USA PATRIOT Act, proclaiming that "not allowing aggressive action relating to the activities of noncitizens and illegal aliens places our nation at greater risk."[647]

When the 109th Congress opened, Tancredo had helped elect new representatives, had recruited long-standing representatives to his cause, and his Immigration Reform Caucus counted eighty-two members. By January 2006 the number had increased to ninety-one. A staggering one-in-five representatives believed strongly enough in what Tancredo is pushing for to become members of his Congressional Immigration Reform Caucus.

Another major victory for the white supremacists in the 2004 election was the successful move of Tom Coburn of Oklahoma into the Senate following his previous three terms in the House. In the House, Coburn had voted for militarizing the border and against birthright citizenship for children of noncitizens. The far Right realizes that their growing support in the House means very little if they cannot match it with support in the Senate.

Tancredo's outspokenness about eliminating immigration highlights the split in the Republican party over the issue. At select moments, the Bush administration has found Tancredo too radical in his anti-immigration crusade, and there have been public spats between Tancredo and the White House. Tancredo was personally rebuked by Karl Rove who called him a "traitor to the president" for his comment to the *Washington Times* editorial board that if there was a second terrorist attack the "blood of the people killed" would be on the hands of President Bush.[648] Clearly, the agenda of President Bush and most Republicans is driven more by the profits of big business rather than by the hate of white supremacists. Nevertheless, more of what Tancredo represents and vociferously argues for—like disallowing citizenship to the children of certain immigrants or denying immigrants access to the courts to appeal a deportation order—is getting put onto the congressional agenda and even passed into immigration law.

Each day more Republicans, and even Democrats, are supporting the ideas of Tancredo, John Tanton, Glenn Spencer, and other prominent white nationalists, whether they publicly align themselves with them or not. Soon after the 9/11 attacks, Senator Dianne Feinstein (D-CA) and Senator Jon Kyl (R-AZ) proposed a centralized database to tabulate biometrics of all noncitizens who enter the United States.[649] Civil libertarians warned that this program would target immigrants and that the information would eventually be used to expel some from the country. With the implementation of US VISIT, some of those worst fears have been realized.[650] Feinstein went further, however, and called for serious changes to the student visa category. This California Democrat echoed the calls of the nativist agenda when she called for a "6-month moratorium on the student visa program"[651] in the aftermath of 9/11. John Tanton must have smiled when he saw that his "pause that refreshes," which he had called for in the WITAN memos, was now on the Democratic agenda. Feinstein justified her proposal with rhetoric that could have come straight from Tancredo: "Our national security depends on our system functioning to ensure that terrorists do not take advantage of the vulnerabilities in the student visa program."[652]

FAIR joined Tancredo in acting strategically to use the 9/11 attacks to impact immigration legislation. In the first year after the attacks, a group called 9/11 Families for a Secure America (9/11 FSA) was formed. The group, including family members of 9/11 victims, directly blame U.S. immigration policies for making the acts of terrorism possible. The group did little to conceal its connections to FAIR, leading the Center for New Community, in a report studying 9/11 FSA, to conclude that the group is "yet another façade created by FAIR."[653] FAIR board member Peter Gadiel is the director of 9/11 FSA. FAIR has orchestrated speaking events for family members in front of state legislatures and 9/11-related events. Illustrating the web of questionable connections among white supremacists and anti-immigrationists, 9/11 FSA's Web site is registered to the head of the Colorado Alliance for Immigration Reform, Fred Elbel. According to the Center for New Community report, "this organization boasts Virginia Abernethy of the white supremacist Council of Conservative Citizens as an advisory board member."[654]

One of the main strategies of the 9/11 "families" group was to produce and air commercials that pushed FAIR's immigration agenda. In March 2003 FAIR produced a radio spot for 9/11 FSA asking the governor of Maryland to veto a bill that would allow all immigrants to get a driver's license. The ad ran more than eighty times.[655] In September 2003 another 9/11 FSA television ad that was "paid for in part by the Federation for American Immigration Reform" ran in Washington, DC. The ad called for an "immigration time-out" and ran more than 350 times, mostly at primetime on major Washington, DC, television stations.[656] The links were clearly being made between immigrants and terrorists, setting the stage for harsh legislation to pass.

Back in the halls of Congress in 2004, there was much controversy as Republican representative James Sensenbrenner attempted to attach extremely anti-immigrant clauses to the so-called 9/11 bill. This intelligence bill came out of the extensive hearings and investigations of the 9/11 Commission. However, attaching immigration status to one's driver's license, one of the provisions of the bill, was never part of the Commission's recommendations. Representative Sensenbrenner, with the backing of Tancredo and the Immigration Reform Caucus, kicked the anti-immigration propaganda machine into action to make it appear that the amendment's provisions were indeed part of the 9/11 Commission recommendations. 9/11 Commission members, however, spoke out against the Sensenbrenner amendment, saying that it would not make any significant contribution to public safety and security.[657]

The driver's license and other anti-immigrant clauses were ultimately removed from the 2004 intelligence bill because of Senate resistance in the bill's Conference Committee. The committee's Republican leadership, including House Republican leader Tom DeLay, House Speaker Dennis Hastert, and Chair of the Armed Services Committee Duncan Hunter, promised Sensenbrenner that they would make sure it passed in 2005 if he agreed to its being cut from the 2004 bill. Hence it was reintroduced in 2005 as the REAL ID Act. Anticipating that it would likely be defeated again in the Senate, Republican House leadership had the inspired idea of attaching it to the mammoth Iraq War and Tsunami Aid Supplemental Bill, so that Senators would also be voting against money for troops and flood victims if they objected to the immigration provisions. It was a masterful plan. Sensenbrenner and Tancredo couldn't have wished for a smoother passage of this bill into law.

Before the immigration bill was attached to the war supplemental, FAIR brought its members to Capitol Hill in a week-long lobbying effort to pressure lawmakers to pass the bill. During this "Feet to the Fire" week, FAIR members were all over the halls of Congress. One of the masterminds behind attaching REAL ID to the war supplemental bill, chair of the House Arms Service Committee Duncan Hunter, was kind enough to provide cookies and coffee in his office for the FAIR members during their busy days of lobbying.[658]

Still more of Tancredo's immigration fantasies have been realized in the second term of the Bush presidency. Tancredo's Immigration Reform Caucus has publicly called for a wide expansion of the powers of expedited removal of incoming undocumented foreign nationals, which deports them *before* they can be entered into the system that allows them access to the courts to prove their right to stay in the United States.[659] A Tancredo caucus member, Representative Pete Hoekstra (R-MI) introduced an amendment to bill HR 10 that called for just such an expansion of expedited removal powers.[660] The White House weighed in: "The Administration strongly opposes the overbroad expansion of expedited removal authorities in H.R. 10 (section 3007)."[661] In 2004 the Hoekstra amendment passed the House. DHS soon accorded these powers to select sectors along the southern border so that Border Patrol officers could quickly remove those they apprehend within one hundred miles of the border. And in direct contradiction to the 2004 statement opposing the expansion of expedited removal, the president announced in his November 2005 immigration speech in Arizona that all Border Patrol officers had been granted the powers of expedited removal. "This program is so successful that the Secretary has expanded it all up and down the border."[662]

Tancredo has also called for giving state and local police the authority to enforce immigration laws, a strategy that is now squarely on the mainstream agenda and that has already been made law in Florida and Alabama.

Despite the public discord between the White House and Tancredo, and the posturing of the Republican Party to sideline him, more anti-immigration legislation that Tancredo supports is ultimately getting passed.

The Nativist Agenda Flourishes: What Does the Future Hold?

The 2005 REAL ID Act was like music to the ears of the Congressional Immigration Reform Caucus and anti-immigration groups. The bill contained many of the provisions that were high on the agenda of Tancredo and his supporters going into the 109th Congress. REAL ID achieved three main platforms that Tancredo had been pushing for. First, REAL ID tied immigration status to a driver's license. Second, it limited noncitizens' access to the federal courts by denying a habeas corpus appeal. Third, REAL ID made claiming asylum all but impossible by placing sharp restrictions on eligibility.[663]

Many equally shocking provisions still remain on the to-do list of Tanton, Tancredo and their supporters. And it must be noted that the legislative priorities for 2005–2006 for FAIR, CIS, the Congressional Immigration Reform

Caucus, NumbersUSA, and many of the white supremacist groups like American Border Patrol and Barbara Coe's CCIR are almost identical.

Imagine the U.S. military patrolling the Mexican border or expanded mandatory detention of foreign nationals. Imagine children born in the United States not qualifying for immediate citizenship. Imagine the denial of the right to appeal a decision made by an immigration judge that could ban a legal permanent resident from the United States for life. Imagine laws to deny the use of Consular-issued identifications, or laws that mandate that all hospitals demand proof of immigration status before treating a person in need. Imagine federal laws to turn all state and local police officers into immigration authorities, so if you are a victim of a crime or are a person reporting a crime, in order to access police services you would have to disclose and prove your immigration status. Far-fetched? Well, some of these are already occurring, perhaps leading even closer to the ultimate goal of the Tancredo Immigration Caucus and, increasingly, of FAIR—a near-complete moratorium on all immigration to the United States.

FAIR, CIS, NumbersUSA, and the other more openly racist groups have put a considerable budget behind their extremist agendas. In 2003 NumbersUSA paid K Street lobbying firm Olive, Edwards & Brinkmann $80,000 to lobby DHS and lawmakers on its behalf.[664] One of the partners, James Edwards, is a well-known anti-immigrationist who has worked closely with Rosemary Jenks on the Hill to keep the pressure on lawmakers to pass their policy proposals. Most recently, in September 2005 James Edwards authored a report calling for the U.S. to implement an "ideological exclusion" screening process in its immigration policy that would serve to exclude or deport those with radical ideologies, among which he lists communism, anarchism, and "Islamism" as examples.[665]

Edwards glorifies the days when the United States practiced ideological exclusion in immigration, arguing that it's necessary today in order to keep the country safe. He describes exactly how the U.S. should achieve this ideological exclusion:

> We should promote intelligence-gathering on aliens abroad and intense investigation by consular officers. The State Department should establish management policies that reward consular officers who ferret out fraud or identify visa applicants who are found to hold anti-American, anti-democratic, anti-Western, anti-Christian, or anti-Jewish views. All diplomatic personnel should be trained to look for such dangerous signs.[666]

In these days, when the Bush administration equates an antiwar stance with being anti-American, such a vague and broad classification is dangerous indeed. And given the monetary power of Edwards's firm and his client NumbersUSA, it may not be long before we see such policies made law. (In 2003 Edwards authored a report calling for state and local police to be accorded the power to enforce immigration laws;[667] in 2005 such a measure was included in the immigration legislation that passed the House. His influence should not be underestimated.)

It remains debatable how responsible Democrats are for the harsh immigration legislation that has recently passed given that Congress has been Republican controlled for much of the last decade. Yet the most serious battle that Democrats have lost—and it is arguable whether they even tried to fight—is the battle for public opinion. Immigrants have been criminalized, and there is a rush to incarcerate and deport them. Worse still, support for dramatically reducing immigration has flourished. Democrats lost the public debate on immigration in the mid-1990s. And today, rather than fight to regain rights for immigrants and convince the American people of the need for more progressive and humane immigration policy, the Democrats are silent at best and complicit at worst.

A Case Study of Extremism in Progress

Yet it is not too late to act. Steps can be taken to stop the further transformation of white nationalist ideology into immigration legislation. There remain ongoing legislative efforts ripe for the stopping. Consider the decades-old, far-Right demand for the U.S. military—and if not the U.S. military, then a volunteer force of armed citizens—to assist a woefully underresourced border patrol in guarding the borders. Crazy as it might seem, the calls for citizen-militia groups are now formally on the mainstream agenda, with legislation pending in Congress and a myriad of prominent supporters backing the proposals.

Border vigilantism is not a new phenomena. In 1977, in a scene all too reminiscent of recent Minutemen antics, David Duke, then head of the Knights of the Ku Klux Klan, organized a "Klan Border Watch" that he said would guard the border from San Ysidro, California, to Brownsville, Texas. The rhetoric and outlaw conduct of the Klan patrollers during the event—which attracted infinitely more journalists than Klan members—were clearly racist.[668]

Then in the 1990s a more open and concerted citizen patrol effort began in Cochise County, Arizona. Roger and Donald Barnett, local ranch owners, gained national attention when they began rounding up at gunpoint hundreds of migrants that they claimed were undocumented and handing them over to authorities. Extremist groups took immediate notice and proclaimed the Barnetts heroes. Reporters came from miles away to cover this new phenomenon, and the Barnetts took them on tours to "hunt" undocumented migrants.

In March 1999 the Barnetts and other fellow landowners, twenty in total, declared their open contempt for the rule of law: "If the government refuses to provide security, then the only recourse is to provide it ourselves."[669] The Barnetts were now making mainstream news with feature stories appearing in the *New York Times* and ABC's *World News Tonight*. Ominously, one of the Barnetts told *USA Today*, "I'm prepared to take a life if I have to."[670]

To date, Roger Barnett claims to have rounded up nearly twelve thousand alleged undocumented immigrants.[671] Barnett and other citizen border-watchers are almost always armed when on patrol. In 2004 there was at least one unsolved murder in the region due to gunshots to the head and body.[672] Ray Ybarra of the ACLU in Texas has learned from a Freedom of Information Act request that there have been thirty other incidents of severe mistreatment of migrants by nonlaw enforcement, with some cases of random shots fired that have resulted in injury and migrants left wounded in the desert. The local police have not investigated the murders or shootings, most often saying that the victims were undocumented and that the killings appeared to have been from rival coyote gangs. Human rights lawyers and even the Mexican consulate have loudly condemned the lack of action, saying that plenty of evidence points to vigilante landowners.[673]

How did the situation go from KKK border patrols to a few avowedly racist ranch owners hunting for "illegals" to mainstream calls for these actions to be legalized in the name of protecting the homeland? It may have started as the outlaw actions of a few, but the likes of John Tanton, Glenn Spencer, and the politically savvy Minuteman leader Chris Simcox saw it as an opportunity and very quickly made the most of it.

The ranch owners' justification for their patrolling actions, which has won mainstream approval, is simply that they are protecting their own property from destruction by the tens of thousands of individuals who trek across their land. Their loftier goals—those of protecting their fellow citizens from an invasion from the South—have struck a chord with white supremacists and racist anti-immigrant groups across the country. Whether patrolling their own land with pistols at the ready or patrolling the highways to snatch nonwhite, migrant-looking people, the Barnetts have started a fad. Now each year hundreds of people flock to Arizona to join in the human hunt and capture of border crossers.

The anti-immigration movement has latched on to vigilante border patrols. Minuteman leader Chris Simcox has emerged as the masterful and friendly face of the growing citizen militia movement. Over the past few years, his month-long Minuteman patrols of the Arizona border have steadily attracted more attention—though not necessarily more members. The Minutemen claim simply to be highlighting how underequipped U.S. Border Patrol is to do its job by acting as backup. Citizens are encouraged to sign up online, but they are not trained or equipped by the Simcox operation to carry out the citizen patrols. Volunteers are left alone to track down immigrants using any means necessary.

Simcox, for his part, spends much of his time talking to reporters and describing his sparse operation as bigger and more mainstream than it is. Simcox ruthlessly blames elected officials for the invasion, as he perceives it coming from the South. He once told the *Washington Times*, "I dare the president of the United States to arrest Americans who are protecting their own country . . . We will no longer tolerate the ineptness of the government in dealing with these criminals and drug dealers. It is a monumental disgrace that our government is letting the American people down, turning us into the expendable casualties of the war on terrorism."[674]

Although President Bush has called the Simcox Minutemen "vigilantes," in the early years the White House refused to condemn their actions. When asked during the first Bush term what the President thought of the actions on the border by the Minutemen, Press Secretary Ari Fleischer's response belied any real condemnation: "The president believes that the laws of the land need to be observed and the laws need to be enforced."[675]

The other leader of the border-militia movement is a California transplant and a prominent supporter of Prop 187, Glenn Spencer. On the one hand, Spencer claims that his organization, American Border Patrol (ABP) is an apolitical nonprofit group whose aim is to make the U.S. a safer place. "By using high tech, innovative equipment, ABP members detect, locate and report illegal immigration as it occurs."[676] On the other hand, Spencer's views on Mexicans are virulent. He believes they are intent on "la Reconquista," the re-conquest, of the United States, and that there is a plot by the Mexican government to send hordes of Mexicans to recolonize land that Mexico lost in the 1848 Treaty of Guadalupe Hidalgo at the end of the U.S.-Mexican War. "This gang is here to subvert our immigration laws," Spencer told *Salon.com* journalist Max

Blumenthal, referring to Mexican immigrants. He concluded by saying that the United States was in danger of losing to "that cesspool of a culture."[677]

Spencer's model of border vigilantism is unique in that he has invested in technology, "from scratch" an unmanned aerial vehicle (UAV) that has heat detection sensors to detect human life. Using his for-profit company, Border Technology Inc., to fund and build UAVs, Spencer is now vying for official government contracts to sell his homemade vehicles to the Department of Defense or Homeland Security.[678]

Spencer, like Simcox, has benefited from the political and financial support of the godfather of the anti-immigrant cause, John Tanton. Spencer says he has solicited Tanton, who sits on American Patrol's advisory board, for funding.[679] According to IRS Form 990 returns, over a three-year period beginning in 1998, two Tanton groups, FAIR and U.S. Inc., have donated $50,050 to Spencer's American Patrol and Voices of Citizens Together.[680] FAIR has also publicly backed the Minutemen. After the much-publicized April 2005 Minuteman border patrols, FAIR hosted a Capitol Hill lobby week in May 2005 called "Feet to the Fire," which many of the Minutemen attended to pressure lawmakers to pass the REAL ID bill. In fact, Minuteman founder James Gilchrist was one of the honored guests, as was Colorado representative Tom Tancredo.[681]

FAIR and vigilante militias have a long history of collaboration. In 1999, John Tanton was so impressed by the Barnett's approach that FAIR brought Roger Barnett to Capitol Hill for its Immigration Awareness Week. Barnett tugged at the heartstrings of lawmakers by telling them of his hardships and the dangers of simply trying to live amid the constant traffic of "illegals."

Following the April 2005 Minuteman patrols of the Arizona border, it was reported that some forty Minuteman-inspired groups in eighteen states had sprung up and into action. In California, a group leading patrols told all volunteers to bring baseball bats, mace, pepper spray, and machetes to patrol the border. When U.S. Border Patrol objected, the group compromised. They said they would carry only one weapon: a gun.[682]

The end result of this dual strategy of political schmoozing and direct action may be dire. Legislation was entered into Congress in the days before the summer recess of 2005 that would allow states to deputize citizens to patrol the border and, according to the language of the bill, "use any means and any force authorized by State law to prevent individuals from unlawfully entering the United States."[683] The governor of the state would control the so-called Corps, and the governor would be "authorized to call United States citizens into service in the militia." Known as the Border Protection

Patrol Act, it was introduced by Texas representative John Culberson and forty-seven other legislators. The legislation came shortly after Customs and Border Protection commissioner Robert C. Bonner publicly stated that he thought it might be viable to designate anti-immigrant vigilante groups an "auxiliary" arm of Border Patrol.[684]

As with many of the harshest clauses of the 1996 immigration legislation and the 2005 REAL ID Act, this citizen militia bill is but one of the many examples of legislation that needs urgent attention before it quietly slips into law. In fact, while many on the Left think this legislation has little chance of passing, Ray Ybarra of the ACLU in Texas has strong words of warning: "The climate is ripe for legislation to pass allowing citizens to patrol the border. When you have a Democratic governor declaring a state of emergency in his border counties, saying Border Patrol is not able to protect the border, when you have the media celebrating the Minutemen, legislation like this seems appropriate."[685]

The Role of the Media

As Ybarra points out, the media has played a distinct role in immigration debates and has enabled anti-immigrant laws to pass. One example is the bounty hunter amendment to the REAL ID Act. In the days following its introduction, the national media barely mentioned it. The last-minute amendment required the Department of Homeland Security to contract out the enforcement of deportations to bail bondsmen. The amendment author, Texas representative Pete Sessions, argued that too many people with deportation orders simply disappear inside the country and never actually leave as per their order. The government was not adequately finding and deporting people. Hence the need, according to Sessions, to contract out the job of finding, rounding up, and then deporting those with orders to go.[686]

This brazen amendment would essentially place a bond on the heads of those with a deportation order and outsource a governmental job to contractors with very little training, oversight, or accountability. The amendment stated, "At any time before a breach of any bond condition, if in the opinion of the bail bondsman the person constitutes a flight risk, that person can be detained."[687] Traci Hong of the Asian American Justice Center worried that the amendment would give strong financial incentive to bondsmen to track down immigrants who had not completed their full appeals process or whose cases were still pending a final decision.[688]

Lone Democrats from the Black Congressional Caucus, including representatives John Conyers Jr., Bernie Thompson, and Sheila Jackson Lee, likened the amendment to the Fugitive Slave Act of 1850. On the House floor, Texas representative Jackson Lee declared that "if we randomly give the opportunity to bondsmen who have no understanding of immigration laws, we can be assured that in a discriminatory fashion they will be rounding up people who look different and speak different languages, and we will be impacted in a very negative way."[689] Evidently, the mainstream media did not find this worthy of coverage.

In fact, the only mainstream national news source to detail Representative Pete Sessions's proposal was the *San Francisco Chronicle*.[690] The *Washington Post* gave it one line, and the *New York Times*, the *Los Angeles Times*, *National Public Radio*, the *Houston Chronicle*, the *Boston Globe*, and most media of record ignored it. *Voice of America* gave it one paragraph, a benign description stating that it would ensure that "once someone is ordered deported, they are speedily returned to their home country."[691] Jim Lehrer's *NewsHour* mentioned this important information in its news headlines, but also gave it the positive spin of simply enacting 100 percent of all deportation orders. There was no mention of the deep concerns being voiced about the amendment.

The only media in the country to give this amendment substantial coverage was Pacifica Radio. Mitch Jeserich covered the story for the national news program Free Speech Radio News on the day it broke and also on the following day. He spoke to the head of the Jail Bondsman's Association who was joyous at the potential windfall for his industry. Jeserich also gave play to the powerful voice of dissent that came from the few lone Democratic House members who spoke out against the bill, like Representative Sheila Jackson Lee.

I was on Capitol Hill watching the proceedings during the days that this bill was being debated. In talking with some of the radio correspondents who cover the Hill for various broadcast outlets—one for Public Radio International and a freelance agricultural reporter—I found it fascinating that they did not cover the critical parts of the bill. Both seemed to be applying a level of self-censorship. One told me that it "was not of interest to my audience"; the other said his editor "would probably just cut it out anyway" and that the driver's license clause was the biggest part of the bill and therefore the most newsworthy.[692]

In the days and weeks after this amendment was introduced, as I spoke before various groups of students and in public forums, I asked audience members what they thought of this amendment. Not one person I spoke to had even heard that such an amendment was pending in Congress. There was unanimous outrage that it could become law, an indication that if only people were informed of it, they might agitate against it. The media must take responsibility for its failure to report on the bounty hunter amendment. Luckily, it was stripped from the bill before it was attached to the Iraq war and tsunami supplemental that made REAL ID law. But that doesn't mean it won't return, buried in some new extensive immigration bill and quietly pass into law.

What the Future Holds

The stealth capturing of the terms of the immigration debate and of immigration policy-drafting by extremist and racist elements needs urgent attention. To win fundamental rights for immigrants and implement a humane immigration policy there needs to be just as calculated and precise a strategy as was designed years ago by John Tanton. It needs to be proactive and not defensive. It needs to be driven by immigrants and their allies, as immigrants know best the shortcomings and hardships of our current policy. Furthermore, there needs to be a fundamental reversal of the criminalization of nonwhite immigrants. And for this to happen at a legislative level, it first needs to happen in the hearts and minds of every American.

Immigrant communities across the U.S. are leading the way in organizing for a society that most of us would probably want to live in. While it is true that many immigrants come to the U.S. for economic reasons, they also come here for the promises of democracy and freedom that are sold to the world as American ideals. For many immigrants these are not abstract principles or commodities to be bought, sold, or imposed. Democracy and freedom are absolutely worth fighting for.

While small victories have been won by immigrant communities over the past few years, the fruits of these struggles burst onto the national agenda with the massive Spring 2006 protests that occurred in big cities and small towns around the country. Students walked out of classrooms despite threats of expulsion. Workers walked off the job despite threats of firing. Immigrants stepped forward to send a loud and clear message to elected representatives that they *will* take part in creating the America they want to live in. Many bring experiences of participatory democracy and a history of movement building to this land of plenty, if only we'd listen and learn.

In New York City, a broad coalition of grassroots groups has come together to educate themselves and others on the legislation before Congress and to write their own legislation that addresses immigrant needs and that acknowledges the huge benefits that immigrants bring to American society. Immigrant

Communities in Action is seizing power from the Democratic Party, the Republican Party, and the anti-immigration lobby. It doesn't have anywhere near the financial power of these groups, but it has people power.

Furthermore, grassroots organizing like that of Immigrant Communities in Action (ICIA) is actively working to build bridges of solidarity with African-American communities. ICIA understands that African Americans have been alienated from supporting the newly emerging and more mainstream immigrant rights movement because there is little acknowledgement of the unemployment and further economic hardship that very cheap immigrant labor has caused this community. ICIA understands well that the claim that immigrants "do the work that no one else will do" is simply wrong and deliberately divisive. It is not that African Americans won't do the work—throughout American history blacks have been forced to work the worst jobs for a pittance—it's that racism in the job market prefers cheap undocumented labor to cheap African-American labor. It is up to immigrant communities to actively build solidarity with African-American communities, as there is so much to learn from their history of struggle. Likewise, immigrant communities need to acknowledge that their struggle for justice is intertwined with that of Native American communities. Inspiring examples of solidarity coalitions between indigenous and immigrant communities are found in Arizona border towns. Together, these communities form a mighty wave of opposition to the agenda of the powerful few.

Yet to support a proimmigrant agenda today is to be attacked as being an open-border advocate or a bleeding-heart liberal. As illustrated in chapter one, the exporting of U.S. economic policies, which further impoverishes poor nations, needs to be fought as well. A movement for immigrant rights must also build solidarity with people around the world who struggle to end crippling neoliberal economic policies, which drive so many to emigrate. It is crucial that the reasons for migration be studied and addressed and not treated as secondary. If Mexico and Central America were viable places to work and raise a family, the traffic coming across the southern border would be dramatically lessened. If Caribbean nations provided decent work opportunities that paid a living wage, fewer would overstay visas. The U.S. must examine its role in impoverishing these nations as a critical element of its immigration debate. And just as important, the United States must listen to the solutions and proposals put forth by immigrants and their advocates, and let these communities lead the way forward to an America where we all want to live.

EPILOGUE

"*You're* the victim, Ma'am," the stocky, gold-suited NYPD detective told me, his dimpled chubby cheeks glowing with an air of smugness. "She entered *YOUR* home without *YOUR* permission and stole *YOUR* wallet and credit cards. I'm just sorry she has any rights at all."

I was sitting in the NYPD transit police precinct at the 145th Street A train subway station in Harlem. It had been a long day of shuttling between precincts in the area to try to recover my personal goods, which had been stolen from my apartment the night before. The detective had just finished questioning the suspect who had been found with my wallet in her possession as she was selling rides from my subway card at a nearby subway station. "I gave her two warnings," the harried arresting officer told me, almost apologetically. "I told her to leave the station, that she wasn't allowed to sell swipes. But she was just trying to get a fix, and I found her in the same spot hours later, so I arrested her."

When the police discovered my wallet in her possession, the woman, Gloria, told police that we were friends, that I had given her my wallet. At that moment I was so relieved that all Gloria had taken was my wallet—she could have easily taken a G4 Mac laptop as well as a DVD player and stereo equipment—I almost wished her to be my friend. "She's a crack addict, Ma'am, and *YOU'RE* the victim of her foul habit."

Somehow I could not feel like the victim. I did desperately need my wallet back, mainly because it contained my INS work permit, and without it I would be without proof that I could work in the country. Therefore, I was at the mercy of the police who very much wanted me to press charges. "How many floors in your building, Ms. Fernandes?" was one of the questions I was asked as I waited on the lone wooden precinct bench that I had been sitting on for large parts of the day. "Do you have security cameras in your building?" I told the police that I live in a four-floor brownstone and that there are no security cameras.

Twelve hours after the arrest, at six in the evening, the gold-suited detective strode out from behind a locked door and triumphantly stuck his stubby and sticky palm into my hand and announced, "We got her to confess, Ms. Fernandes, you can rest easy now!"

"Got her to confess?" I asked, and the detective looked me directly in the eye and told me about his victory.

"Uh huh. I got it out of her, Ma'am. Told her we had her fingerprints from the scene, that she had been caught on video camera in your building, and that we had witnesses. She crumpled in a minute!" On seeing my brow distort and my eyes open wide at the obvious lies he had just told to extract the confession, the detective quickly added, "It's all part of the job, Ma'am. Just remember, *YOU'RE* the victim, Ma'am."

To me, the victim was clearly the woman who was caught with my wallet. Gloria told police she had entered the gate of my brownstone for some privacy while she smoked her crack and found the front door ajar. Gloria grabbed my wallet and walked a mere four blocks to the train station, where she attempted to sell subway rides for a buck a piece. The most she could have made was five dollars. And for a possible five bucks she stood there from three in the morning, when the officer gave her the first warning, to six, when the officer finally arrested her. Gloria had had ample time to run up many charges on one of my credits cards, yet had not.

Gloria was obviously desperate for a small amount of quick cash. I believed she needed public health intervention, not a jail cell. As I tried to ascertain whether I knew her from around the neighborhood, I asked police to describe her. "Black . . . Haitian, I think," was the response. Suddenly, the irony was too great for me to bear. I was about to leave on another trip to Port-au-Prince to visit people who had been deported after serving time in U.S. jails for offenses such as lifting someone's wallet to pay for a drug habit. Gloria's conviction would be based on my police report and testimony. I was now part of the arsenal that not only busts and imprisons drug users and addicts, but my testimony—which the police pressured me to give for the return of my wallet—was going to be used to deport a woman to a notorious Haitian prison, where I knew grave human rights abuses were routinely committed.

In the days following the break-in, during one of the media classes I teach at various high schools around New York, I told my students what happened with Gloria. There was a very mixed reaction. This New York City public school is home to a large immigrant and native-born population. Each year my classes have a distinct United-Nations feel, and I find myself teaching students who come from countries like Guinea-Bissau, Bangladesh, and Israel. When I recounted my break-in story, making sure to reiterate that I indeed left my front door ajar, a fascinating discussion ensued.

One student was puzzled by my decision not to give my testimony to the police, because after all, he reminded me, Gloria had entered my apartment and could have killed me. He believed that the police were only trying to help me by telling a few little lies to get Gloria to confess. He said that she deserved to be punished, even if it meant she would be deported. Another student, one of the smartest and most focused students in the class, said that he thought Gloria was the victim of racism. The first student shook his head emphatically and said that people like Gloria give all immigrants a bad name. He added that all immigrants should learn English, like his family did, and find a job rather than steal from people who worked hard.

There was a moment of silence as most of the students nodded in agreement with their classmate's definition of the role of immigrants in society. Then in heavily accented yet grammatically flawless English, a female student said quietly that not all immigrants *can* learn English, like her mother. With her head down, she told the class how her family had come to the U.S., how they had been forced to leave all of their possessions in the African country she called home because their lives were threatened. Her family simply had to flee for their lives. I knew this girl had recently been granted asylum but did not know any of the details. She went on to tell us that since coming to America, her parents had been trying to learn English, trying to find work, trying to find housing. She had been lucky to be accepted to this high school, she told us, because she had tried at least ten other schools that refused to enroll her. One student responded that despite all they had been through, her parents hadn't taken to robbing people to survive. The refugee student didn't respond—she just heaved a long breath and appeared to be fighting back tears.

Then another student spoke up, timidly, like he was confessing a secret. He said that he was scared that he and his parents might be deported, even though they had done nothing wrong. My instinct was to ask him if he was undocumented, but I caught myself, realizing the intrusiveness of my question. So instead I asked him why he feared deportation, and he told me that he was *not* "illegal," that he was a citizen, but that his parents were only green-card holders. Yet he said he was frightened because his boss at the deli where he works regularly threatens the staff by saying that he will call immigration. My student honestly believed that citizens could be deported.

My story about Gloria led to a wide-ranging discussion among immigrant and nonimmigrant students about the current climate of fear, the role of immigrants in society, and the costs versus benefits of current immigration policies. Many stereotypes were reinforced and burning secrets revealed.

Some time later, with another class of students at a different public school,

I was reviewing interviews that the students had done with each other. I heard real fear in the voice of one student as he talked about how he was petrified that the government was going to deport his mother. He said that he didn't know what he would do if that happened and kept repeating that his mother was a good person. I was surprised to hear this because I had no idea that his family might have questionable status. On investigating, I discovered that his family is perfectly documented, but because of all the discussion he had been hearing about the deportation of immigrants, he had assumed that his mother was at risk.

Immigration is a hot issue right now. And as my students' fears and my apartment break-in experience proved to me, we are all part of the system that is criminalizing immigrants and forcing many to live in a state of fear. Even if we are sympathetic to the situation that immigrants face, our sympathies accomplish little. Laws need to be changed, and public discourse needs to be seized back from its current place, so that immigrant no longer equals terrorist.

Gloria should receive medical treatment and social services for her drug addiction and, at worst, should serve prison time for her theft. But if you believe that Gloria does not deserve to be permanently removed from the country on the completion of her jail term, then you must act. Noncitizens like Gloria are being removed from the country every day, and it will not stop until the laws are changed.

Never in U.S. history has there been such a deliberate moral and legal divide between immigrant communities and citizens. It hasn't happened overnight, nor is it simply the result of 9/11. Families are being torn apart by the nation's immigration policies. Today's divide threatens to irreparably crack the foundations of American society, because at the heart of what is essentially a low-intensity war against immigrants is the future of the nation. Most people probably do not think too much about the differences between citizens and noncitizens, yet day by day, the gulf between these two groups grows. It is a divide that has been quietly and systematically engineered. Two systems of justice, two systems of social services, two economies.

The census bureau estimates that our country gains an immigrant every thirty-one seconds. That works out to be just over one million immigrants per year. Many of these immigrants are black- and brown-skinned, contributing to the ethnic and cultural diversification of the country. It is this shift in demographics that frightens a small but well-organized sector of the citizen population. It is too easy to dismiss their moves to halt immigration as simply anti-immigration, for many of the leading proponents are themselves descendants of recent immigrants. In fact, it is their deep-rooted fear of democracy—the core American ideal itself—the sharing of power and privilege—that drives the racist's immigration agenda. Because their views and efforts, which are based on their doomed schemes to achieve racial and political domination in America, are fundamentally antidemocratic, they are also, therefore, anti-American. Anti-democracy networks like Tanton's and others—fueled on fear, exclusion, and hate—are the real threat to America, and one sees signs of their embarrassing presence as surely as one still sees the Confederate flag. Unfortunately, lawmakers long ago ceded the debate to a white nationalist agenda that wants to reverse immigration, and today we are seeing the results of that loss. Despite the past decade's rollback of rights, advocates of democracy, human rights, peace, and social justice are organizing with immigrants to overcome the politics of exclusion. Far from being a small, invisible, or voiceless presence, first-generation immigrants—those with documents and those hoping to gain status—dwarf the white nationalists in raw numbers and are increasingly organizing to participate in and improve democracy in the United States.

What we saw in Spring 2006, when massive numbers took to the streets and shut down businesses and schools, is that immigrants are turning the target around. Their demands are concrete: legalization; a path to citizenship; an end to criminalization, detention, and deportation; and the ability to participate fully in society without fear. As illustrated throughout this book, immigrants are not a static, homogenous group. They come to America for widely different reasons, they bring with them vastly different histories and cultures, and they promise incredible diversity to society. Hence it cannot be underestimated just how significant the masses organizing across all these lines are. Who better to propose solutions to the multitude of questions that immigration raises than those who live the reality? There *is* legislation written by those directly affected, and communities *are* seizing the moment to carefully craft their valid life experiences into future laws that should be high on the agenda in Congress.

Immigration is crucial to the U.S.; only a few deny this. Yet our reasons for valuing immigration vary widely. For those of us who believe in a just society, which should strive continually to make room for new people, new ideas, new cultures, new philosophies, and new ways of living, we must join the community-organizing efforts that are happening all around us. From the nannies who care for our children to the busboys who clear our tables; from the IT specialist who helps us resolve a personal computer issue to the laborer who picks the tomato that colors our salad: immigrants are not simply service providers and cheap labor. They are, in fact, engaged in vital civic engagement as they mobilize to change the course of history. And if we truly believe in democratic principles, we must watch, learn, and participate, for this is democracy in action.

There are certain non-negotiable elements to our democracy. One of the first is that we are an open society. Therefore, to use immigration policy and social welfare policy to target certain groups of people is fundamentally undemocratic and necessarily anti-American. We have the moral high ground, and we mustn't cede an inch.

It has been argued that our immigration system is broken and open for exploitation by any potential immigrant. In fact, our immigration system is cruel and contravenes basic ethical principles of an open society. We must use international law and international standards of human rights to reinforce that feeling in our heart that we are right on this one. Because we are.

Today's immigration movement reminds us of America's history and its pride in being a great melting pot. Everyone here today, apart from Native Americans and the descendants of African people who were forcibly brought to the United States as slaves, is an immigrant or the descendant of an immigrant. Yet when one considers that history has been successfully rewritten by the conquerors to remove from public consciousness the fact that all the borders of this country were violently imposed, and that the wealth of the land was extracted over the bodies of entire indigenous nations and successive generations of enslaved Africans, it cannot be doubted that the abhorrent attempt will be made to write certain groups of immigrants out of history as well. Today, the descendants of those same conquerors have made it cliché—even worse than cliché, irrelevant—to say that America is a country of immigrants and that we are all richer for it. But if we believe in the fundamental open and participatory nature of democracy—that immigrants deserve the opportunity to participate in our work force, society, and culture—then we must fight for them with the same intensity and passion with which we fight for democracy itself.

AFTERWORD

As journalists we cover stories at a particular moment in time, without following up to document their evolution over longer periods. In the case of our nation's immigration policies, I believe we absolutely must study their long-term impact.

In the course of writing this book, many courageous individuals shared their stories with me. This is where they are today:

Chapter 1

Maria and her Mexican-born children: Lupita, Juan, and Javier
Maria's husband continues to work as a cook for below minimum wage at a New York City restaurant. Javier, although undocumented, is enrolled in school. Juan has a job and is going to a local community college, where he is learning English. Lupita got married and in December 2005 had a baby boy.

Chapter 2

Samir Hussain
Hussain lives and works in Miami. He is taking legal action against the government for his wrongful imprisonment.

Allah Dita
Dita was deported to Pakistan. Further information is not available.

Kamal Essaheb
In July 2005 the cases of Kamal and his brother Hassan were "administratively closed." The third Essaheb brother won the diversity lottery and was granted a green card. In December 2005 Kamal wrote me that "this is all, of course, good news as we are no longer facing the chance of imminent deportation." The family continues to live in Queens, New York.

Veronica
Her whereabouts are unknown. She was likely deported.

Hamza Zakir
His whereabouts are unknown. DHS officials at the Krome Detention Center will not disclose information on Zakir. The telephone number he gave me for his family was changed six months ago. He is most likely still at Krome.

Suzette Fertil
Her whereabouts are unknown. DHS officials at the Broward Transitional Center will not disclose information on, when, or if Suzette was transferred out of the facility. On my December 2005 trip to Haiti, I asked the prison warden of the main women's prison if she knew Suzette, and the warden told me that a woman by that name had passed through the prison some months earlier and was then released. Suzette may be living in Haiti. Her husband, Frederick, and daughter, Sara, still live in Miami.

Majid and his brother Ali
Majid was deported in 2003 to Pakistan, and his brother accepted voluntary departure. Both now live back in Pakistan. Their families were also forced to return to Pakistan, as they could not make ends meet in New York.

Chapter 3

Vimral
She continues to work as a hairdresser in New York, and is doing well.

José Inez Rodriguez Cruz
His whereabouts are unknown. DHS officials at BTC will not disclose information on his case. I was once in regular contact with Rodriguez Cruz's wife in Managua, Nicaragua, but her telephone is no longer being answered.

David
He attends the College of Staten Island and is expected to graduate in June 2007. He is a member of the refugee rights group Nah We Yone.

Michael Knowles
Knowles continues his work as an asylum officer with U.S. Citizenship and Immigration Services and as Vice President at Large of AFGE Council 117,

which represents immigration workers within the Department of Homeland Security.

Chapter 4

Oladokun Sulaiman
He was deported to Nigeria on a U.S. Marshall's flight from an unknown location and was handcuffed the entire flight. On arriving in Nigeria, Sulaiman attempted to have his case resolved by contacting his college, which had given false information to the U.S. Embassy, but his efforts and the college's cooperation were unsuccessful. He is currently working in Malaysia, as employment opportunities in Nigeria are slim. He hopes to have his case reopened and to be given the chance to return to the United States to finish his studies and graduate.

Vasant Mehta
In April 2006 Mehta finally managed to take a vacation and visit his family in India after being away for five years. He continues to work for Pixil Systems and is constantly struggling to get a fairer wage.

Philippe Louis Jean
Studying full time in San Diego and working two jobs, Louis Jean plans to begin the process of reapplying for his green card in early 2007. He is afraid to visit his family in New York because he is vulnerable to rearrest, detention, and deportation for the same case that was dismissed in California.

NOTES

1. In a nationally televised speech on May 15, 2006, President Bush promised that "up to 6,000 [National] Guard members will be deployed to our southern border." A complete transcript of the speech is available on the White House web site here: http://www.whitehouse.gov/news/releases/2006/05/20060515-8.html.
2. Nina Bernstein, "Judge Rules that U.S. Has Broad Powers to Detain Noncitizens Indefinitely," *New York Times*, June 15, 2006. Article posted here: http://www.nytimes.com/2006/06/15/nyregion/15detain.html.
3. Andrew Ryan, "ICE Arrests About 2,000 Illegal Immigrants," Associated Press, June 14, 2006. Full article posted here: http://www.breitbart.com/news/2006/06/14/D8I84S980.html.
4. Marc, interview by the author, December 12, 2005.
5. Beriberi is a vitamin deficiency disease caused by inadequate bodily stores of thiamine (vitamin B1). It can damage the heart and nervous system. See http://www.nlm.nih.gov/medlineplus/ency/article/000339.htm.
6. Brad Heath, "Students Slip Past Visa Check. National Program Finds 36,000 Immigration Violations, but Only 1,600 Are Investigated," *Detroit News*, September 19, 2005. See http://www.detnews.com/2005/schools/0509/19/A01-319221.htm.
7. Maria, interview by the author, February 27, 2005.
8. Maria, interview by the author, January 29, 2005.
9. J. Durand and D. S. Massey, "The Costs of Contradiction: U.S. Border Policy 1986–2000," *Latino Studies*, 1, no. 2 (July 2003): 233–52.
10. Leslie Berestein, "Ariz., Imperial Valley Shoulder Unexpected Social, Financial Costs," *San Diego Union-Tribune*, August 1, 2004, http://www.signonsandiego.com/news/reports/gatekeeper/20040801-9999-1n1econ.html.
11. "President Addresses American Society of Newspaper Editors Convention, J. W. Marriott Hotel, Washington, D.C.," Office of the Press Secretary, the White House, April 14, 2005, http://www.whitehouse.gov/news/releases/2005/04/20050414-4.html.
12. Robert Longley, "Border Security Gets $6.7 Billion in Bush 2006 Budget. Includes $137 million to detect WMD's," February 2005, U.S. Government Info/Resources, http://www.usgovinfo.about.com/od/defenseandsecurity/a/homeland06.htm.

13. Isabel García, Tucson Public Defender and Co-chair of Derechos Humano, interview by the author, April 15, 2005.
14. Miguel, interview by the author, April 12, 2005.
15. Mario, interview by the author, April 12, 2005.
16. See chapters 2 and 6 for a full breakdown of the rollbacks to the rights of green-card holders—formally known as legal permanent residents—that have occurred over the past decade.
17. Michael E. Fix and Wendy Zimmermann, "All Under One Roof: Mixed-Status Families in an Era of Reform," Urban Institute, October 6, 1999, http://www.urban.org/url.cfm?ID=409100.
18. "INS Issues Foreign Travel Advisory for Aliens with Pending Immigration Applications," Immigration and Naturalization Service, December 13, 2000, http://uscis.gov/graphics/publicaffairs/advisories/advisory.htm.
19. José, interview by the author, April 13, 2005.
20. Ibid.
21. "FY 2004: U.S. Customs and Border Protection Apprehends Large Amount of Narcotics, Thousands of Undocumented Migrants," U.S. Customs and Border Protection, January 18, 2005, http://www.customs.gov/xp/cgov/newsroom/news_releases/archives/2005_press_releases/0012005/01182005_3.xml.
22. Kweisi Mfume, "Protecting Immigrant Children," National Association for the Advancement of Colored People Action Alert Report, April 1, 2004, http://www.naacp.org/inc/docs/washington/108/108_aa-2004-01-04.pdf.
23. Christopher Nugent, "Protecting Unaccompanied Immigrant and Refugee Children in the United States," *Human Rights*, Winter 2005, http://www.abanet.org/irr/hr/winter05/immigrant.html.
24. Thomas Allen, "The Gangs of ORR," VDARE.com, June 1, 2005, http://www.vdare.com/allen/050601_orr.htm.
25. BICE later changed its name to Immigration and Customs Enforcement (ICE).
26. Victoria López, Executive Director of the Florence Project, interview by the author, April 14, 2005.
27. Maria, interview by the author, October 20, 2004.
28. "U.S. Customs and Border Protection, Border Agency Reports First-Year Successes," January 11, 2005, www.cbp.gov/xp/cgov/newsroom/news_releases/archives/2005_press_releases/0012005/01112005.
29. Isabel García, interview by the author, April 15, 2005.
30. Brenda Norrell, "Tohono O'odham and Yaqui: 'No More Walls,'" *Indian Country Today*, July 20, 2004, http://www.indiancountry.com/content.cfm?id=1090337206.
31. Norrell, "Tohono O'odham and Yaqui."
32. Angelita Reno Ramo, interview by the author, November 29, 2005.
33. José, interview by the author, April 13, 2005.
34. Jeffrey S. Passel, Randy Capps, and Michael Fix, "Undocumented Immigrants:

Facts and Figures," Urban Institute Immigration Studies Program, January 12, 2004, http://www.urban.org/UploadedPDF/1000587_undoc_immigrants_facts.pdf.

35. Bill Richardson, governor of New Mexico, on *NewsHour* with Jim Lehrer, August 18, 2005, http://www.pbs.org/newshour/bb/latin_america/july-dec05/borders_8-18.html. "The Comprehensive Enforcement and Immigration Reform Act of 2005," Senator John Cornyn's address to Congress, http://www.cornyn.senate.gov/index.asp?f=record&lid=l&oid=17&rid=236985&pg=2.
36. B. Lindsay Lowell and Roberto Suro, "How Many Undocumented: The Numbers Behind the U.S.-Mexico Migration Talks," The Pew Hispanic Center Report, March 21, 2002, http://pewhispanic.org/files/reports/6.pdf.
37. Ibid.
38. Maria, interview by the author, February 27, 2005.
39. Ruth Morris, "As Construction Business Climbs, Wages Are Falling," *Sun Sentinel*, August 14, 2005, A1.
40. "Rural America Grapples with Diversity," *Rural Migration News*, http://migration.ucdavis.edu/rmn/more.php?id=209_0_2_0.
41. "Injury and Injustice—America's Poultry Industry," United Food and Commercial Workers, http://www.ufcw.org/press_room/fact_sheets_and_back grounder/poultryindustry_.cfm.
42. Andrew Stelzer, "'Truth Tour' Highlights Poverty Wages," *Indymedia.us*, March 7, 2005, http://indymedia.us/en/2005/03/5371.shtml.
43. John Ross, "Teoti-Wal-Mart," *The Progressive*, 69, no. 3 (March 2005).
44. http://www.census.gov/PressRelease/www/releases/archives/facts_for_features_special_editions/004707.html.
45. "Hispanic Population Reaches All-Time High of 38.8 Million, New Census Bureau Estimates Show," U.S. Census Bureau, June 18, 2003, http://www.census.gov/PressRelease/www/releases/archives/hispanic_origin_population/001130.html.
46. http://www.census.gov/PressRelease/www/releases/archives/facts_for_features_special_editions/004707.html.
47. Rebecca Jannol, Deborah Meyers, and Maia Jachimowicz, "U.S.-Canada-Mexico Fact Sheet on Trade and Migration," Migration Policy Institute, November 2003, http://www.migrationpolicy.org/pubs/US-Canada-Mexicofact%20sheet.pdf.
48. Maria, interview by the author, February 27, 2005.
49. Ibid.
50. Senator Larry Craig, interview by the author broadcast on Free Speech Radio News as part of the report "UFW Supports Temporary Workers Bill," February 10, 2005, http://www.fsrn.org/news/20050210_news.html.
51. Ibid.
52. Isabel García, interview by the author, April 15, 2005.
53. Timothy A. Wise, "A Fate Worse than NAFTA: Mexico's Failure to Implement Farm Protections," *The Ultimate Field Guide to the U.S. Economy*, November 17,

2003, http://www.fguide.org/Bulletin/mexico.htm.

54. John Ross, "NAFTA and Zapatistas Both Reach 10-Year Anniversaries," latinamericapress.org, January 19, 2004, http://www.latinamericapress.org/article.asp?IssCode=&IanCoade=1&ar+Code=3612.

55. "President Addresses American Society of Newspaper Editors Convention, J. W. Marriott Hotel Washington, D.C.," Office of the Press Secretary, the White House, April 14, 2005, http://www.whitehouse.gov/news/releases/2005/04/20050414-4.html.

56. Census-bureau-alert mailing list: CB05-FFSE.03, April 20, 2005, Special Edition, Cinco de Mayo, http://www.census.gov/Press-Release/www/releases/archives/facts_for_features_special_editions/004707.html.

57. John Ross, "NAFTA and Zapatistas."

58. David Bacon, *The Children of NAFTA: Labor Wars on the U.S./Mexico Border* (Berkeley: The University of California Press, 2004). Also see John Ross, "Nafta and Zapatistas."

59. John Ross, "May Day '96 in Mexico—Angry Workers, Decrepit Leaders, Divided Unions," *Mexico Barbaro*, May 5–15, 1996, #14. Archived at http://flag.blackened.net/revolt/mexico/reports/unionros.html.

60. David Bacon, "NAFTA at Ten," LaborNet Germany, November 16, 2003, http://www.labournet.de/internationales/la/naftabilanz.html.

61. Ibid.

62. Paul Blustein, "World Bank Questions Free Trade's Benefits. Global Agreement May Do Little to Relieve Poverty, Economic Body Finds," *Washington Post*, December 17, 2005, D1, http://www.washingtonpost.com/wp-dyn/content/article/2005/12/16/AR2005121601689.html.

63. Isabel García, interview by the author, April 15, 2005.

64. Ibid.

65. Katherine McIntire Peters, "Up Against the Wall," *GovExec.com*, October 1, 1996, http://www.govexec.com/archdoc/1096/1096s1.htm.

66. Thomas Jiménez, interview by the author, April 11, 2005. The offices of U.S. Representatives Jim Kolbe and Jeff Flake provided information to the newspaper the *Tucson Citizen* that begins: "According to Border Patrol Apprehension statistics, 1 percent of those apprehended crossing the border are criminals . . . the other 99 percent are immigrants coming to the United States for work." http://www.tucsoncitizen.com/index.php?page=opinion&story_id=073003_borderqaonline.

    "McCain Introduces Comprehensive Immigration Reform," John McCain's official Web site, http://mccain.senate.gov/index.cfm?fuseaction=Newscenter.ViewPressRelease&Content_id=1148.

67. Kat Rodriguez, interview by the author, April 12, 2005.

68. This number is provided by Wayne Cornelius, Director of the Center for Comparative Immigration Studies, University of California, San Diego. Cited

on the No More Deaths Web site, http://www.nomoredeaths.org/CallToAction.html.

69. Ignacio Ibarra, "'No More Deaths Camp' an Oasis for Migrants," *Arizona Daily Star*, March 2, 2005, http://www.azstarnet.com/dailystar/dailystar/63746.php.

70. Sixty-seven deaths were reported by Pima County Medical Examiner, eight by Yuma County Medical Examiner, and four by the Cochise County Medical Examiner. Derechos Humanos press release, August 10, 2005, http://www.derechoshumanosaz.net/DOCS/List_of_dead_2004_2005.pdf.

71. James Pinkerton, "In One Year, 473 Migrants Perish along Busy Border," *Houston Chronicle*, November 19, 2005, A1.

72. Ibid.

73. In many of his public remarks, President Bush often acknowledges that the majority of those who are crossing the border are doing so for work. Here is one example from statements he made at the American Society of Newspaper Editors Convention (J.W. Marriot Hotel, Washington, D.C., April 14, 2005):

"It would be better if our Border Patrol agents were chasing down drugs and guns than trying to chase down people. And by that I mean, it would be a much more efficient use of taxpayer's money if the system were legal, the worker system was legal so that the Border Patrol could focus on other issues. In other words, if it were legal, people wouldn't have to get in the back of an 18-wheeler. If it were legal to come here and work, you wouldn't have to walk miles across the hot desert. And it would make it easier to protect our border with an immigration system that worked on legalizing work." A full transcript is available at http://www.whitehouse.gov/new/releases/2005/04/20050414-4.html.

74. "DHS Begins Second Phase of Arizona Border Effort," U.S. Customs and Border Protection, March 30, 2005. http://www.customs.gov/xp/cgov/newsroom/news_releases/archives/2005-press-releases/03302005_dpr.xml.

75. Maria, interview by the author, July 12, 2005.

76. Maria, interview by the author, February 27, 2005.

77. Ibid.

78. Ibid.

79. Renee Downing, "Border Control? What We See Here Is Anything But," *Washington Post*, May 1, 2005, B1.

80. "Highlights of the President's FY 2006 Budget for CBP," U.S. Customs and Border Patrol, February 10, 2005, http://www.cbp.gov/xp/cgov/newsroom/commissioner/messages/archives/2005/highlights_2006budget.xml. See http://www.cbp.gov/xp/cgov/newsroom/commissioner/messages/highlights_2006budget.xml.

81. "DHS Begins Second Phase of Arizona Border Effort," U.S. Customs and Border Protection, March 30, 2005, http://www.customs.gov/xp/cgov/newsroom/press_releases/departmental_press_releases/03302005_dpr.xml.

82. Gloria Chávez, spokeswoman for the U.S. Customs and Border Protection Agency as quoted in Eliza Barclay, "Mexico Angry Over Border Weapons," *Washington*

Times, August 5, 2005, http://washingtontimes.com/upi-breaking/20040805-060338-8314r.htm.
83. Ibid.
84. "Other FAQ's," United States Border Patrol Unofficial Web Site, http://www.honorfirst.com/otherfaq.htm.
85. U.S. Border Patrol, San Diego Sector, Regional Emergency and Crisis Team (REACT), http://www.specwarnet.com/taclink/Federal/REACT.htm.
86. Thomas Jiménez, interview by the author, April 11, 2005.
87. Ibid.
88. "Goy Ridge Addresses U.S. Conference of Mayors," Office of the Press Secretary, the White House, January 23, 2002, http://www.whitehouse.gov/news/releases/2002/01/20020123-23.html.
89. Francisco Javier García Arten, interview by the author, April 13, 2005.
90. House Report 104-863 - MAKING OMNIBUS CONSOLIDATED APPROPRIATIONS FOR FISCAL YEAR 1997, Section 102c, http://thomas.loc.gov/cgi-bin/cpquery/?&dbname=cp104&sid=cp104yWjtd&refer=&r_n=hr863.104&item=&sel=TOC_1810919&
91. Stephen Siciliano, "Environmental Groups Sue Customs Agency over Proposal for Reinforcing Border Fence," *Daily Report for Executives*, February 18, 2004.
92. Ibid.
93. REAL ID Act of 2005, Sec. 102, Waiver of Laws Necessary for Improvement of Barriers at Borders, http://thomas.loc.gov/cgi-bin/query/F?c109:1:./temp/~c109GN7cpC:e8964:.
94. Thomas Jiménez, interview by the author, April 11, 2005.
95. "Spotlight on Surveillance: Surveillance at Our Borders," Electronic Privacy Information Center, March 2005, http://www.epic.org/privacy/surveillance/spotlight/0305.html.
96. Eric Lipton, "Despite New Efforts along Arizona Border, 'Serious Problems' Remain," *New York Times*, March 14, 2005, http://www.nytimes.com/2005/03/14/politics/14border.html?ex=1114315200&en=19bcbd4199a35bba&ei=5070.
97. U.S. Customs and Border Protection, FY 2004: "U.S. Customs and Border Protection Apprehends Large Amount of Narcotics, Thousands of Undocumented Migrants," January 18 2005, http://www.cbp.gov/xp/cgov/newsroom/news_releases/archives/2005_press_releases/0012005/01182005_3.xml.
98. Wayne Cornelius, "Evaluating Enhanced U.S. Border Enforcement," Migration Policy Institute, May 1, 2004, http://www.migrationinformation.org/feature/display.cfm?ID=223.
99. Robert Longley, "Border Security Gets $6.7 Billion in Bush 2006 Budget, Includes $137 Million to Detect WMDs," *About.com*, February 2005, http://usgovinfo.about.com/od/defenseandsecurity/a/homeland06.htm.
100. Mike Madden, "Sensors along the Border Wasting Agents' Time," *Arizona*

Republic, January 21, 2006.

101. Kat Rodriguez, interview by the author, April 14, 2005.
102. Thomas Jiménez, interview by the author, April 11, 2005.
103. Isabel García, interview by the author, April 14, 2005.
104. "Economic Impact of the Mexico-Arizona Relationship: An Academic Research Project, May 2003," Thunderbird, The Garvin School of International Management, pg. 9, www.thunderbird.edu/pdf/about_us/econ_impactAZ.pdf.
105. Eduardo Porter, "Illegal Immigrants Are Bolstering Social Security with Billions," *New York Times*, April 5, 2005, http://www.nytimes.com/2005/04/05/business/05immigration.html?
106. *Larry D. Hiibel v. Sixth Judicial District Court of Nevada, Humboldt County, et al.*, brief of Amici, Curiae Electronic Privacy Information Center (EPIC) and Legal Scholars and Technical Experts to the Supreme Court, no. 03=5554, December 13, 2003, p. 13, http://www.epic.org/privacy/hiibel/epic_amicus.pdf.
107. Ibid. The opinion is *Arizona v. Evans*, 514 U.S. 1 (1995).
108. "Deadlines Approach for Ashcroft Immigrant Fingerprinting Program; ACLU Says Plan Is Full of Holes, Advises Immigrants to Seek Counsel," ACLU, December 13, 2002, http://www.aclu.org/ImmigrantsRights/ImmigrantsRights.cfm?ID=11479&c=22.
109. Isabel García, interview by the author, April 14, 2005.
110. Ibid.
111. "Fact Sheet: Arizona Border Control Initiative–Phase II," Department of Homeland Security, March 30, 2005, http://www.dhs.gov/dhspublic/display?content=4415.
112. Isabel García, interview by the author, April 14, 2005.
113. Marisa Dersey, interview by the author, April 9, 2005.
114. Ibid.
115. Marisa Dersey, interview by the author, April 10, 2005.
116. Ibid.
117. Judith Greene, "Bailing Out Private Prisons," *The American Prospect*, pg. 23, September 10, 2001.
118. Isabel García, interview by the author, April 14, 2005.
119. *9/11 and Terrorist Travel: A Staff Report of the National Commission on Terrorist Attacks Upon the United States* (Franklin, TN: Hillsboro Press, 2004), 11.
120. Ibid., 6 and Chap. 2.
121. Ibid, Chap. 2.
122. "Border Agency Reports First-Year Successes," U.S. Customs and Border Protection, January 11, 2005, http://www.customs.gov/xp/cgov/newsroom/news_releases/archives/2005_press_releases/0012005/01112005.xml.
123. Demetrios G. Papademetriou and Deborah Waller Meyers, eds., *Caught in the Middle: Border Communities in an Era of Globalization* (Washington, DC: Carnegie Endowment for International Peace, 2001), 62.

124. Isabel García, interview by the author, April 14, 2005.
125. Eric Lipton, "Despite New Efforts along Arizona Border, 'Serious Problems' Remain," *New York Times*, March 14, 2005, http://www.nytimes.com/2005/03/14/politics/14border.html?ex=1114315200&en=19bcbd4199a35bba&ei=5070.
126. See chapter 5 for a fuller breakdown of these actions as they pertain to DHS.
127. Frank Tiboni, "Border UAVs Take Off," *FCW.com*, June 28, 2004, http://www.fcw.com/article83404-06-28-04-Web.
128. Ibid.
129. Eric Lipton, "Despite New Efforts along Arizona Border, 'Serious Problems' Remain," *New York Times*, March 14, 2005, http://www.nytimes.com/2005/03/14/politics/14border.html?ex=1114315200&en=19bcbd4199a35bba&ei=5070.
130. Chris Halsne, "Failure of High-Tech Border Cameras Threaten National Security," *KIRO 7 Eyewitness News*, broadcast November 25, 2002.
131. John Mintz, "Defective Equipment 'Guards' U.S.-Mexican Border," *Washington Post*, April 11, 2005.
132. Brendan I. Koerner, "The Security Traders," *Mother Jones*, September/October 2002.
133. U.S. General Services Administration, "Compendium of Audits of the Federal Technology Service Regional Client Support Centers," December 14, 2004, pp. 173–77, http://www.gsa.gov/gsa/cm_attachments/GSA_DOCUMENT/COMPENDIUM_R2-sM2T_0Z5RDZ-i34K-pR.pdf.
134. "U.S. Department of Homeland Security Awards Two Contracts Totaling $33.1 Million to ManTech," ManTech International Corporation, January 12, 2004, http://phx.corporate-ir.net/phoenix.zhtml?c=130660&p=irol-newsArticle&ID=483866&highlight=.
135. See chapter 5 for a fuller breakdown of Cross Match's contract and performance record with DHS.
136. "Department of Homeland Security Testifies on U.S.-Visit Program," United States Mission to the European Union, March 4, 2004, http://www.useu.be/Terrorism/USResponse/Mar0404HutchinsonUSVISIT.html.
137. Daniel González, "Wilson 4 Avoid Deportation," *Arizona Republic*, July 22, 2005.
138. Neoliberal market reform, also known as structural adjustment, was carried out in two stages during the 1980s and 1990s. It is a process of economic restructuring based on privatization of the state sector; an end to numerous price controls, subsidies, and protectionist measures; and significant lowering of barriers for trade.
139. In fact, according to Benita Jain of the Immigrant Defense Project of the New York State Defenders Association, "people who testify are often deported to countries where the people they informed on threaten to kill them." Interview by the author, April 7, 2006.

140. Samir Hussain, interview by the author, May 10, 2005.
141. Ibid.
142. Detention 101: Detention, Deportation, and the Criminal Justice System, Workshop held at New York University by Families for Freedom and the Immigrant Defense Project, February 26, 2005. See http://www.familiesfor freedom.org and http://www.immigrantdefenseproject.org.
143. U.S. Citizenship and Immigration Services, "Yearbook of Immigration Statistics: 2003," table 43 (aliens removed by criminal status and region and country of nationality, fiscal years 1993–2003), http://uscis.gov/graphics/shared/statistics/yearbook/YrBk03En.htm.
144. "Department of Justice Inspector General Issues Report on Treatment of Aliens Held on Immigration Charges in Connection with the Investigation of the September 11 Terrorist Attacks," June 2, 2003, http://www.usdoj.gov/oig/special/0306/press.pdf.
145. *In Liberty's Shadow: U.S. Detention of Asylum Seekers in the Era of Homeland Security* (New York and Washington, D.C.: Human Rights First, 2004), 18–19.
146. Nina Bernstein, "Judge Supports Broad Powers of Detention," *New York Times*, June 15, 2006, B1.
147. "Amnesty International's Concerns Regarding Post September 11 Detentions in the USA," Amnesty International, March 14, 2002, http://web.amnesty.org/library/Index/ENGAMR510442002.
148. Adem Carroll, interview by the author, January 12, 2002.
149. Allah Dita, interview by the author, August 10, 2002.
150. Attorney General John Ashcroft, memorandum to the U.S. Attorney's office entitled "Anti-Terrorism Plan," September 17, 2001. See http://www.usdoj.gov/usao/paw/task_forces.html#atac.
151. Quoted in Kareem Fahim, "Endgame," *Village Voice*, March 6, 2002.
152. "Department of Justice Inspector General Issues Report on Treatment of Aliens Held on Immigration Charges in Connection with the Investigation of the September 11 Terrorist Attacks, June 2, 2003, http://www.usdoj.gov/oig/special/0306/press.pdf.
153. Attorney General John Ashcroft, press conference, March 20, 2002. See http://www.yale.edu/lawweb/avalon/sept_11/ashcroft_018.htm.
154. Lynn Waddell, "Special Report: Immigration Law. Elusive refuge. Detention Rates Increase in Name of Homeland Security, but Advocates on Both Sides Worry about Tactics," Florida Immigrant Advocacy Center, January 27, 2005, http://fiacfla.org/printable.php?id=79.
155. Cheryl Little and Kathie Klarreich, "Securing Our Borders: Post 9/11 Scapegoating of Immigrants," Florida Immigrant Advocacy Center, April 2005, Chapter 3.
156. Quoted in Sandra Hernández, "Haitians, Latinos Fear They're Profiling's New Faces," *Florida Immigrant Advocacy Center*, January 15, 2005, http://www.fiacfla.

org/inthenews.php#78.

157. *Border Protection, Antiterrorism, and Illegal Immigration Control Act of 2005*, HR 4437, 109th Cong., http://thomas.loc.gov/cgi-bin/query/F?c109:4:./temp/~c109xyRmH6:e108_366:.

158. Dorothy Harper, interview by the author, May 15, 2005.

159. In NY State, there are also hotline numbers to call; the state the number is 1-888-SAFENYS and in New York City 1-888-NYCSAFE. The line is staffed by New York police and the Joint Terrorism Task Force. See http://www.security.state.ny.us/hotline.html.

160. Ritt Goldstein, "US Planning to Recruit One in 24 Americans as Citizen Spies," *Sydney Morning Herald*, July 15, 2002, http://www.smh.com.au/articles/2002/07/14/1026185141232.html.

161. See interviews by the author in "The Justice Department's Detention Secret," a radio documentary that aired on Pacifica Radio's Free Speech Radio News on September 11, 2002, http://www.fsrn.org/news/20020911b_news.html.

162. Dorothy Harper, interview by the author, May 15, 2005.

163. Philippe Louis Jean, interview by the author, March 16, 2005.

164. Bill Goodman, interview by the author, August 2002.

165. Benita Jain, interview by the author, May 23, 2005.

166. Suzanne Brown, interview by the author, May 16, 2005.

167. See http://www.fairus.org/site/PageServer?pagename=research_researchb150_sup.

168. Dorothy Harper, interview by the author, May 15, 2005.

169. Veronica, interview by the author, May 16, 2005.

170. Suzanne Brown, interview by the author, May 16, 2005.

171. "Department of Justice Inspector General Issues Report on Treatment of Aliens Held on Immigration Charges in Connection with the Investigation of the September 11 Terrorist Attacks," June 2, 2003, http://www.usdoj.gov/oig/special/0306/press.pdf.

172. Suzanne Brown, interview by the author, May 16, 2005.

173. "Number of Detainees under the Jurisdiction of the U.S. Marshals Service and Immigration and Naturalization Service, by Location of Facility, Fiscal Year-End 2002," U.S. Department of Justice, Office of the Federal Detention Trustee, http://www.usdoj.gov/ofdt/stsref4.htm, http://www.usdoj.gov/ofdt/statistics.htm.

174. Judith Greene, "Bailing Out Private Jails," *The American Prospect*, September 10, 2001. http://www.prospect.org/print/V12/16/greene-ju.html. "The private-prison industry is in trouble. For close to a decade, its business boomed and its stock prices soared because state legislators across the country thought they could look both tough on crime and fiscally conservative if they contracted with private companies to handle the growing multitudes being sent to prison under the new, more severe sentencing laws. But then reality set in with accumulating

press reports about gross deficiencies and abuses at private prisons; lawsuits; million-dollar fines. By last year, not a single state was soliciting new private-prison contracts. Many existing contracts were rolled back or even rescinded. The companies' stock prices went through the floor." The article goes on to explain how the federal government, rather than let failing businesses accept a market-dictated demise, actively bailed them out.

175. On any given day there are twenty-three thousand immigration detainees being held in U.S. prisons. "Commission on Immigration," report to the House Delegates by the American Bar Association, p. 2, http://www.abanet.org/publicserv/immigration/107e_detention.pdf.
176. See the author's "The Justice Department's Detention Secret," Free Speech Radio News special documentary, broadcast September 11, 2002, http://www.fsrn.org/news/20020911b_news.html.
177. Farouk Abdel-Muhti, interview by the author, April 2002.
178. Daniel Zwerdling, "Immigrant Detainees Tell of Attack Dogs and Abuse," National Public Radio's *All Things Considered*, broadcast November 17, 2004, http://www.npr.org/templates/story/story.php.?storyid=4170152.
179. Karen Keller, "Detainees Accuse Jail of Retaliation," *NorthJersey.com*, December 31, 2005.
180. Brian Donohue, "Passaic to Stop Holding Immigrant Detainees at Jail," *Newark Star Ledger*, December 28, 2005.
181. Karen Keller, "Passaic Jail Ends Housing Immigrant Detainees," *NorthJersey.com*, December 29, 2005.
182. Ewa Kern-Jedrychowska and Nowy Dziennik, "Doing Time at a Detention Center: Abu Ghraib Comes Home," *Polish Daily News*, January 9, 2005. An English translation is available at http://www.indypressny.org/article.php3?ArticleID=1856. See the part of the article headed "More People than Beds."
183. Nancy Morawetz, "Detention Decisions and Access to Habeas Corpus for Immigrants Facing Deportation," Boston College, *Boston College Third World Law Journal*, http://www.bc.edu/schools/law/lawreviews/meta-elements/journals/bctwj/25_1/25_1_toc.htm.
184. The decision is available at http://supct.law.cornell.edu/supct/html/99-7791.ZO.html, Section IV.
185. Office of the Inspector General, U.S. Department of Justice, "The September 11 Detainees: A Review of the Treatment of Aliens Held on Immigration Charges in Connection with the Investigation of the September 11 Terrorist Attacks," 110–16, http://www.fas.org/irp/agency/doj/oig/detainees.pdf.
186. "USA: Amnesty International to Tour Jails Housing Post-September 11 Detainees—but Access to Federal Detention Facility 'stonewalled,'" Amnesty International, February 5, 2002. See http://web.amnesty.org/library/Index/ENGAMR510252002.

187. "Presumption of Guilt: Human Rights Abuses of Post September 11 Detainees," Human Rights Watch Report, August 2002. See http://www.usdoj.gov/oig/special/0312/chapter5.htm , Supplemental Report on September 11 Detainees' Allegations of Abuse at the Metropolitan Detention Center in Brooklyn, New York, December 2003, Office of the Inspector General.
188. "Statement of Glenn A. Fine, Inspector General, U.S. Department of Justice, before the Senate Committee on the Judiciary Concerning 'Detainees,'" June 15, 2005, http://www.usdoj.gov/oig/testimony/0506b.htm.
189. Ibid.
190. Hamza Zakir, interview by the author, May 18, 2005.
191. Jodi Wilgoren, "Refugees in Limbo, Ordered Out but with Nowhere to Go," *New York Times*, June 4, 2005, A1.
192. United States General Accounting Office, "Immigration Enforcement: Better Data and Controls Are Needed to Assure Consistency with the Supreme Court Decision on Long-Term Alien Detention," May 2004, http://www.gao.gov/cgi-bin/getrpt?GAO-04-434.
193. "President Discusses Border Security and Immigration Reform in Arizona," Office of the Press Secretary, White House, November 28, 2005, http://www.whitehouse.gov/news/releases/2005/11/20051128-7.html.
194. *Border Protection, Antiterrorism, and Illegal Immigration Control Act of 2005*, HR 4437. See section 404, Denial of Admission to Nationals of Country Denying or Delaying Accepting Alien, http://thomas.loc.gov/cgi-bin/query/F?c109:3:./temp/~c109YvFUK4:e138567:.
195. http://www.ice.gov/graphics/dro/opsmanual/work.pdf.
196. Craig Hanley, PhD, "Study on Asylum Seekers in Expedited Removal" (report given to supplement congressional testimony), February 2005, http://www.uscirf.gov/countries/global/asylum_refugees/2005/february/conditionConfin.pdf.

See also Rajeev Goyle and David A. Jaeger, PhD, "Deporting the Undocumented: A Cost Assessment," Center for American Progress, July 26, 2005, 6, http://www.americanprogress.org/site/apps/nl/content3.asp?c=biJRJ8oVF&b=1002793&ct=1223773.
197. See chapter 5 for a fuller breakdown of Wackenhut/GEO's record.
198. Suzette Fertil, interview by the author, May 18, 2005.
199. Joan Friedland, "Official Crime Information Should Be Accurate," *Miami Herald*, April 28, 2003.
200. "Jury Finds Former Federal Contractor Guilty on Two Counts of Shredding Immigrants' Documents," Department of Justice, Central District of California, http://www.usdoj.gov/usao/cac/pr2003/177.html.
201. Suzette Fertil, interview by the author, May 18, 2005.
202. For a further breakdown of the private immigrant prison industry, see chapter 5.
203. Philippe Louis Jean, interview by the author, March 16, 2005.

204. Ibid.
205. Ibid.
206. Interview by the author, May 18, 2005.
207. Suzette Fertil, interview by the author, May 18, 2005.
208. Bill Goodman, interview by the author, August 2002.
209. Letter dated April 27, 2002, provided to the author by Adem Carroll of The Islamic Circle of North America.
210. Ali, interview by the author, August 16, 2002. Included in "FBI and INS Arrests of South Asians and Muslims Continue," a news report by the author aired nationally on Pacifica Radio's Free Speech Radio News on August 16, 2005, http://www.fsrn.org/news/20020816_news.html.
211. Benita Jain, interview by the author, May 23, 2005.
212. "Video Conferencing Technology: Where and How Is It Being Used?" American Immigration Law Foundation, June 2001, http://www.ailf.org/lac/lac_lit_071601a.pdf.
213. J. Traci Hong, "Objecting to Video Merits Hearings," American Immigration Law Foundation, July 31, 2002, http://www.ailf.org/lac/lac_pa_080902.asp.
214. Ibid.
215. Marisa Dersey, interview by the author, April 9, 2005.
216. Diane, an officer of the DHS office at BTC, in conversation with the author, December 8, 2005.
217. Ibid.
218. U.S. Citizenship and Immigration Services, "Yearbook of Immigration Statistics: 2003," tables 36, 40, and 42, http://uscis.gov/graphics/shared/statistics/yearbook/YrBk03En.htm.
219. Collection of extensive news reporting from various Caribbean news outlets about the problems of the U.S. deportees: http://www.caribbeannews.com/previous_NOVEMBER_2002.html.
220. David Bulbulia, representative of the Barbadian Embassy, interview by the author, August 26, 2005.
221. Jenny Cuffe, "Asylum Questions for DR Congo," *BBC News*, December 1, 2005, http://news.bbc.co.uk/2/hi/africa/4483364.stm.
222. Lemy Seraphin, Wilbur's sister, interview by Kody Emmanuel.
223. Philipe Denoso, Director of the International Red Cross in Haiti, interview by the author, May 9, 2005.
224. Father Jean Juste, interview by the author, May 10, 2005. Months after this interview about his imprisonment in the National Penitentiary, Father Jean Juste was again arrested, and was accused of murder (he was in Miami when the murder occurred).
225. See "Haiti," Bureau of Democracy, Human Rights, and Labor, U.S. Department of State, February 23, 2001, http://www.state.gov/g/drl/rls/hrrpt/2000/wha/795.htm; Nina Bernstein, "Deportation Case Focuses on Definition of Tor-

ture," *New York Times*, March 11, 2005, B1.

226. In January 2002 then White House Counsel Alberto Gonzales wrote a memo condoning elements of torture. The document is available at http://lawofwar.org/Yoo_Delahunty_Memo.htm.

227. "In re J-E, Respondent," U.S. Department of Justice Executive Office for Immigration Review Board of Immigration Appeals, March 22, 2002, http://www.immigrationlinks.com/news/Matter%20of%20J-E.pdf. Following is the definition of torture put forth in the decision:

 4) According to 8 C.F.R. § 208.16(c)(3) (2001), in adjudicating a claim for protection under Article 3 of the Convention Against Torture, all evidence relevant to the possibility of future torture must be considered, including, but not limited to: (1) evidence of past torture inflicted upon the applicant; (2) evidence that the applicant could relocate to a part of the country of removal where he or she is not likely to be tortured; (3) evidence of gross, flagrant, or mass violations of human rights within the country of removal, where applicable; and (4) other relevant information regarding conditions in the country of removal.

228. David C. Brotherton, "Exiling New Yorkers," National Immigration Project of the National Lawyers Guild, http://www.nationalimmigrationproject.org/KHA/Exiling%20New%20Yorkers.html.

229. Ibid.

230. Carla Kiiskila, "Kandler Rules Haitian Prison Conditions Torture per se," American Immigration Lawyers Association, Washington State Chapter mailing list, January 26, 2006.

231. The term "aggravated felony" was initially added to immigration law in 1988 to cover the offenses of murder, illicit drug trafficking, and firearms trafficking. Since 1988 Congress has amended this term several times, vastly expanding the offenses it covers and expanding the immigration consequences of being deemed an "aggravated felon." For example, a person found guilty of an aggravated felony is barred from citizenship, asylum, and voluntary departure. The last major expansion of this term was in 1996 when AEDPA and IIRAIRA added a broad range of minor offenses and barred immigrants who had committed an aggravated felony from applying for Cancellation of Removal, a one-time pardon from deportation for lawful permanent residents who have exhibited strong equities (such as close family ties in the U.S. and rehabilitation). See Socheat Chea, "The Evolving Definition of an Aggravated Felony," FindLaw, 1999, http://library.findlaw.com/1999/Jun/1/126967.html.

232. *Immigration and Nationality Act* (INA), section 101 (a) (43), http://uscis.gov/graphics/lawsregs/INA.htm.

233. See the Supreme Court opinion *Leocal v. Ashcroft*, 03-583, *United States of America v. German Palacios-Suarez*, 04-4187. Also available at http://a257.g.akamaitech.net/7/257/2422/09nov20041130/www.supremecourtus.gov/opinions/04pdf/03-583.pdf.

In this case, Josue Leocal, who had been a lawful permanent resident for almost twenty years, had been ordered deported based on a DUI conviction under a Florida statute that punishes drivers for negligently causing injury. The government had argued, and the immigration and a lower federal court had agreed, that this offense was a "crime of violence," that is, an aggravated felony requiring mandatory deportation. In a unanimous opinion, the Supreme Court decided that this offense was not an aggravated felony and that Mr. Leocal had not been deportable as an "aggravated felon" after all.

There have been cases where, on appeal, noncitizens with a deportation order have had a court decide that the crime for which they are being deported or for which they received a sentence enhancement does not constitute an aggravated felony. See the opinion of Sixth Circuit Court of Appeals, which vacated a sentence on the grounds that "prior state felony convictions are not 'aggravated felonies'" (*United States of America v. German Palacios-Suarez*, decided and filed July 22, 2005).

234. Ibid.
235. *Gonzales-Gomez v. Achim* (Docket No. 05-2728), 6. There is no official legal reporter citation yet, but the Lexis citation is 2006 U.S. App. LEXIS 7066 at *9 (7th Cir. 2006) (J. Posner). See also http://www.ca7.uscourts.gov/fdocs/docs.fwx?caseno=05-2728&submit=showdkt&yr=05&num=2728.
236. Former inmates, human rights lawyers, and the Red Cross representative in Haiti told me this in interviews. A prison guard and Haitian Coast Guard officers told me the same off the record.
237. Claire Anderson, "New Initiative Provides Immigrants with Legal Advice and Representation," *Amsterdam News*, October 14, 2004, http://www.amsterdamnews.com/News/article/article.asp?NewsID=49342&sID=4.
238. Mary Dougherty, Denise Wilson, and Amy Wu, "Immigration Enforcement Action: 2004," November 2005, pg. 1, http://uscis.gov/graphics/shared/statistics/publications/AnnualReportEnforcement2004.pdf.
239. Vimral, interview by the author, February 16, 2005.
240. Ibid.
241. Ibid.
242. José Inez Rodriguez Cruz, interview by the author, May 18, 2005.
243. Ibid.
244. Michael Knowles, interview by the author, February 24, 2005.
245. "Advance Parole" is the government re-entry permission for those who are pursuing a change-of-status process, usually those awaiting a green card, to be able to leave and reenter the U.S. See "INS Issues Travel Advisory for Aliens with Pending Immigration Applications," U.S. Citizenship and Immigration Services, December 13, 2002, http://uscis.gov/graphics/publicaffairs/advisories/advisory.htm.
246. Credible Fear Interview of José Inez Rodriguez Cruz, May 2, 2005, Miami

International Airport. Provided to author by José Inez Rodriguez Cruz.

247. Marc Seitles, interview by the author, July 9, 2005.
248. Credible Fear Interview of José Inez Rodriguez Cruz, May 2, 2005, Miami International Airport. Provided to author by José Inez Rodriguez Cruz.
249. Designating Aliens for Expedited Removal, 69 Federal Regulation 48,877 (2004). Federal Register: August 11, 2004 (Volume 69, Number 154), pp. 48877–48881, http://cryptome.quintessenz.at/mirror/bcbp081104.txt.
250. "Asylum Seekers in Expedited Removal," U.S. Commision on International Religious Freedom, February 8, 2005, 4, http://www.uscirf.gov/countries/global/asylum_refugees/2005/february/execsum.pdf.
251. Ibid.
252. Nina H. Shea, "Human Rights Ignored," *Wall Street Journal*, August 24, 1990.
253. Credible Fear Interview of José Inez Rodriguez Cruz, May 2, 2005, Miami International Airport. Provided to author by José Inez Rodriguez Cruz.
254. Juan Mann, "Detention Rates Increase in Name of Homeland Security, but Advocates on Both Sides Worry About Tactics," *Miami Daily Business Review*, January 27, 2005, http://www.vdare.com/mann/050207_fl_business.htm.
255. See article 31, paragraph 1 of the 1951 Refugee Convention. Available online at http://unhchr.ch/html/menu3/b/o_c_ref.htm.
256. Lynn Waddell, "Special Report: Immigration Law, Elusive Refugee, Detention Rates Increase in the name of Homeland Security, but Advocates on Both Sides Worry about Tactics," *Daily Business Review*, January 27, 2005.
257. Cheryl Little and Kathie Klarreich, "Securing Our Borders: Post 9/11 Scapegoating of Immigrants," Florida Immigrant Advocacy Center, 2005.
258. Ibid, 23.
259. Ibid, 23.
260. Marc Seitles, interview by the author, July 9, 2005.
261. Ibid.
262. *Border Protection, Antiterrorism, and Illegal Immigration Control Act of 2005*, section 213, Reform of Passport, Visa, and Immigration Fraud Offenses.
263. David, interview by the author, February 17, 2005
264. Marc Seitles, interview by the author, August 29, 2005.
265. *In Liberty's Shadow: U.S. Detention of Asylum Seekers in the Era of Homeland Security*, (New York: Human Rights First, 2004), 28–29, http://www.humanrightsfirst.org/asylum/libertys_shadow/Libertys_Shadow.pdf.
266. Vimral, interview by the author, February 16, 2005.
267. See Gary Pierre-Pierre, "A Death Bares America's Biased Policy," *New York Daily News*, November 28, 2004, pg. 45.
268. Ibid.
269. Jacqueline Charles, "Courts Quick to Reject Applications," *Miami Herald*, December 22, 2002.
270. "INS Invoking Post 9/11 Regulation against Haitian Asylum Seekers:

Controversial Regulation Was Intended to Target Terrorists," *Human Rights First*, November 7, 2002, http://www.humanrightsfirst.org/media/2002_alerts/1107.htm.

271. Steven Forester, interview by the author, January 21, 2006.
272. Ibid.
273. Edward Neepaye, quoted in, "Save Asylum, Save Lives—Say 'No' to the REAL ID Act," Human Rights First, http://www.humanrightsfirst.org/asylum/realid/asylum_stop_realid.htm.
274. The treatment of children is extensively documented in the publications of Human Rights First, Florida Immigrant Advocacy Center, Women's Commission for Refugee Women and Children, Amnesty International, and Human Rights Watch. There is also extensive media documentation; see footnotes 107–113 in *In Liberty's Shadow: U.S. Detention of Asylum Seekers in the Era of Homeland Security*, (New York: Human Rights First, 2004), http://www.humanrightsfirst.org/asylum/libertys_shadow/Libertys_Shadow.pdf.
275. Ibid., 10–11.
276. "Testing Community Supervision for the INS: An Evaluation of the Appearance Assistance program," Vera Institute of Justice, August 1, 2000, pg. 72, http://www.vera.org/publication_pdf/aapfinal.pdf.
277. Cheryl Little and Kathie Klarreich, "Securing Our Borders: Post 9/11 Scapegoating of Immigrants," Florida Immigrant Advocacy Center, April 2005, 16.
278. Luisa Yañez with Cindy Kent, "Wackenhut's Record Questioned Performance at Work-Release Center Studied," *Sun-Sentinel*, August 12, 1999.
279. Alvin Reid, "Dark Day for Black Business Looms," *St. Louis American*, March 17, 2005.
280. Sherrie Gossett, "Lawsuits Plague Chip-Implant Company," WorldNetDaily.com, June 11, 2002, http://www.worldnetdaily.com/news/article.asp?ARTICLE_ID=27917.
281. "BI Finds a New Owner," *Denver Business Journal*, August 11,2000, http://www.bizjournals.com/denver/stories/2000/08/07/daily28.html.
282. Michael Knowles, interview by the author, February 24, 2005.
283. Joseph Club, interview by the author, May 8, 2005.
284. Merrill Smith, "Warehousing Refugees: A Denial of Rights, a Waste of Humanity," *World Refugee Survey, 2004*, U.S. Committee For Refugees and Immigrants, pg. 38, http://www.refugees.org/article.aspx?id=1156.
285. Ibid.
286. Joseph Club, interview by the author, May 8, 2005.
287. "11 Haitian Migrants Drown in Bahamian Waters," Hot Calaloo, July 2001, http://www.hotcalaloo.com/july2001.htm.
288. Kathleen Newland, "Troubled Waters: Rescue of Asylum Seekers and Refugees at Sea," Migration Policy Institute, January 1, 2003, http://www.migration

information.org/Feature/display.cfm?ID=80.

289. Jonathan Cunningham, "The Real Fugee-La," WireTap, January 5, 2004, http://www.alternet.org/wiretap/17481/.
290. Filipe Denoso, interview by the author, May 7, 2005.
291. See www.uscg.mil/hq/g-o/g-opl/mle/amiostats1.htm.
292. Jocelyn MaCalla, interview by the author, February 28, 2005.
293. Filipe Denoso, interview by the author, May 7, 2005.
294. Ibid.
295. Michael Smith, "U.S. Coast Guard increases patrols off Haiti to halt any boat people," Associated Press, March 7, 2004.
296. "Report on the Situation of Human Rights in Haiti," Chapter 3, Inter-American Commission on Human Rights, March 9, 1993, http://www.cidh.oas.org/countryrep/EnHa93'/chap.3.htm.
297. "FIAC Urges U.S. Officials Not to Repatriate Haitians Aboard Coast Guard Cutters and Requests Access to Haitians," Florida Immigrant Advocacy Center, February 26, 2004, http://www.fiacfla.org/pressreleases.php#6.
298. Richard Bouzl, interview by the author, May 9, 2005.
299. Joseph Club, interview by the author, May 8, 2005.
300. "Haiti—Country Assistance Evaluation," World Bank (report no. 23637), February 12, 2002, http://lnweb18.worldbank.org/oed/oeddoclib.nsf/DocUNIDViewForJavaSearch/718D6FBC34815E5685256B7A007F32F0/$file/haiti_cae.pdf.
301. Filipe Denoso, interview by the author, May 7, 2005.
302. Jocelyn MaCalla, interview by the author, February 28, 2005.
303. Ibid.
304. Ibid.
305. Ibid.
306. "Refugee Policy Adrift: The United States and Dominican Republic Deny Haitians Protection," Women's Commission for Refugee Women and Children, January 2003, 14–15, http://www.womenscommission.org/pdf/ht.pdf.
307. Ibid., 14.
308. "President Bush Welcomes Georgian President Saakashivili to White House," White House, Office of the Press Secretary, February 25, 2004, http://www.whitehouse.gov/news/releases/2004/02/20040225-1.html.
309. See http://abcnews.go.com/wire/World/reuters20040211_588.html.
310. Rachel Swarns, "Halliburton Subsidiary Gets Contract to Add Temporary Immigration Detention Centers," *New York Times*, February 4, 2006, A7.
311. Cheryl Little and Charu Newhouse al-Sahli, "Haitian Refugees: A People in Search of Hope," Florida Immigrant Advocacy Center, May 2004, 31.
312. Article 33 of "Convention Relating to the Status of Refugees," Office of the High Commissioner for Human Rights, July 28, 1951, http://www.unhchr.ch/html/menu3/b/o_c_ref.htm.

313. "Haiti's Aristide Defiant in Exile," *BBC News*, March 8, 2004, http://news.bbc.co.uk/1/hi/world/americas/3543355.stm. See also "The Haiti Coup One Year Later: A Look Back at the U.S. Role in the Overthrow of Aristide," *Democracy Now!*, February 28, 2005, http://www.democracynow.org/article.pl?sid=05/02/28/1456242.
314. Adam Entous, "U.S. to Pay Haitian Coast Guard to Curb Refugees," Reuters, March 5, 2004, http://www.reuters.com/newsArticle.jhtml?type=domesticNews&storyID=4509955.
315. In some cases where a mass outflow of refugees is expected, there has been an in-country screening process set up by the U.S. government to screen people so they do not have to leave the country and risk their life trying to get to the U.S. to apply for asylum.
316. "Response to Congresswoman Ros-Lehtinen's 7 November Questions Regarding Haitian Refugees," submitted by Paul V. Kelly, Assistant Security for Legislative Affairs, U.S. Department of State, November 22, 2002, http://www.womenscommission.org/pdf/ht.pdf.
317. "Refugee Policy Adrift: The United States and Dominican Republic Deny Haitians Protection," Women's Commission for Refugee Women and Children, January 2003, 33, http://www.womenscommission.org/pdf/ht.pdf.
318. White House press conference, November 7, 2002, http://www.whitehouse.gov/news/releases/2002/11/20021107-2.html.
319. Eleanor Acer and Archana Pyati, "In Liberty's Shadow: U.S. Detention of Asylum Seekers in the Era of Homeland Security," pg. 24, Human Rights First, February 2004. See http://www.humanrightsfirst.org/asylum/libertys_shadow/LS_4_Security_Env.pdf.
320. Ibid., 24.
321. "Operation Liberty Shield: Press Briefing by Secretary Ridge," Department of Homeland Security, March 18, 2003, http://www.dhs.gov/dhspublic/display?content=525.
322. Lynn Waddell, "Elusive Refuge: Detention Rates Increase in Name of Homeland Security, but Advocates on Both Sides Worry about Tactics," Florida Immigrant Advocacy Center, January 27, 2005, http://fiacfla.org/printable.php?=79.
323. Kyle Horst, interview by the author, May 12, 2005.
324. "Population, Refugees and Migration," U.S. Department of State, 2002.
325. Erin Corcoran, interview by the author, June 3, 2005.
326. Lavinia Limón, "Lives Unlived," *World Refugee Survey 2004*, U.S. Committee for Refugees, 18, http://www.refugees.org/data/wrs/04/pdf/18-20.pdf.
327. Erin Corcoran, interview by the author, June 3, 2005.
328. See http://thomas.loc.gov/cgi-bin/query/z?c109:H.R.418.
329. "*REAL ID* Endangers People Fleeing Persecution," Human Rights First, http://www.humanrightsfirst.org/asylum/asylum_10_sensenbr.asp.
330. Coalition of the faith-based organizations to Senator, April 11, 2005, http://www.

humanrightsfirst.org/asylum/pdf/realid/faith-based-041105.pdf.
331. "F1" is the name of the student visa.
332. "Record Total of 547,867 International Students on U.S. Campuses, Enrollment Rises 6.4%, Largest Increase Since 1980," Institute of International Education, November 13, 2001, http://opendoors.iienetwork.org/?p=25089.
333. Tanya Schevitz, "Huge Drop in Foreign Students on Campus, Post 9-11 Security Discourages Many from Coming to U.S.," *San Francisco Chronicle;* September 9, 2003, A1.
334. "International Student Enrollments Declined by 2.4% in 2003/04," Institute of International Education, November 10, 2004, http://opendoors.iienetwork.org/?p=50137.
335. Sam Dillon, "U.S. Slips in Attracting the World's Best Students," *New York Times*, December 21, 2004, A1.
336. William Fisher, "Give Us Your Huddled Masses . . .," *The Modern Tribune*, February 10, 2005, http://www.themoderntribune.com/give_us_your_tired_and_huddled_masses.htm.
337. Juan Gabriel Valdés, *Pinochet's Economists: The Chicago School of Economics in Chile* (Cambridge: Cambridge University Press, 1995).
338. David Harvey, *A Brief History of Neoliberalism* (Oxford: Oxford University Press, 2005), 54.
339. Yomi Ademuwagun, interview by the author, June 12, 2005.
340. Dan Eggen, "FBI Seeks Data on Foreign Students Colleges Call Request Illegal," *Washington Post*, December 25, 2002, A1.
341. Ibid.
342. See http://www.ice.gov/pi/news/factsheets/0212FINALRU_FS.htm.
343. "Foreign Students Jailed in Colorado," Associated Press, December 27, 2002, http://www.why-war.com/news/read.php?id=2666.
344. Immigration and Naturalization Form I-831, signed by Special Agent Eric Wein, March 6, 2003, case number NYC0303000415.
345. Sherri Powar, "U.S. Government Report Criticizes Visa Delays for International Students and Faculty," Alliance for International Educational Exchange, March 15, 2004, http://isss.binghamton.edu/new/visadelaycriti.htm.
346. Victoria Gilman, "State Department Extends Mantis, New Clearance Period Announced for Foreign Students and Researchers," *Chemical & Engineering News*, 83, no.8 (February 21, 2005), 12. See www.gao.gov/new.items/d04371.pdf.
347. "Border Security: Improvements Needed to Reduce Time Taken to Adjudicate Visas for Science Students and Scholars," February Government Accountability Office Report, 2004, http://www.gao.gov/new.items/d04371.pdf.
348. Immigration and Naturalization form I-831, signed by Special Agent Eric Wein, March 6, 2003, case number NYC0303000415.
349. "Fraud Prevention Program: Report of Investigation," U.S. embassy in Lagos,

case no. 03-6201, February 28, 2003.

350. Office of the registrar of the Nigerian College of Fisheries and Maritime Technology to the U.S. embassy in Lagos, March 11, 2004, REF: S/F 1907/Vol. 1/5.
351. Immigration and Naturalization form I-831, signed by Special Agent Eric Wein, March 6, 2003, case no. NYC0303000415.
352. Yomi Ademuwagun, interview by the author, June 12, 2005.
353. Oladokun Sulaiman, e-mail message to the author, July 20, 2005.
354. Christi Hegranes, "Student of Concern," *San Francisco Weekly*, May 18, 2005, http://www.sfweekly.com/Issues/2005-05-18/news/feature.html.
355. "Considering the Impact of Proposed Changes in Deemed Export Regulations," Stanford University, www.stanford.edu/dept/DoR/exp_controls/comments.html.
356. Christi Hegranes, "Student of Concern," *San Francisco Weekly*, May 18, 2005, http://www.sfweekly.com/Issues/2005-05-18/news/feature.html.
357. Kelly Field, "Proposed Federal Rules on Equipment Licenses for Foreign Researchers Would Be Costly, Scientists Say," *Chronicle of Higher Education*, May 9, 2005.
358. "Security Controls on Scientific Information and the Conduct of Scientific Research," The Commission on Scientific Communication and National Security, established by Center for Strategic and International Studies in collaboration with the National Academies, June 1, 2005, 5.
359. Ibid., 7.
360. Ibid., 12.
361. Ibid., 13.
362. William Fisher, "On Immigration the U.S. Shoots Itself In the Foot," *The Daily Star*, February 14, 2005.
363. Ibid.
364. An H-1B is a work visa that allows an individual to work for a particular company for a limited period of time, after which they must return home.
365. Sangeeta Kamat, Biju Mathew, and Ali Mir, "Producing High Tech: Globalization, the State and Migrant Subjects," Globalization Societies and Education, vol. 2, no. 1, March 2004, 5-23.
366. Javed, interview by the author, July 10, 2005.
367. Vasant Mehta, interview by the author, June 17, 2005.
368. See http://www.pixelsystemsinc.com.
369. Vasant Mehta, interview by the author, August 30, 2005.
370. See http://www.pixelsystemsinc.com/site/whats_new.asp?WhatsNewId=13.
371. Vijay Prasad quoted in Monica Gutierrez, "Coming to (Work in) America," *VisaPortal.com*, http://www.visaportal.com/page.asp?page_id=112.
372. Philippe Louis Jean, interviews by the author, March 15, 2005 and August 30, 2005.

373. Ibid.
374. Ibid.
375. "Fact Sheet: Military Naturalizations," U.S. Citizenship and Immigration Services, March 7, 2005, http://www.ilw.com/immigdaily/news/2005,0309-military.pdf.
376. "Bush Speeds Citizenship for Military," *CNN.com*, July 3, 2002, http://archives.cnn.com/2002/US/07/03/bush.military.citizenship/.
377. Philippe Louis Jean, interview by the author, March 15, 2005.
378. Louis Jean was charged with adultery because his superior discovered that his separation from his wife was not a formal divorce. He was charged with sodomy because under military law, any sexual act that is not intercourse in the missionary position, with the man on top of the woman, is classified as sodomy and a crime.
379. "Proud to be an American: Immigrant Soldier Granted American Citizenship in Death," *Veterans Today*, August 30, 2004, http://www.veteranstoday.com/article56.html.
380. Ibid.
381. Rainer Sabin, "Military Recruiters Turn Out in Full Force at Convention," *Arkansas Democrat Gazette*, July 2, 2005.
382. Olivia J. Quinto, "Immigrant Soldiers in Iraq Get Citizenship," *Philippine News*, July 8, 2005.
383. Brandon Bain, "Federal Law Offers posthumous citizenship for Soldiers," *Newsday*, March 25, 2006.
384. Gregg Zoroya, "Troops Put Lives on the Line to Be Called Americans," *USA Today*, June 30, 2005, A1.
385. See chapter 2.
386. Traci Hong, interview by the author, January 30, 2006.
387. Ibid.
388. See http://www.iava.org/index.php?option=com_content&task=view&id=43&Itemid=66.
389. Swire, who advised President Clinton on privacy issues, has said that many technology firms or dot-com companies that survived the IT bust of 2000 recast themselves as homeland security companies in the aftermath of the 9/11 attacks. Many companies quickly acquired homeland security departments, and Swire questions whether the need for profits or the country's need for homeland security protection was paramount. Peter Swire, interview by Jessica Silver-Greenberg, May 3, 2005. See also Brendan I. Koerner, "The Security Traders," *Mother Jones*, September/October 2002.
390. "Department of Homeland Security," Office of Management and Budget, Executive Office of the President, http://www.whitehouse.gov/omb/budget/fy2004/homeland.html.
391. Ibid.

392. From section 101(b) of the Homeland Security Act of 2002:
    The Primary Mission of the Department is to:
    - prevent terrorist attacks within the United States;
    - reduce the vulnerability of the United States to terrorism;
    - minimize the damage, and assist in the recovery, from terrorist attacks that do occur within the United States;
    - carry out all functions of entities transferred to the Department, including by acting as a focal point regarding natural and manmade crises and emergency planning;
    - ensure that the function of the agencies and subdivisions within the Department that are not related directly to securing the homeland are not diminished or neglected except by a specific explicit Act of Congress; and
    - monitor connection between illegal drug trafficking and terrorism, coordinate efforts to sever such connections, and otherwise contribute to efforts to interdict illegal drug trafficking.

    See http://www.whitehouse.gov/deptofhomeland/bill/title1.html#101.
393. Christopher Logan, "Inside the White House Advisory Group: Influential Business Leaders, Former Officials, Sit at the Homeland Security Table," *Congressional Quarterly*, October 18, 2002.
394. Ibid.
395. Bob Herbert, "Whose Hands Are Dirty?" *New York Times*, November 25, 2002, A21.
396. Daneille Brian, executive director of the Project on Government Oversight, to Tom Ridge, Homeland Security secretary, July 8, 2003, http://www.pogo.org/p/government/go-030702-homeland.html.
397. Anne-Marie Cusac, "Open to Attack," *The Progressive*, October 29, 2003, http://www.alternet.org/story.html?StoryID=16968.
398. See http://corzine.senate.gov/press_office/record.cfm?id=189735.
399. "Senate Declines to Act on Corzine's Chemical Security Amendment," OMB Watch, October 4, 2004, http://www.ombwatch.org/article/articleview/2444/1/1?TopicID=1.
400. "Corruption Probe Hits U.S. Insurers," *BBC News*, October 15, 2004, http://news.bbc.co.uk/2/hi/business/3745334.stm.
401. Monica Langley and Theo Francis, "Insurers Reel from Spitzer's Strike," *Wall Street Journal*, October 18, 2004, A1.
402. "MMC Reaches Settlement Agreement with New York State Attorney General and Superintendent of New York State Insurance Department," Marsh & McLennan Companies Inc., January 31, 2005, http://www.mmc.com/news/pressReleases_222.pdf.
403. Eliot Spitzer quoted in Associated Press, "Marsh & McLennan Chairman Resigns Post," SmartPros, October 26, 2004, http://accounting.smartpros.com/x45640.xml.

404. Wayne Madsen, "Homeland Security, Homeland Profits," CorpWatch, December 21, 2001, http://www.corpwatch.org/article.php?id=1108.
405. "Margie Burns, "The Strange Career of 'Homeland Security,'" *Online Journal*, June 29, 2002, 1, http://www.onlinejournal.com/archive/06-29-02_Burns.pdf.
406. "Summary Proceedings—'Balancing Security and Mobility: A Symposium on Innovative Approaches to Transportation Security,'" Volpe Center, May 6, 2004, 6, http://gulliver.trb.org/publications/security/proceedings_may604.pdf.
407. "Homeland Security Act of 2002: Section 312, Homeland Security Institute," Homeland Security Institute, http://www.homelandsecurity.org/LegislativeFoundation.asp.
408. Thomas Maier, "Questions on Kerik's Two Roles," *New York Newsday*, December 11, 2004.
409. Jonathan Karp, "Bikers' water backpack now a soldiers' essential," *The Wall Street Journal*, July 19, 2005, B1.
410. Ibid.
411. Veronique de Rugy, "Bad News for Homeland Security," *TCSDaily.com*, June 8, 2005, http://www.tcsdaily.com/Article.aspx?id=060805B.
412. Angie C. Marek, "Security at Any Price? Homeland Protection Isn't Just Job 1 in Washington; It's More Like a Big Old Government ATM," *U.S. News & World Report*, May 30, 2005, pg. 22.
413. The Armed Forces Communications and Electronics Association—a private association, not at all connected to the government.
414. "U.S. Department of Homeland Security Awards Two Contracts Totaling $33.1 Million to ManTech," ManTech, January 12, 2004, http://phx.corporate-ir.net/phoenix.zhtml?c=130660&p=irol-newsArticle&ID=483866&highlight=.
415. "Homeland Security Information Network to Expand Collaboration, Connectivity for States and Major Cities," Department of Homeland Security, February 24, 2004, http://www.dhs.gov/dhspublic/display?content=3350.
416. John Foley, interview by the author, February 22, 2005.
417. Ibid.
418. "Pakistani Video Maker Pleads Guilty in U.S.," *Daily Times Monitor Pakistan*, October 9, 2004, http://www.dailytimes.com.pk/default.asp?page=story_9-10-2004_pg7_44.
419. John Foley, interview by the author, February 22, 2005.
420. "Fact Sheet: Company Description," ManTech, http://phx.corporate-ir.net/phoeniz.zhtml?c=130660&p=irol-newsArticle&ID=820636&highlight=.
421. Eric Lipton, "Former Anti-terror Officials Find Industry Pays Better," *New York Times*, June 18, 2006, 1. See also Angie C. Marek, "Security At Any Price? Homeland Protection Isn't Just Job 1 in Washington; It's More Like a Big Old Government ATM," *U.S. News & World Report*, May 30, 2005, http://www.usnews.com/usnews/news/articles/050530/30homeland.htm.

422. Katharine Mieszkowski, "Passport to Pry," *Salon.com*, April 7, 2005, http://dir.salon.com/story/tech/feature/2005/04/07/savi/index.html.
423. Ange C. Marek, "Security at Any Price? Homeland Protection Isn't Just Job 1 in Washington; It's More Like a Big Old Government ATM," *U.S. News & World Report*, May 30, 2005, http://www.usnews.com/usnews/news/articles/050530/30homeland.b1.htm.
424. Elizabeth Brown, "More Than 2000 Spin Through Revolving Door," Center for Public Integrity, April 7, 2005, http://www.publicintegrity.org/lobby/report.aspx?aid=678.
425. "How the Revolving Door Undermines Public Confidence in Government, and What To Do About It," Revolving Door Working Group, October 2005, http://www.revolvingdoor.info.com.
426. It is not known exactly how much was spent on homeland security lobbying, but the defense lobbyists, with a quarter of the budget, spent $44 million in 2003. One can only imagine how much more was spent on DHS.
427. Alice Lipowicz, "Defense, Homeland Security Industries Rack Up Lobbying Dollars," *Washington Technology*, April 11, 2005, http://www.washingtontechnology.com/news/1_1daily_news/25975_1.html.
428. Tim Starks, "Security 'Gold Rush' Yields Nuggets for Some," *Congressional Quarterly Weekly*, January 22, 2005, http://www.globalsecurity.org/org/news/2005/050122-security-gold.htm.
429. Peter Swire, interview by Jessica Silver-Greenberg, May 3, 2005.
430. "Federal Contracting and Iraq Reconstruction," Project on Government Oversight, October 27, 2003, http://www.pogo.org/p/contracts/co-031001-iraq.html.
431. Robert O'Harrow Jr. and Scott Higham, "U.S. Border Security at a Crossroads; Technology Problems Limit Effectiveness of US-VISIT Program to Screen Foreigners," *Washington Post*, May 23, 2005, A1.
432. Ibid.
433. Adam M. Forman, interview by the author, February 23, 2005.
434. "US-VISIT: How It Works," Department of Homeland Security, http://www.dhs.gov/dhspublic/interapp/editorial/editorial_0525.xml.
435. Marcia Heroux Pounds, "Lasting Impression Cross Match Tech of Palm Beach Gardens is Working to Reach a Wider Market with its Forensic-Quality Tools," *Sun-Sentinel.com*, July 11, 2004, 1E.
436. Cynthia L. Webb, "US VISIT Launch Met with Criticism," *Washington Post*, January 8, 2004.
437. Adam M. Forman, interview by the author, February 23, 2005.
438. Marcia Heroux Pounds, "Lasting Impression Cross Match Tech of Palm Beach Gardens is Working to Reach a Wider Market with its Forensic-Quality Tools," *Sun-Sentinel.com*, July 11, 2004, 1E.
439. Adam M. Forman, interview by the author, August 16, 2005.

440. "US-VISIT: Goals," Department of Homeland Security, http://www.dhs.gov/dhspublic/display?content=4257.
441. Adam M. Forman, interview by the author, August 16, 2005.
442. Ibid.
443. "US-VISIT: Goals," Department of Homeland Security, http://www.dhs.gov/dhspublic/interapp/display?content=4257.
444. Barbara M. Harrison, Freedom of Information Act Officer, Department of Homeland Security, e-mail message to Joshua Chaffin, December 7, 2005.
445. See chapter 1.
446. The DHS Web site lists examples of US VISIT's big catches. There is no listing of a suspected terrorist. See "U.S. Entry-Exit System Hailed for 'Unprecedented Results,'" U.S. Department of State, May 18, 2005, http://usinfo.state.gov/gi/Archive/2005/May/19-588378.html.
447. The response to my US-VISIT FOIA request offered to provide a list of each of the 1,091 cases, detailing what each person had been stopped for, but there was a $28-per-hour charge for the work. DHS estimated that it would cost $13,958 to complete the FOIA request. It also advised that the results would contain "very incomplete data on the specific information of interest to you."
448. "Department of Homeland Security Testifies on U.S.-VISIT Program," United States Mission to the European Union, March 4, 2004, http://www.useu.be/Terrorism/USResponse/Mar0404HutchinsonUSVISIT.html.
449. Ibid.
450. "United States Visitor and Immigrant Status Indicator Technology," Electronic Privacy Information Center, http://www.epic.org/privacy/us-visit/.
451. Letters of complaint from travelers whose information was taken under US VISIT to the Department of Homeland Security, Electronic Privacy Information center, http://www.epic.org/foia_notes/usvisit1.pdf.
452. Ibid.
453. Joan Friedland, "Official Crime Information Should Be Accurate," *Miami Herald*, April 28, 2003.
454. *Border Protection, Antiterrorism, and Illegal Immigration Control Act of 2005*, section 410, Listing of Immigration Violators in the National Crime Information Center Database, provision (a) (3).
455. "Major Management Challenges Facing the Department of Homeland Security," DHS Office of the Inspector General Office of Audits, OIG-05-06, December 2004.
456. See http://www.gao.gov/pas/2005/dhs.htm.
457. For a full list of Office of the Inspector General and General Accounting Office reports on INS data inaccuracies, see "INS Data: The Track Record," from the National Immigration Law Center, http://www.nilc.org/immlawpolicy/misc/INS%20data%20accuracy.pdf.
458. "Biometric Identifiers," Electronic Privacy Information Center, http://www.

epic.org/privacy/biometrics/.

459. Sara Michael, "US-VISIT Lacks Privacy Requirement, Lieberman Says," *FCW.com*, December 4, 2003, http://www.fcw.com/article81563-12-4-03-Web.
460. Peter Swire, interview by Jessica Silver-Greenberg, August 19, 2005.
461. Marcia Heroux Pounds, "Lasting Impression Cross Match Tech of Palm Beach Gardens is Working to Reach a Wider Market with its Forensic-Quality Tools," *Sun-Sentinel.com*, July 11, 2004, 1E.
462. *United States v. Scheffer*, 523 U.S. 303, 118 S. Ct. 1261, 140 L. Ed. 2d 413, 419 (1998).
463. Peter Swire, interview by Jessica Silver-Greenberg, May 3, 2005.
464. Ibid.
465. Glenn Spencer, interview by Jessica Silver-Greenberg, July 21, 2005.
466. Daniel Sheehy, quoting Glenn Spencer, *Fighting Immigration Anarchy: American Patriots Battle to Save the Nation* (Bloomington, IN: AuthorHouse, 2005), 64.
467. *Los Angeles Times*, October 25, 1996, p.B1.
468. Glenn Spencer, interview by Jessica Silver-Greenberg, July 21, 2005.
469. Jerry Seper, "Border Hawk Hunts Illegals," *Washington Times*, April 24, 2005, A1.
470. Glenn Spencer, interview by Jessica Silver-Greenberg, July 21, 2005.
471. Daniel Sheehy, quoting Glenn Spencer, *Fighting Immigration Anarchy: American Patriots Battle to Save the Nation* (Bloomington, IN: AuthorHouse, 2005), 89.
472. Ibid.
473. See http://fpc.state.gov/documents/organization/54514.pdf, pg. 42.
474. See http://www.fcw.com/fcw/articles/2004/0628/web-uav-06-28-04.asp.
475. Eric Lipton, "Despite New Efforts Along Arizona Border, Serious Problems Remain," *New York Times*, March 14, 2005, http://select.nytimes.com/gst/abstract.html?res=F20B14F93E580C778DDDAA0894DD404482.
476. "Budget-in-Brief Fiscal Year 2006," Department of Homeland Security, February 7, 2005, pg. 51, http://www.dhs.gov/interweb/assetlibrary/Budget_BIBFY06_2-7-05.pdf.
477. "President Discusses Border Security and Immigration Reform in Arizona," Office of the Press Secretary, White House, November 28, 2005, http://www.whitehouse.gov/news/releases/2005/11/20051128-7.html.
478. Glenn Spencer, interview by Jessica Silver-Greenberg, July 21, 2005.
479. "Spotlight on Surveillance," Electronic Privacy Information Center, August 2005, http://www.epic.org/privacy/surveillance/spotlight/0805/#20.
480. Steven Ware, interview by author, January 30, 2006.
481. Susan Carroll quoting Walker Butler, "Ground radar may find border crossers. Congressmen, feds want to buy system from Scottsdale firm," *Arizona Republic*, May 16, 2005.
482. Robert Longley, "Border Security Gets $6.7 Billion in Bush 2006 Budget," *About.com*, February 2005, http://usgovinfo.about.com/od/defenseandsecu-

rity/a/homeland06.htm.

483. Steven Rosenfeld, "Forget Halliburton," *TomPaine.com*, January 16, 2004, http://www.tompaine.com/Archive/scontent/9781.html.
484. See http://www.corpwatch.org/article.php?list=type&type=11.
485. Quoted in "Alabama State Troopers Said to Receive 'Clear Authority' in Civil Immigration Enforcement," *Immigrants' Rights Update* 17, no. 7 (November 24, 2003), http://www.nilc.org/immlawpolicy/arrestdet/ad075.htm.
486. Ibid.
487. "State and Local Police Enforcement," National Immigration Forum, May 2004, http://www.immigrationforum.org/DesktopDefault.aspx?tabid=572.
488. Mutty Strulovic, interview by the author, August 15, 2005.
489. Dan Waxwell, interview by the author, August 18, 2005.
490. "Blanket Purchase Agreements (BPAs)," Naval Air Warfare Center Training Systems Division, http://www.ntsc.navy.mil/Resources/Library/Acqguide/sap-bpa.htm.
491. Dan Waxwell, interview by the author, August 18, 2005.
492. Victoria López, interview by the author, April 15, 2005.
493. Alisa Solomon, "Detainees Equal Dollars: The Rise in Immigrant Incarcerations Drives a Prison Boom," *Village Voice*, August 14, 2002.
494. Judith Greene, "Bailing Out Private Jails," *The American Prospect*, September 10, 2001, http://www.prospect.org/print/V12/16/greene-ju.html.
495. Kelly Lytle, "Constructing the Criminal Alien: A Historical Framework for Analyzing Border Vigilantes at the Turn of the 21st Century," Center for Comparative Immigration Studies, University of California, San Diego, October 2003, 6, http://www.ccis-ucsd.org/PUBLICATIONS/wrkg83.pdf.
496. These laws mandated the detention of any arriving foreigner without a visa or valid documentation and also widely expanded the offenses for which a noncitizen could be put into deportation proceedings. A noncitizen would therefore be jailed while the deportation case ran its course. See chapters 1, 3, and 6 for fuller explanation.
497. See chapter 1.
498. Victoria López, interview by the author, April 14, 2005.
499. Craig Hanley, PhD, "Study of Asylum Seekers in Expedited Removal," (report given to supplement congressional testimony), pg. 184, February 2005, http://www.uscirf.gov/countries/global/asylum_refugees/2005/february/conditionConfin.pdf; Rajeev Goyle and David A. Jaeger, PhD, "Deporting the Undocumented: A Cost Assessment," Center for American Progress, July 26, 2005, 6.
500. Alisa Soloman, "Detainees Equal Dollars: The Rise in Immigrant Incarcerations Drives a Prison Boom," *Village Voice*, August 14–20, 2002.
501. See chapters 1 and 2 for a evidence of zealous detention, prosecution, and lengthy sentences for minor offences.

502. "Major Management Challenges Facing the Department of Homeland Security," Department of Homeland Security, Office of the Inspector General, Office of Audits, OIG-05-06, December 2004, http://www.mipt.org/pdf/DHS-OIG-05-06.pdf.
503. Rajeev Goyle and David A. Jaeger, PhD, "Deporting the Undocumented: A Cost Assessment," Center for American Progress, July 26, 2005, pg. 6, http://www.americanprogress.org/atf/cf/%7BE9245FE4-9A2B-43C7-A521-5D6FF2E06E03%7D/DEPORTING_THE_UNDOCUMENTED.PDF.
504. Kelly Brewington, "PA Volunteers Reach Out to Asylum-Seekers; York Residents Provide Necessities to Those New to U.S.," *Baltimore Sun*, December 5, 2005.
505. "Audit of the Department of Justice, Office of the Federal Detention Trustee," Office of the Inspector General, December 2004, http://www.usdoj.gov/oig/reports/OBD/a0504/exec.htm.
506. Alisa Soloman, "Detainees Equal Dollars. The Rise in Immigrant Incarcerations Drives a Prison Boom," *Village Voice*, August 14, 2002.
507. Judith Greene, "Bailing Out Private Jails," *The American Prospect*, September 10, 2001, http://www.prospect.org/print/V12/16/greene-ju.html.
508. Phillip Mattera, Mafruza Khan, and Stephen Nathan, "Corrections Corporation Of America: A Critical Look at Its First Twenty Years," Open Society Institute, December 2003, pg. vi, 25, http://www.soros.org/Staging/initiatives/justice/articles_publications/publications/cca_20_years_20031201/CCA_Report.pdf.
509. Associated Press, "Corrections Corporation 2Q Profits Rise," August 4, 2005, http://news.moneycentral.msn.com/ticker/article.asp?Symbol=US:CXW&Feed=AP&Date=20050804&ID=5019357.
510. Corrections Corporation of America financial report, second quarter 2005, pg. 8, http://www.shareholder.com/Common/Edgar/1070985/950144-05-8173/05-00.pdf.
511. Ibid.
512. Scott Pelley, "Locked Inside a Nightmare," *60 Minutes II*, May 2000, http://www.cbsnews.com/stories/2000/05/09/60II/main193636.shtml.
513. Ibid.
514. Judith Greene, "Bailing Out Private Jails," *The American Prospect*, September 10, 2001, http://www.prospect.org/print/V12/16/greene-ju.html.
515. "The GEO Group Inc. Celebrates Name Change," NYSE Group, January 21, 2004, http://www.nyse.com/Frameset.html?displayPage=/events/1074166229819.html.
516. See http://www.bizjournals.com/southflorida/stories/2005/07/18/daily29.html.
517. See chapter 2.
518. "The GEO Group Inc.: Key Developments," MSN Money, http://news.moneycentral.msn.com/ticker/sigdev.asp?Symbol=GGI.
519. Ibid.
520. See http://news.moneycentral.msn.com/ticker/article.asp?Symbol=US:GGI&

Feed=PR&Date=20050714&ID=4963516.

521. "Private and Public Prisons: Studies Comparing Operational Costs and/or Quality of Service," U.S. General Accounting Office, GAO/GGD-96-158, August 1996.
522. See chapter 4 for more details on Philippe Louis Jean's case.
523. Philippe Louis Jean, interview by the author, March 15, 2005.
524. Ibid.
525. Released June 2, 2003: See http://www.fas.org/irp/agency/doj/oig/detainees.pdf.
526. See http://www.ice.gov/doclib/partners/dro/oopsmanual/work.pdf.
527. See http://www.ccr-ny.org/v2/reports/report.asp?ObjID=4mORdJEVGx&Content=330.
528. See http://www.ccr-ny.org/v2/reports/report.asp?ObjID=2FhipyPsQJ&Content=620.
529. "Federal Judge Rules on Constitutionality of Kickback in Contract between New York State Prisons and MCI," Center for Constitutional Rights, http://www.ccr-ny.org/v2/reports/report.asp?ObjID=2FhipyPsQJ&Content=620.
530. Paul Duggan, "Captive Audience Rates High. Families Must Pay Dearly When Inmates Call Collect," *Washington Post*, January 23, 2000, A03.
531. May 18, 2005, visit.
532. See http://www.brennancenter.org/programs/cj/coalition_fcc_comments.pdf.
533. Loie Fecteau, "Prison Phone Kickbacks Alleged," *Albuquerque Journal*, January 4, 2000.
534. Dannie Martin, "Private Jailer Reaches Out to Gouge Convicts," New America Media, January 27, 2005, http://crm.ncmonline.com/news/view_article.html?article_id=db9150c4841f2e5bb6ca33139b3f5143.
535. Isabel García, interview by the author, April 15, 2005.
536. Mark Potok, interview by the author, September 2, 2005.
537. Mark Potok and Heidi Beirich, "The Puppeteer," *Intelligence Report*, a publication of the Southern Poverty Law Center, Summer 2002, http://www.splcenter.org/intel/intelreport/article.jsp?aid=93.
538. From comments made during a public forum on immigration held in Las Vegas over the 2005 Memorial Day Weekend, quoted in Leonard Zeskind, "The New Nativism: The Alarming Overlap Between White Nationalists and Mainstream Anti-Immigrant Forces," *American Prospect Magazine*, November 10, 2005, http://www.prospect.org/web/page.ww?section=root&name=viewPrint&articleID=10485.
539. Anne C. Mulkern, "Firebrand Tancredo Puts Policy Over Party Line," *Denver Post*, November 27, 2005, http://www.denverpostbloghouse.com/washington/?p=320.
540. "A Statement of the Principles of the Council of Conservative Citizens," http://www.cofcc.org/manifest.htm.

541. See http://www.patriotic-flags.com/tshirt/white_pride.htm.
542. Mark Potok, "One More Enemy," *Intelligence Report*, Winter 2002, http://www.splcenter.org/intel/intelreport/article.jsp?aid=72.
543. Mark Potok, "The New Internationalism," *Intelligence Report*, Fall 2001, http://www.splcenter.org/intel/intelreport/article.jsp?aid=175.
544. Nancy Hill-Holtzman, "Sybert's Ties to Group Called Racist at Issue," *Los Angeles Times*, Oct 25, 1996, B1.
545. Mark Potok and Heidi Beirich, "Blood on the Border," *Intelligence Report*, Spring 2001, http://www.splcenter.org/intel/intelreport/article.jsp?pid=420.
546. American Immigration Lawyers Association, "Restrictionist Watch," Volume 1, Number 2, March 19, 2004, http://www.aila.org/content/default.aspx?docid=10307.
547. Mark Potok and Heidi Beirich, "Blood on the Border," *Intelligence Report*, Spring 2001, http://www.splcenter.org/intel/intelreport/article.jsp?pid=419.
548. Ibid., 3.
549. Ibid.
550. Peter Smith, interview by the author, July 16, 2005.
551. Mark Potok and Heidi Beirich, "Blood on the Border," *Intelligence Report*, Spring 2001, http://www.splcenter.org/intel/intelreport/article.jsp?pid=420.
552. Leonard Zeskind, "The New Nativism: The alarming Overlap Between White Nationalists and Mainstream Anti-Immigrant Forces," *American Prospect Magazine*, November 10, 2005, http://www.prospect.org/web/page.ww?section=root&name=ViewPrint&articleId=10485.
553. Max Blumenthal, "Vigilante Injustice," *Salon.com*, May 22, 2003, http://dir.salon.com/story/news/feature/2003/05/22/vigilante/index3.html?pn=1.
554. Ibid.
555. Peter Smith, interview by the author, July 16, 2005.
556. Rick Swartz, interview by the author, August 12, 2005.
557. Ibid.
558. Ibid.
559. Ibid.
560. Illegal Immigration Reform and Immigrant Responsibility Act of 1996, Public Law 104-208, Div. C, 110 U.S. Statutes at Large 3009-546 (1996). See http://thomas.loc.gov/cgi-bin/query/z?c104:H.R.2202.
561. Antiterrorism and Effective Death Penalty Act of 1996, Public Law 104-132, 110 U.S. Statutes at Large 1214 (1996). See http://thomas.loc.gov/cgi-bin/query/z?c104:S.735.
562. Immigration and Naturalization Service Statistical Yearbook, 1996–2002, tables 36 and 43, http://www.USCIS.gov/graphics/shared/statistics/yearbook/2003/Table36D.xls/Table430.xls.
563. See chapter one for a fuller breakdown of the effects of mass deportations.
564. Rick Swartz, interview by the author, August 12, 2005.

565. The 1996 Personal Responsibility and Work Opportunity Reconciliation Act, Public Law 104-193, 110 U.S. Statutes at Large 2168 (1996). See http://thomas.loc.gov/cgi-bin/query/F?c104:5:./temp/~c104TNIguX:e142080.
566. Amanda Levinson, "Immigrants and Welfare Use," Migration Policy Institute, August 1, 2002, http://www.migrationinformation.org/feature/display.cfm?ID=45.
567. California Proposition 187, http://www.americanpatrol.com/REFERENCE/prop187text.html.
568. "Issue & Debate: Immigration," a debate between Berman and Dan Lungren, California attorney general, moderated by Jeffrey Kaye on PBS's *NewsHour*, October 22, 1996, http://www.pbs.org/newshour/bb/election/october96/immigration_10-22.html.
569. A transcript is available at http://clinton4.nara.gov/WH/New/other/sotu.html.
570. Bill Clinton, *Between Hope and History: Meeting America's Challenges for the 21st Century* (New York: Random House, 1996), 134.
571. Lance Hill, "The Politics and Background of David Duke. Resource Packet," Louisiana Coalition against Racism, December 1991.
572. Ibid.
573. Leonard Zeskind, "Searchlight on the States: Duke Conference Draws European Racists," *International Searchlight*, no. 361 (July 2005): 33.
574. Tyler Bridges, *The Rise of David Duke*, (Jackson: University Press of Mississippi, 1995), 67. See also United Press International, "Klan Leader Egged During Tour," October 16, 1977, reprinted in *The Crusader*, no. 27, 1977, 2; Frank Del Olmo, "'Border Watch' by Klan Called a Media Event," *Los Angeles Times*, October 27, 1977, 3; and Luke Cannon, "The 'Border Patrol' that Wasn't," *Washington Post*, November 8, 1977, A19.
575. Frank Del Olmo, "'Border Watch' by Klan called a Media Event," *Los Angeles Times*, October 27, 1977, 3.
576. David Duke, *My Awakening: A Path to Racial Understanding* (Free Speech Press, 1998).
577. Ibid.
578. John Tanton, memorandum to FAIR, 1986. Memo one available at http://www.splcenter.org/intel/intelreport/article.jsp?sid=123&printable=1. See also memo two, http://www.splcenter.org/intel/intelreport/article.jsp?sid=124&printable=1; and memo three, http://www.splcenter.org/intel/intelreport/article.jsp?sid=125&printable=1.
579. Paragraph 14 under section II of John Tanton, memorandum to WITAN IV Attendees, October 10, 1986, http://www.splcenter.org/intel/intelreport/article.jsp?sid=125.
580. Ray Ybarra, interview by the author, August 12, 2005.
581. John Tanton, memorandum to WITAN IV Attendees, October 10, 1986, http://www.splcenter.org/intel/intelreport/article.jsp?sid=125.

582. James Crawford, *Hold Your Tongue: Bilingualism and the Politics of English Only*, "Hispanophobia," From chapter 6, (Boston: Addison-Wesley, 1992), http://ourworld.compuserve.com/homepages/JWCRAWFORD/HYTCH6.htm.
583. Ibid.
584. "John Tanton's Network," *Intelligence Report*, Summer 2002, http://www.splcenter.org/intel/intelreport/article.jsp?sid=72.
585. Mark Potok and Heidi Beirich, "The Puppeteer," *Intelligence Report*, Summer 2002, http://www.splcenter.org/intel/intelreport/article.jsp?aid=93.
586. Ibid.
587. John Tanton, "International Migration 1975," published in 1975, is reprinted in John Rohe, *Mary Lou and John Tanton: A Journey into American Conservation* (FAIR Horizon Press, 2002), 194.
588. Mark Potok and Heidi Beirich, "The Puppeteer," *Intelligence Report*, Summer 2002, http://www.splcenter.org/intel/intelreport/article.jsp?aid=93.

    For an idea of the kind of material the *Citizens Informer* publishes, the *Intelligence Report* offers this example: "One of the group's featured columnists, who identifies himself as H. Millard, recently wrote there on his view on the likely effects of immigration and intermarriage. Millard, who refused to be interviewed, is a Costa Mesa, Calif., real estate agent whose full name is Martin H. Millard. 'What will emerge will be just be a slimy brown mass of glop,' Millard wrote. The columnist goes on to say that intermarriage will bring about 'genocide.'" From Mark Potok and Trish O'Kane, "Sharks in the Mainstream," *Intelligence Report*, Winter 1999, http://www.splcenter.org/intel/intelreport/article.jsp?pid=621.
589. "Federation for American Immigration Reform (FAIR)," Center for New Community, November 2004, 3–4, http://www.newcomm.org/fair2004.pdf.
590. Mark Potok, editor of the *Intelligence Report*, to Larry Fahn, president of the Sierra Club, October 23, 2003.

    See also "Federation for American Immigration Reform (FAIR)," Center for New Community, November 2004, http://www.newcomm.org.
591. Center for New Community, "White Nationalist Staffing U.S. Immigration Reform Pact," Center for New Community, http://www.newcomm.org/index.php?option=com_content&task=view&id=9&Itemid=2.
592. "Extremist Leads New Arkansas Anti-Immigrant Group," Southern Policy Law Center, January 25, 2005, http://www.splcenter.org/intel/news/item.jsp?aid=8.
593. "Federation for American Immigration Reform (FAIR)," Center for New Community, November 2004, 7–9, http://www.newcomm.org/fair2004.pdf.
594. Figure is as of the October 15, 2004, FEC filing deadline. See http://www.newcomm.org/fair2004.pdf.
595. Ira Kurzban, attorney in the case *Jean v. Nelson*, interview by the author, January, 30, 2006.
596. Heidi Beirich, "Defending Immigrants," *Intelligence Report*, Summer 2002,

http://www.splcenter.org/intel/intelreport/article.jsp?aid=91.

597. Mark Potok and Heidi Beirich, "The Puppeteer," *Intelligence Report,* Summer 2002, http://www.splcenter.org/intel/intelreport/article.jsp?pid=181.
598. John Tanton, "End of Migration Epoch?" reprinted in John Rohe, *Mary Lou and John Tanton: A Journey into American Conservation* (FAIR Horizons Press, Washington, D.C.: 2002), 226.
599. John Tanton, memorandum to FAIR, 1986, Available at http://www.splcenter.org/intel/intelreport/article.jsp?sid=123&printable=1.
600. "Head of Legislative Affairs Named," The Third Branch 37, no. 8 (August 2005), http://www.uscourts.gov/ttb/aug05ttb/leg_affairs/.
601. Rick Swartz, interview by the author, August 12, 2006.
602. Doris Meissner, interview by the author, August 25, 2005.
603. Ira Kurzban, interview by the author, November 2005; Jake Bernstein, "Lamar's Alien Agenda," *Texas Observer,* October 25, 2002.
604. Ibid.
605. James Crawford, *Hold Your Tongue,* "Hispanophobia."
606. Al Kamen, "Time is Slater's Co-pilot," *Washington Post,* October 2, 2000, A23.
607. Ibid.
608. Rick Swartz, interview by the author, August 12, 2005.
69. Heidi Beirich, "Defending Immigrants," *Intelligence Report,* Summer 2002, http://www.splcenter.org/intel/intelreport/article.jsp?pid=177.
610. "Head of Legislative Affairs Named," *The Third Branch* 37, no. 8 (August 2005), http://www.uscourts.gov/ttb/aug05ttb/leg_affairs/.
611. Ray Ybarra, interview by the author, August 24, 2005.
612. The hearing was called "War on Terrorism: Immigration Enforcement Since September 11, 2001."
613. See http://commdocs.house.gov/committees/judiciary/hju86954.000/hju86954_0.HTM.
614. See "Alleged Deception of Congress: The Congressional Task Force on Immigration Reform's Fact-finding Visit to the Miami District of INS in June, 1995," Office of the Inspector General, U.S. Department of Justice, June 1996, http://www.usdoj.gov/oig/special/9606/miafile2.htm.
615. John Tanton, ed., "Common Sense on Mass Immigration" (Petosky, MI: Social Contract Press, 2004), http://www.commonsenseonmassimmigration.org/index.html.
616. Peter Brimelow, author of *Alien Nation,* is another overtly white supremacist who pushes an end to immigration. See Heidi Beirich and Mark Potok, "Keeping America White," *Intelligence Report,* Winter 2003, http://www.splcenter.org/intel/intelreport/article.jsp?aid=152.
617. See her testimony to the U.S. House of Representatives Judiciary Subcommittee on Immigration, Border Security, and Claims, April 30, 1997, http://www.cis.org/articles/1997/jenks43097.htmpg.

618. Mark Potok and Heidi Beirich, "The Puppeteer," *Intelligence Report*, Summer 2002, http://www.splcenter.org/intel/intelreport/article.jsp?aid=93.
619. Rosemary Jenks and David Simcox, "Refugee and Asylum Policy: National Passion Versus National Interest," Negative Population Growth Forum Series, February 1992, http://www.npg.org/forum_series/ref&asylum_policy.htm.
620. Ibid.
621. Ibid.
622. See details regarding Numbersusa.com in the Center for Public Integrity's LobbyWatch database, http://www.publicintegrity.org/lobby/profile.aspx?act=clients&year=2003&cl=L018444.
623. See, for example, e-mail alert from Anne Manetas of NumbersUSA, April 10, 2002, http://www.americanpatrol.com/245i/VoteNxtWk245iSen020410.html.
624. Ray Ybarra, interview by the author, August 12, 2005.
625. American Immigration Lawyers Association, *Restrictionist Watch* 2, no. 1, February 2005.
626. "Ninth Circuit Court of Appeals Rejects Bid by Illegal Aliens to Overturn Arizona's Proposition 200," FAIR, August 9, 2005, http://www.fairus.org/site/PageServer?pagename=media_release080905.
627. Ibid.
628. David Kelly, "Colorado Activists Push Immigration Initiative," *Los Angeles Times*, March 13, 2005.
629. Arkansas Taxpayer and Citizen Protection Act, 85th General Assembly, regular session, senate bill 206 (2005), http://www.arkleg.state.ar.us/ftproot/bills/2005/public/SB206.pdf.
630. Joe McCutchen, letter to the editor, *Southwest Times Record*, June 21, 2003.
631. "Extremist Leads New Arkansas Anti-Immigrant Group," Southern Poverty Law Center, January 25, 2005, http://www.splcenter.org/intel/news/item.jsp?aid=8.
632. Heidi Beirich, "Xenophobia," *Intelligence Report*, Spring 2005, http://www.splcenter.org/intel/intelreport/article.jsp?aid=530.
633. Associated Press, "Arkansas immigration lobbyist tied to alleged hate groups," January 27, 2005.
634. Leonard Zeskind, "The New Nativism: The Alarming Overlap Between White Nationalists and Mainstream Anti-Immigrant Forces," *American Prospect Magazine*, November 10, 2005, http://www.prospect.org/web/page.ww?section-root&name-ViewPrint&articleId-10485.
635. M. E. Sprengelmeyer, "Tancredo Gets Back on Track," *Rocky Mountain News*, August 3, 2005, http://www.tancredo.org/news/art2005aug03.html.
636. Michael Scherer, "Scrimmage on the Border," *Mother Jones*, July/August 2005.
637. Ibid.
638. Mark Potok, "The Party of Fear," *Intelligence Report*, Spring 2004, http://www.splcenter.org/intel/intelreport/article.jsp?aid=381
639. Ibid.

640. Tanton's contributions are listed on the Federal Election commission's Web site. Search by individual contributor at http://www.fec.gov/.
641. Max Blumenthal, "Vigilante Injustice," *Salon.com*, May 22, 2003, http://dir.salon.com/story/news/feature/2003/05/22/vigilante/index3.html?pn=1.
642. Ibid.
643. "Team America PAC," Tom Tancredo's official Web site, http://www.tancredo.org/info/team_america_pac.html.
644. Ibid.
645. American Immigration Lawyers Association, *Restrictionist Watch* 1, no. 4, July 21, 2004.
646. American Immigration Lawyers Association *Restrictionist Watch* 1, no. 5, September 9, 2004, http://www.aila.org/content/default.aspx?docid=11420.
647. "Price Statement on the Patriot Act," Tom Price's official Web site, July 22, 2005, http://tomprice.house.gov/html/release.cfm?id=63.
648. Michael Scherer, "Scrimmage on the Border," *Mother Jones*, July/August 2005.
649. Albert Baldero and Annan Boodram, "Immigration and Terrorism: The U.S. Responds to Attacks," *Caribbean Voice*, October 2001, www.catibvoice.org/Immigration/terrorism/html.
650. See chapter 5.
651. "Senator Feinstein Urges Major Changes in U.S. Student Visa Program," September 27, 2001, http://www.senate.gov/~feinstein/releases01/stvisas1.htm.
652. Ibid.
653. Center for New Community, "9/11 Families for a Secure America," http://www.newcomm.org.
654. Ibid.
655. *9/11 Families for a Secure America Newsletter*, April 18, 2003, 1, http://www.911fsa.org/newsletters/newsletters.html.
656. *9/11 Families for a Secure America Newsletter*, January 30, 2004, 2, http://www.911fsa.org/newsletters/newsletters.html.
657. "Leiberman Says Real ID Act Would Make Nation Less Safe by Repealing Terrorist Safeguards Enacted Upon Recommendation of 9/11 Commision," April 20, 2005, http://lieberman.senate.gov/newsroom/release.cfm?id=23669&&. See also the following passage from a letter from 9/11 Commission members Governor Thomas Kean and Congressman Lee Hamilton to members of the bill's Conference Committee: "We believe strongly that this bill is not the right occasion for tackling controversial immigration and law enforcement issues that go well beyond the Commission's recommendations. We note in this regard that some of these provisions have been advocated in response to Commission recommendations. They are not Commission recommendations." Kean and Hamilton then added, "We believe we are better off with broad bipartisan agreement on key recommendations of the Commission in support of border security than taking up a number of controversial provisions that are

more central to the question of immigration policy than they are to the question of counterterrorism."

See http://www.aila.org/content/default.aspx?bc=6729%7C11693.

658. Mitch Jeserich, Pacifica Radio's FSRN Capitol Hill correspondent, interview by the author, August 25, 2005.
659. See chapter 3 for more details on expedited removal.
660. The amendment is available at http://thomas.loc.gov/cgi-bin/bdquery/D?d108:9:./temp/~bdJuMa::.
661. White House to the Hon. Peter Hoekstra, October 18, 2004, http://www.globalsecurity.org/intell/library/congress/2004_rpt/041018-whitehouse01.htm.
662. "President Discusses Border Security and Immigration Reform in Arizona," Office of the Press Secretary, the White House, November 28, 2005, http://www.whitehouse.gov/news/releases/2005/11/20051128-7.html.
663. See chapter 3.
664. See details regarding NumbersUSA.com in the Center for Public Integrity's LobbyWatch database, http://www.publicintegrity.org/lobby/profile.aspx?act=clients&year=2003&cl=L018444.
665. James R. Edwards Jr., "Keeping Extremists Out. The History of Exclusion and the Need for It's Revival," Center for Immigration Studies, September 2005, http://www.4acloserlook.com/back1005.pdf.
666. Ibid., 16.
667. "James R. Edwards Jr., "Officers Need Backup: The Role of State and Local Police in Immigration law Enforcement," Center for Immigratin Studies, April 2003, http://www.cis.org/articles/2003/back703.html.
668. United Press International, "Klan Leader Egged During Tour," October 16, 1977, reprinted in *Crusader*, no. 27 (1997): 2. See also "'Border Watch' by Klan called a Media Event," *Los Angeles Times*, October 27, 1977, 3, and Luke Cannon, "The 'Border Patrol' That Wasn't," *Washington Post*, November 8, 1977, A19.
669. Max Blumenthal, "Vigilante Injustice," Salon.com, May 22, 2003, http://dir.salon.com/story/news/feature/2003/05/22/vigilante/index3.html?pn=1.
670. Ibid.
671. "Activist cleared of Trespassing in Immigrant Detention Case," Associated Press, June 24, 2006, www.620ktar.com/?nid=6&sid=19044.
672. Ray Ybarra, interview by the author, August 24, 2005.
673. Ibid.
674. Max Blumenthal, "Vigilante Injustice," Salon.com, May 22, 2003, http://dir.salon.com/story/news/feature/2003/05/22/vigilante/index3.html?pn=1.
675. Ibid.
676. "American Border Patrol Story," American Border Patrol, http://www.americanborderpatrol.com/abpstory.html.
677. Max Blumenthal, "Vigilante Injustice," Salon.com, May 22, 2003, http://dir.salon.com/story/news/feature/2003/05/22/vigilante/index3.html?pn=1.

678. See chapter 5.

679. Max Blumenthal, "Vigilante Injustice," Salon.com, May 22, 2003, http://dir.salon.com/story/news/feature/2003/05/22/vigilante/index3.html?pn=1.

680. Ibid.

681. Mitch Jeserich, "The Reality Behind the REAL ID Act," *Commondreams.org*, May 5, 2005, http://www.commondreas.org/views05/0505=30.htm.

682. Duncan Mansfield, "Anti-immigration Groups Head to Interior," Associated Press, July 17, 2005.

683. *Border Protection Corps Act of 2005*, HR3622,109th Cong., 1st sess. (July 29, 2005), http://thomas.loc.gov/cgi-bin/query/z?c109:H.R.3622.IH.

684. Brendan Coyne, "Border Patrol to Turn Down Vigilante Help," *The New Standard*, July 22, 2005, http://newstandardnews.net/content/?action=show_item&itemid=2130.

685. Ray Ybarra, interview by the author, August 24, 2005.

686. See http://www.sfgate.com/cgi-bin/article.cgi?file=/c/a/2005/02/11/MNG3HB99O41.DTL.

687. Traci Hong, interview by Mitch Jeserich in "Critics Denounce the REAL ID Act," Free Speech Radio News, February 11, 2005.

688. Ibid.

689. Edward Epstein, "House OKs Ban on Licenses for Illegal Immigrants, Bill Also Encourages Bounty Hunters to Track Down Those Ordered Deported," *San Francisco Chronicle*, February 11, 2005, http://www.sfgate.com/cgi-bin/article.cgi?file=/c/a/2005/02/11/MNG3HB99O41.DTL.

690. Ibid.

691. Dan Robinson, "US House Passes Tough Immigration Law," *Voice of America*, February 10, 2005, http://www.voanews.com/english/archive/2005-02/2005-02-10-voa72.cfm?CFID=8542579&CFTOKEN=84044044.

692. Interviews by the author, February 11, 2005.

INDEX

ABOUT THE AUTHORS

Deepa Fernandes is the host of *Wakeup Call*, the popular morning show on Pacifica radio station WBAI in New York City. Her award-winning radio features have aired on the BBC World Service and Public Radio International. Her writing has appeared in the *Village Voice*, *In These Times*, and *Amsterdam News*.

Howard Zinn grew up in the immigrant slums of Brooklyn, where he worked in the shipyards in his late teens. During World War II he served as an air force bombardier. Later, Zinn received a doctorate in history from Columbia University and was a postdoctoral fellow in East Asian studies at Harvard University. He is the author of numerous books, including his epic masterpiece, *A People's History of the United States*.